The
cool fire

The cool fire

how to make it in television

by Bob Shanks

W·W·NORTON & COMPANY·INC.

New York

Library of Congress Cataloging in Publication Data

Shanks, Bob.
  The cool fire.

  Includes index.
  1. Television broadcasting—United States.
I. Title.
PN1992.3.U5S53   791.45   75-37521
ISBN 0-393-08363-2

Printed in the United States of America

1 2 3 4 5 6 7 8 9 0

Because of their love, laughter,
and inexplicable understanding,

This book, with all else I have,
belongs to
my wife, Ann
and
children—
Jennifer, Anthony, John

contents

preface

For so long that it seemed like always, we gathered around the fire. The fire was human central—warmth and light, food and solace. It is only when you count the small change of time jingling in the pockets of our own memories that need for the fire has diminished.

The fire is out of sight now. We have moved it to the basement and enclosed it; we regulate it by thermostats or third persons. In our time, the event and the presence of the fire, which caused a thousand generations to seek it for survival and then to make it social, are gone.

But the attendant rituals of so long a learning die hard. Recently, I saw a fireplace in the fortieth-floor executive suite of a climate-controlled office tower. That hearth, of course, is a cosmetic vestige and holds no fire. Nobody really needs it, except to answer some ancestral yearning. A yearning which I believe is in us all, as strongly as ever. Of course, most of us do not have fireplaces today, even fake ones. Only the Marlboro Man and kids at summer camp ever build an open fire.

Most of us satisfy the need with something else: the new hearth —electronic and in living color. That is where we gather now— around the cool fire of television.

In America, the cool fire shines from 950 television stations aimed at 100 million sets in 68.5 million homes. Americans, on the average, spend 6 hours and 15 minutes a day watching it flicker. You have heard it said, and the Bureau of Statistics confirms it, there are more television sets than bath tubs in this country.

Television is pervasive, relentless, commonplace, irresistible. "Electronic wallpaper," one television executive called it, as he contemplated a scuff mark on his Gucci loafers. "It's the worst in us that uses it most often. When we pay attention at all, that is. Mostly, it's just there."

Others have claimed that it is unmatched in its power to bring us together. Marshall McLuhan, a kind of media messiah, has declared that all the tribes of the world will one day gather around the cool fire in a common "global village."

Either way, it cannot be ignored. At its worst, television will make you want what you do not need and vote for men who are not what they seem. ("Television never lies," say people who lie on it all the time.) At its best, television can instruct and inspire.

Leave it for now that television is monstrous in its realities, in its reach and its implications. But regardless of the moral arguments about television—who should control it and for what ends—I consider it to be my profession. I loathe the incompetency and carelessness in television as much as a lawyer or a doctor would in his profession.

Since you will be taking my word for a lot, I think it is fair and necessary to tell you about myself.

I have been a professional in television for sixteen years. Before that, I graduated in theatre and television from Indiana University and got through two years in the Army in special services by writing speeches for a general and putting on plays and a weekly television show.

Coming on to New York, I began and quickly ended a career as an actor. I got killed on "Love of Life" and died in several other shows. As boring as I was as an actor, I have never regretted this experience; it gave me insight and sympathy for performers and, thus, valuable rapport with them.

Next, I worked as coffee boy on a show called "America after Dark." (We called it "America *in* the Dark.") This was a mercifully short-lived program on NBC between the original "Steve Allen Tonight Show" and the old "Jack Paar Tonight Show." My salary as coffee boy was $150 a week and out of that I had to pay for the coffee and pastries. After the first week, I learned by accident—my supplier was out of fresh—that day-old pastries cost only half as much and nobody noticed the difference. From then on, I bought them regularly. I had taken my first step toward becoming a producer.

For six months, after "America after Dark" was canceled, I worked as a waiter in a theatrical saloon (another lesson), until I got a job as talent coordinator for the "Jack Paar Tonight Show."

I got the chance for this job on the Paar show by maintaining friendships with two carry-over staff members whom I had met during my coffee-boy days. The job was "temporary," I was told; ninety days only, they said, since the regular man was sick, but would be coming back. This job also paid $150 a week but carried with it a $50 a week expense account! When I got my first $100,000 a year job, the thrill was not equal.

The first week on the Paar staff, I shared an office with another talent coordinator, and it was sheer panic for me. I didn't know anyone and the other man spent the entire day talking to powerful agents and famous performers. He ate at Sardi's and Toots Shor's and 21 and had no trouble at all making out his expense account. Mine could have won a fiction prize. It contained the names of a lot of out-of-work actors whom I knew from my days at Stella Adler's acting school. I think I even wrote down Stella's name. In absolute desperation about the telephone, I used to dial my own apartment number and talk to the incessant ringing. My old army buddy, who worked as a copy boy for the New York *Times,* got called several times a day and he in turn would call and leave various names for me to call back.

All along, though, I knew I would have to book somebody for the show. It would have to be somebody impressive, if I wanted to keep the job. Certainly, I had no intention of remaining temporary. But who? I was shut out from all the normal channels by the other more experienced talent coordinators.

For some reason I remembered that the playwright, George S. Kaufman, had been witty on a show called "This Is Show Business." Kaufman had been absent from the tube for a long time, after confessing on the air at Christmas time that if he heard "Silent Night" once more, he would throw up. Quaintly enough, this caused a national scandal and Kaufman was banished from television. He would be perfect, I knew, but (A) I wasn't sure he was still alive, and if he was, (B) how to contact him?

In the beginning, one is frequently intimidated about approaching the famous. They seem unreachable without some magical process or, at the least, "knowing somebody."

Being from Indiana, I was naïvely unaware of this phenomenon and simply looked Kaufman up in the New York phone book. There he was. I called, got him, and arranged a meeting. He was an enormous hit on the show and appeared often. Moreover, he was grateful, he told me, for the public opportunity to prove that he was still alive; Paar was happy because Kaufman always got big, biting laughs. I was happy because Paar was happy.

The talent coordinator who had been ill returned, another got fired for falling asleep drunk in the front row at one telecast, and I stayed on—in various advance jobs for four years. During that time, I booked the first-time appearances on television of Woody Allen, Bob Newhart, Dick Gregory, the Smothers Brothers, Aretha Franklin, Buck Henry, Renee Taylor, Alan Arkin, Nipsey Russell, George Segal, Joan Rivers; and later, when I produced the "Merv Griffin Show," Stiller and Meara, Redd Foxx, George Carlin, Dick Cavett, Lily Tomlin, Richard Pryor, David Steinberg, John Denver, and Bette Midler.

I also auditioned and turned down a young girl named Barbra

Streisand! Who knew she would turn out to be Barbra Streisand?

Barbra realized that I was the one keeping her off the "Tonight Show," which was and is powerful exposure for a young performer. She called and asked to see me about a personal and career problem, since she just *knew* I was the *only* one in the business *sensitive* enough to help her. *Everybody* in the business said that about me, she said. Who could resist? Of course, I said, "Come in."

When we met, Barbra explained that she was from Cleveland, Ohio! (I have always admired this double gamble: She counted on my being from the Midwest, thus more sympathetic, and on my inability to recognize her Brooklyn accent.) She said her mother was suffering from cancer and was putting tremendous pressure on her to come home, get a job, and get married in Cleveland, since she was having such thin success in show business in New York.

What did I think, honestly, were her chances in the business? Her career was in my hands. Should she go home and give it all up, or was there a way she could prove to herself and to her dying mom in Cleveland ("Gee, if she could only see me on TV.") that it wasn't all a useless dream?

Well, what would you do? I had grown up on movies with plots like that one. Of course, Barbra got her "Tonight Show" bookings.

I went on in the business to become at various times, an associate producer, producer, writer, and director for NBC, CBS, ABC, PBS, and Group W-Westinghouse. Currently, I am a vice-president of ABC. I have been fired twice, canceled three times, won some prizes, owned my own company, and made more money in a single year than the president of the United States does. I have also stood behind the white line waiting for my unemployment check.

Through television, I met my wife, traveled from the Pacific to the Soviet Union, and worked with everyone from President John F. Kennedy and Bertrand Russell to Miss Nude America and a guy who played *Melancholy Baby* by beating on his head.

With it all, I have never lost my fascination for television nor exhausted my frustration. I know a lot about it and I will put down here as much of what I know as I can.

acknowledgments

I owe more thank yous than you will hear in a season of awards shows. In particular, I thank my parents; I thank my wife, Ann Shanks, for her enthusiasm, endurance, and editorial comments; my editor, Ed Barber, for his faith in this project and for his wise red pencil; Wally Weltman for his technical evaluation; Linda Finson for her research assistance; Jorn Winther for production pages; Lee Adams and Charles Strouse, the Frank Music Company, Jacqueline Babbin, Pete Hamill, Herbert Leonard, Carolyn Raskin, and Eric Lieber for allowing me to use certain materials of theirs; Marcy Olive and Susan Pomerantz for their preparation of the manuscript.

Also, I am grateful for information and assistance from ABC, ABC Press Information, ASCAP, BMI, Camera Mart, Laurence S. Dickter at the Cable Television Information Center, CBS Press Information, Eastman/Kodak and Richard L. Thomas, The National Association of Broadcasters, NBC Press Information, RCA, and Leslie Slocum at the NAB's Television Information Office, as well as the publications, *Broadcast* magazine, the *Hollywood Reporter,* and *Variety.*

I gained valuable insight from three books: *Television: The Business Behind the Box,* Les Brown (Harcourt, Brace, Jovanovich, Inc., 1971); *TV, the Big Picture,* Stan Opotowsky (E. P. Dutton & Co., Inc., 1961); *Television and Radio,* Giraud Chester, Garnet R. Garrison, and Edgar E. Willis (Appleton-Century-Crofts, Educational Division, Meredith Corporation, 1971).

If a man is judged truly by his friends, I am content. I have so many helpful and good ones.

The
cool fire

Chapter **1**
the producer

"Film is a director's medium," nearly everyone has said. You can, with the same authority and a good deal more freshness, say, "Television is a producer's medium." Of course, some rather neck-bulging arguments will ensue about both of these oversimplifications. Granite proclamations of this kind have little real value, but in motion pictures and television, these two stand up as solid points of truth.

I don't know all the reasons why. Perhaps in film it began at the beginning, when the director was usually brought from *theatre* and was considered an *artiste,* or was a cameraman who had unique technical skills. There is also the tyranny of "looking through the lens" in film. Only one person at a time can see the image as it is being recorded, and even during rehearsal or setup, it is awkward for more than a very few to have a look. This gives the film cinematographer and, by evolvement, the director, exclusive power.

In television, everyone involved can see the main image instantly and usually three or four other simultaneous camera inputs that the director could be choosing. No wonder that the television director is more frequently second-guessed.

Most of the early film producers were businessmen who saw Edison's toy as the way to riches and seldom thought of their activity in terms of art or even craft. I don't think this has been true in television. With television packagers, this businessman role is a function fulfilled by the programmers—the network or local station executives—while the producer has evolved as a vital member of the creative team.

Furthermore, a film happens once; a television show may take place daily or weekly or monthly, which requires that the director be a different person for each episode in the series. Also, the director of a film is involved with the making of his project over a much longer period of time; he usually comes into the process earlier and stays until the project is completed and ready to be seen.

A television director may be brought in only on the day of taping or a few days before. Even for large-scale dramas, the director is seldom around for more than three or four weeks. When the shooting is finished, so, ordinarily, is he. The producer and an assistant director, with editors, finish the project.

All of this makes the producer the continuum on a television project. Most often, the project has been his from the initial idea—either out of his own head or in seeing a property worthy of adaptation—straight through to the end. Even when he has been assigned the project by a programmer, a network or local station, or major packaging company, he is always the first member of the creative team to be called. On a minute-to-minute basis, the producer is on the set or in the control room, exercising final and active authority over the entire production.

Some big-name television directors have resisted this producer control. A few, a very few, have been able to overcome it. The rest have left television for films, or have accepted the producer as the ultimate authority. Of course, frequently, in both films and television, functions have merged within one person—a producer-director, or a producer-writer, or a director-writer, or the producer-director-writer. We call these hyphenates, and I will discuss this phenomenon in more detail as we go along.

Suffice it for now to say, rule number one for a good producer is that he has the right to the power and the responsibility to use that power. When all the others have gone home, the producer alone will be blamed—or applauded.

How a producer uses his authority will, of course, be controlled by his experience in the profession and, even more, by the kind of person the producer is. Whether your childhood has shaped you into Attila the Hun or Martin Milquetoast, with professional self-awareness, you can learn to moderate the extremes of those qualities and leave the excesses at the door during production. Sigmund Freud notwithstanding, the producer is not preordained to fail. However, a producer's personal colors may well be his key to success, giving him a unique vision. There is no single producer type. Producers Bob Banner and Alan Landsburg are so soft-spoken, I have often had difficulty hearing them in face-to-face meetings; yet both are tough, efficient professionals with taste and judgment. Jerry Lewis and Dan Curtis come on like a Ringling Brothers parade, but underneath they are two of the gentlest, most sensitive men I know. Joe Hamilton wears sweaters and red socks; David Susskind is never without a suit and tie. Aaron Spelling is a health-food nut; Jacqueline Babbin chain-smokes. To Barry Shear, everything is "chaos"; to David Frost, everything is "lovely." X is an alcoholic; Y is on skimmed milk and tea. A bribes you with pro basketball tickets; B won't wish you Happy New Year if it might cost him a penny. C was the son of a studio head; D came from South Dakota and didn't know a soul. I know one woman producer who begins every encounter so defensively that you would think you had already told her to dispose of her show in a rude but colorful manner; on the other hand, one male producer deplores meeting except over lunch and vintage wine in a three-star restaurant, and will discuss everything but the show. That always seems to embarrass him.

A wise and confident producer will be himself and will use his power prudently and privately. He will never humiliate a director or any other member of the team in public (exceptions come later), nor will he second-guess decisions. Such negative behavior is poisonous and usually indicates an insecure producer or one who is on the ultimate ego-trip, a journey that only the most masochistic would wish to make with him.

Even if a producer does force a director to submit by degrading him in public (and when a director does submit he will always be looking for ways to get even; and there are lots of them), the crew and cast will still resist. This can cost not only money, but faulted quality in the product, and it most certainly will jeopardize a producer's chances of future work. There is nothing more damaging to a production than the tense and polluted atmosphere which a producer can create. I have seen it scores of times. All right, even in this climate, I have seen shows turn out to be hits. I am convinced, however, that these exceptions would have been still bigger hits if that toxin had not been in the air.

On the other hand, a producer whose only aim is "to be liked" or to have peace at any price, is in still bigger trouble. I have cursed myself, many times, in the editing room or while watching a show of mine on the air, for not having stepped in when my instincts told me, "That's not right." "They're taking too long." "The lighting is awful." "The star's off the mark." "The joke was missed in the wide shot." "Discipline that unruly son of a bitch." And so on. A producer should never say, "Don't bother," or "It's only a television show." If that is his attitude, he should join a commune. You have to fight for everything you get and want in a production.

Overall, the most difficult aspect of a producer's job is to know when to fight, when to step in, and when not to and how to do it. Of course, the decision is never a crisp one; that is, with only the immediate factor weighing in the judgment. Every time a producer is about to intercede, he must go through a mental check list, weighing alternatives. First, is the current problem a pound of trouble or ten pounds or a ton?

As an example, let us say I have a girl singer, downstage, fore-ground, and there is a palm tree, upstage, background, which appears to be growing out of her head. I want to stop the number and reposi-tion either the girl singer or the palm tree. Good. But now comes the check list. The tree growing out of her head looks silly—but *how* silly? Have only I noticed it? Will an audience? But more importantly, what are the other considerations? Does the girl singer have to leave in ten minutes to make a plane for Las Vegas? Is this the first take or the fortieth? What are the mental and physical states of the girl and of the rest of the cast? How big a star is the girl? When is the orchestra due for a break or a meal or overtime? Am I behind schedule? Will it cost me $5 or $5,000 to redo it? Is it an "event" show where this is the only performance? (I could still find ways of shifting her position during the one take.) Have I overshot and perhaps don't need this number for the final cut?

Depending on my quick answers to these and other questions, I may decide that the tree growing out of the girl singer's head doesn't look *that* silly; I may even convince myself that the tree is enhancing her performance!

I offer you a few examples out of my own career as to this business of stepping in. Overall, I consider myself—and most others confirm it—to be a low-key, "polite" producer, preferring to work by persuasion. I am normally willing, in fact eager, to let each member of the team do his job and exercise his own creative judgments. But, I think I am tough as hell underneath and unshakable in getting what I want in a production. Here is how I dealt with a couple of situations of which I am proud. I will also tell about another time when I think I failed.

I was producing a "Jerry Lewis Muscular Dystrophy Telethon" that, at the point of the story, was in its seventeenth hour on the air, not to mention the hours everybody had been working prior to the show on preproduction. Everyone involved was on the edge of ex-haustion (though it is astonishing how exhilarating this kind of intense production can be).

Joan Crawford, who had behaved generously throughout the show and whom I admire as a consummate professional, had come to loggerheads with Jerry, for whom I have the deepest affection and respect. The substance of the matter escapes me. I simply remember that two big egos were meeting head on. That is all right. I understand these ego problems and am usually tolerant of them. So, I went back and forth between Jerry and Joan, on opposite sides of the backstage area (mind you, the show was going on throughout all of this), first, trying to keep them apart, and, second, trying to negotiate some face-saving compromise between them. My relationships with both were excellent and my credibility intact. They were both somewhat embarrassed by the positions they were taking, but holding firm. No fights yet, just polite intransigence; when a big star is intransigent, he is harder to move than a Russian Army in Czechoslavakia.

Because the moment of truth was coming quickly—I think now the whole problem had to do with positions on stage for the finale, or something like that—and because my own patience was tattered by fatigue, I resolved finally to bring them together. Perhaps this might moderate their positions. But the meeting backstage had just the opposite, inflammatory effect. Both Jerry and Joan threatened to walk off the show. By that time it was critical for me to have at least one of them out on stage (a girl singer with a potted palm growing out of her head was just finishing her number), so I began to boil.

I thought, "Damn these people! I am the producer of this show! How dare they! It has been a good show for seventeen hours and I am not going to let them muck up the end!" I told myself, "I have treated both of them with respect, affection, and high professionalism throughout. I have made them look good. Damn them for this ingratitude! And what about the children? Those with Muscular Dystrophy? Have these two superstar juveniles forgotten about them?!'' All these thoughts burst through and, even if I had wanted to, I was no longer able to control them. I was furious, tired, disgusted—and right. There is nothing more delicious than moral indignation or a sense of righteousness. So I screamed at both of them. I was, I thought, Patrick Henry, Winston Churchill, and, I'm afraid, Abbie Hoffman, rolled into one. I called them babies, selfish, superficial cardboards who didn't give a damn about the children. I shouted one obscenity after another until tears came into my voice. Finally—I said, if anyone was going to walk off this show, it was going to be me.

Joan and Jerry were dumb struck. They had never heard me swear or even raise my voice. The effect was perfect. They both did exactly what I wanted them to do. Even better, we have, all of us, remained good friends ever since.

Another time; more exhaustion. I was producing a variety color special on location around New York City, and through six days of production, it had rained every day. This particular day, I had Dionne Warwick in front of the Pulitzer Fountain by the Plaza Hotel. It was raining Biblically. Dionne was wonderfully patient and good-natured about working at all in such brutal weather, and we had to finish. The show had an air date in two weeks; Dionne had only this one day to give me. She was due to fly out the following morning to open in Las Vegas for three weeks.

Struggling, we had been able to get our "master" shot (I will explain all the terms later) in at least one acceptable "take". In fact, the shot was lovely. The song was "Alfie" and the effect of the rain and Dionne in yellow rain gear, walking along at night holding an umbrella, was beautifully heightened by the poignancy of the song and her performance.

For two hours we had been trying to get just one take of the same song in "medium close" and "close-up." Without these shots, the master shot was meaningless. Dionne Warwick could have been Deanna Durbin, we were so far away.

There was a staff and crew of forty. There were half a dozen cops, blocking off two streets of traffic. There was the remote truck and the generator truck and tons of lighting equipment. The setup, if I recall correctly, was costing $15,000. Everyone wanted to give up, "strike" the location, abandon the song, since we were already well into over-time and there appeared to be no letup in the rain or wind. I kept stalling or disappearing from one spot on the location to another, trying to avoid the pressure to quit and scanning the sky, hoping for a break. I could not accept losing the song. The bloody thing only ran three minutes. Three minutes—that's all I needed! We were in over-time anyway, I thought; the money was already spent and to spend it all and have nothing to show for it was killing me. Even worse, I could see from the master how beautiful the number would be if we could only get it. The pressures to give up became enormous, from my own people and from Dionne's manager, whom I did not blame. He had Las Vegas to think about and the prospect of a wet and weary star getting ill.

Dionne, bless her, never wavered. "I don't mind. I'd like to get it." Finally, around 3:00 in the morning, the rain let up. It did not stop, but it did diminish and so did the wind. We went for a take.

Dionne went to her mark, the lights sizzled on, and I ran into the control truck to watch. She got her cue and began her walk. Eight bars, beautiful. Sixteen bars, still beautiful. Then—I was standing right over the director's shoulder—I could see the umbrella begin-ning to turn inside-out. "That's that," the director moaned. Nobody moved. "Oh, God, no," I thought, "This is our only chance!" Now what? Suddenly, I had an idea. Risky, stupid, and odds on against it, but I went with it.

"Zoom it up her nostrils." I barked at the director, who was wanting to cut. "Don't you dare cut. Tight, go in tight on her—tight as you can. I'm going out there. Hold a wide shot on number 2. You'll be able to see if I can save the damn umbrella."

We had to have the umbrella in the medium and close shots or they would not "cut" with the master shot. In one she would have the umbrella, in the others she wouldn't. That would be ridiculous, unless we called it "The Disappearing Umbrella Act" or something.

I banged out of the control truck and raced to Dionne. When I thought I was in picture range, I dropped to my hands and knees. Dionne must have thought I had gone crazy, but some professional instinct in her told her not to stop singing or take notice of me. When I got to her, I reached up for the umbrella and straightened its bent ribs. Slowly, I handed it back up to her. Now she could manage it. Even the wind helped by subsiding a bit. She kept walking and the umbrella seemed to be holding. I sneaked back out, still on my hands and knees, and Dionne went on to the end of the song. We had gotten the medium and close-up shots and they were gorgeous.

In the cutting room, we covered the few seconds in which the umbrella was missing with the extreme close-up the director had gone in for, "supered" over the wide, or master, shot. For the rest of the song, we were able to use the marvelous medium close-ups in which that blasted umbrella was framing Dionne's beautiful face.

Small things, and audiences never see them. Instead of these two solutions, I am sure we could have found others, but I am proud of both of those moments. There are more than a couple I would rather not recall, but here is one of them.

Things were going beautifully. I was producing the "Merv Griffin Show"—five ninety-minute programs a week; my private company was producing two separate pilot programs, one on location in Europe and another in California, and then I sold a documentary. With all of the other activity, there was no way I could also produce and direct the documentary, so I hired another man, whom I had known, mostly over amusing lunches, and had liked.

I was fascinated by the topic of the documentary; he said he was, too, and, though the budget was tight, it seemed reasonable and worth doing. He handled the preproduction and the shooting adequately and he had four weeks to finish and deliver the show. I saw no cause for alarm. I spoke to him daily on the telephone, while I went about my work with Griffin and on the editing at night of the European pilot. On the phone he was always cheerful and sounded knowing. We agreed that I would look at a "rough cut" of the show in about ten days. When I came to the cutting room, I was aghast. He was nowhere to be found. Moreover, he had not been around much. It flashed through my mind that *he* had always called *me* when we spoke, and had always been "out" when I had tried to reach him. The editor had no rough cut. He had nothing. No plan, no cut sequences. He had not seen nor even heard about our outline for the show, and he had not been told what his deadline dates were! (I should have fired the editor, since a good one would have learned these things for himself.)

I tracked down the producer-director and expressed my dismay. He had a number of reasonable and reassuring excuses. "Relax. I've had a few personal problems, but they're cleared up now. (He was going through a divorce.) I know exactly what you want. It's all in the footage."

Foolishly, I believed him. We agreed that he would go on working and that by the first of the following week, we would look at the rough cut together.

This time when I arrived he was there, but still without a rough cut. Out of eight acts required in the show, the editor had only two assembled. Even these were rambling, boring, and too long. He had cut out of them some of the best footage, which I had seen in "the rushes."

This story is very painful to me, so I will cut it short. Incredibly, I gave him another chance. It was not until a week before the delivery date that I actually fired him. By that point, he had hired three additional editors, without my okay. All of them were making four different shows, since there was no direction or viewpoint from the top.

I brought in my own editor, kept on the others, wrote an outline of the show, and assigned each of them segments to work on with clear goals in mind. One said it just wasn't in the footage to make her sequence. I said it has to be, it is due Wednesday; if you can't find it, leave. We'll finish it. She did and we did. The rest of us worked twenty-eight hours straight, completely cutting and recutting the show and preparing it for the sound mix which had to take place the next day.

We made my delivery date and the show was well-received, but the emotional and physical damage was immense and the budget was a shambles—$20,000 over! Which I had to pay out of my own pocket.

In every way, it was an expensive education and I tried hard to absorb the mistakes: (1) Too many good things happening to me had made me overconfident and, therefore, careless. (2) I had never seen this man's work or taken the trouble to look at a single frame of any show he had ever made. (3) I had not bothered to check with any of the people he had worked for in the past. (When I did, later, several of them told me, "I could have told you. He talks a great show, but can't deliver. Especially in postproduction.") (4) After seeing the rushes, I did not look at the work on a daily basis. (5) When I did see that things were wrong, I still did not fire him immediately.

Overall, I had allowed myself with no concrete evidence and

finally, with negative evidence, to be talked into and talked out of the truer evidence of my instincts and knowledge. In retrospect, it seems astonishing.

Out of it, however, came two good things: The people who had hired me never knew there was any trouble or that I had taken a financial bath. They got their show trouble-free and on time, and they liked it. They hired me to do several more. Second, I have hired lots of producers and directors since then, and have never made those same mistakes again; on the contrary, I make new ones each time.

I hope many of the nuances of producing are becoming clear, but I will try to define them more formally: What is a producer?

In television, he is certainly the commander of the show. Ultimately, he is responsible for every detail. While David O. Selznick seldom produced for television, he was a giant producer of films, and his thoughts about his role are valid for the television producer: "The difference between myself and other producers is I am interested in the thousands and thousands of details . . . the sum total. The way I see it, my function is to be responsible for everything." He is absolutely right.

Most often, the television producer will have had the idea or will at least have acquired the rights to the idea for the show. He will probably have been instrumental in the sale of the idea and then gone on to get the script written or the show outlined. He must hire and fire the staff, the crew, the stars, and the cast. He must order the facilities, sets, and equipment, and set the schedules for preproduction, shooting, and postproduction. If there are locations, he must survey and choose them. He must determine the budget or work with one that he has been assigned. He must negotiate salaries and hours and contracts, conform to union regulations, arrange for the star's dressing room, limousine, or whatever. He must pay the bills, turn out the lights, and make sure the coffee boy doesn't serve day-old pastries.

Most importantly, he must be the audience until an audience sees the show. I am quite serious about this. It is a good producer's ultimate gift and responsibility. He must use his eyes and ears and taste and judgment to view a show as a kind of supersensitive distillation of the waiting millions, guiding and shaping every element to achieve clarity and satisfaction for the viewer. Are those the right colors in the set? Was this character clearly introduced? Do we know what time of day, year, which decade it is? Can I understand what the character is thinking by that expression? Has there been any character motivation to prompt this kiss, killing, or what-have-you? Do I mind that my weatherman is drunk on the air? Is that joke really funny, tasteless, obscure?

A person with no creative talent or technical skill or particular business acumen can still be a good and working producer if he is a good audience. But it is not as easy as it may sound (though, in my experience everyone considers himself a producer). First, one may be too good an audience for the real audience's taste (this happens frequently, by the way), or not good enough.

In the matter of the producer serving as audience, there is a high risk of bruising necessary objectivity by getting too close to a production. A producer must learn to protect his senses. The first and best advice is to let the other people do their jobs. If a producer is writing the joke, mouthing the dialogue, painting the set, adjusting the lights, moving the props, and seating the audience, he is likely to develop callouses on his sensitivity. Of course, one should meet with all the members of the team at the start and make sure that they are clear on goals and tastes where the production is concerned. The show should be an expression of the producer's vision. He should have working knowledge of each of their areas, but he should also let the specialists work and evolve their interpretations of his vision. Unless a producer is an overriding genius (or a boor), this will get him the best the team has to offer, and will provide the individuals on it with the self-esteem which they deserve.

Next, I create distractions during the production as often as I can, since television can generate more tension than a ten-month pregnancy. Even if I cannot walk away from the set or the cutting room or the office, I leave it mentally. I play chess or poker, phone my wife, interview a crew member about his job, his personal history, his family; talk about the president or Napoleon's Russian campaign—anything to let my senses rest and revitalize themselves.

One producer I know keeps a basketball on hand. Another has a baseball and two mitts for pitch and catch. Still a third brings binoculars into the cutting room and watches the occupants in a hotel across the street.

Is all this a contradiction of Selznick's advice? Not really. Yes, *be* involved in every detail, but, when possible, without anesthetizing your audience senses, or letting your tension infect others. In fact, Selznick was never the same after *Gone with the Wind*. He got so embroiled in minutiae—and with his leading lady—that he began to produce one unsatisfying picture after another as well as alienating most members of his splendid team.

Similarly, I know one television producer who became so enmeshed in the writing, directing, the choosing of locations, the caressing of his star, and the editing, that he worked twenty hours a day and went around in a kind of ambulatory stupor. Thus, he abdicated all perspective on his project. The resulting show had a few glittering moments here and there, but, in the sand around them, even these became rhinestones.

Those who have the gifts to direct (Bud Yorkin, Dwight Hemion, Jorn Winther), write (Norman Lear, Paul Keyes, Carolyn Raskin), design (Herbert Brodkin, Gary Smith, Bob Markell), or perform other functions as they produce—or as they are forced by circumstances to do—often handle double or triple duty. Some of the best work I have seen comes from these single-vision, many-talented producers. All of them, however, are on guard against themselves. They are no less forgiving than if their tasks were performed by others. Such hyphenates further protect themselves by consulting a good backup in each area. They demand honestly of an associate producer or director, or writer, or designer, what he thinks of the work they should be doing in the various categories.

I spoke earlier of hyphenates, that is, producer *hyphen* writer, director, designer, and so on. This is an increasingly populous tribe in television. I was one myself: producer-director-writer, and I am sure my motives for becoming so were much like those of all hyphenates.

This phenomenon of hyphenates has evolved because the producer is the final power. Any writer, director, or designer who sees his vision constantly reordered by the producers he works for, (and theirs by the networks they have to please), begins to realize that he is living in a creative iron lung. This is especially true if the producer has apprenticed as an agent, advertising man, salesman, research, and numbers man, lawyer, or accountant. In any case, it occurs to many in the iron lung that if they themselves are the producer as well, they will breathe more freely and they will eliminate at least one choking layer of the committee process. (You know the old joke: What is a camel? A horse made by a committee.)

If creative control is the legitimate parentage in the birth of a hyphenate, the midwife is money—in the form of ownership of the work. If I have designed a graphics look, written the characters, or set a visual stamp on a show as a director, but do not produce or package the project, I will be paid salary (in some cases, percentages) as required, and that will be that. On the other hand, if I am the producer/packager, I will have equity in my creation and will increase my profit potential dramatically. I will also participate in decisions regarding all subsequent uses of the project (overseas, theatrical, syndication, books, records, educational) and share more substantially in the profits from these.

The hyphenate process also works in reverse. Producers get frustrated, too—by directors, writers, and designers who leave them wanting. Some producers who became directors are Harold Prince in the theatre, Stanley Kramer in films, and Dan Curtis in television.

I like the hyphenate phenomenon, for the reasons I have stated, but also for the singularity that it stamps on a project. The more individual the expression is in the work of art, successful or disastrous, the more fascinating I find it. This way of working has come to full flower in contemporary music, where so many of the artists write and produce their material as well as perform it.

Readers starting out in television are probably already impatient with this chapter. I have not said a word yet about how to become a producer. How *do* you start? What do you need?

First, there is desire. Anyone who wants to be a good producer must be eager, hungry, even driven. It is a perilous and difficult field with enormous competition—and not always from the nicest people. Even with the Devil's own fire in you, it is unlikely that you will become a producer of any kind, never mind the kind I am talking about. There are only about two hundred working and successful producers in the whole business of television. If it is not already clear, I should explain that I am discussing not the relatively safe and secure jobholders in local station or staff situations, but those in what used to be called "the big time"—producers who are working at the top of the tent, without a net, the producers in Hollywood and New York who work in national television.

If your nascent perception of a television producer has him constantly in situations like those depicted in Scotch whiskey ads, you have much to learn. Yes, the pay is good and there is glamour, if one perceives those props and settings as being valuable. Surely, there is always a sizable pride of producers at 21 or Sardi's or the Polo Lounge or Chasen's, and they do travel, have fine homes and clothes and cars, and they do get their names in print in disproportion to the rest of society. They do meet more celebrities, have more romances, and they do appear, visibly, to exert some influence in the society.

Of course, this picture of a television producer is promoted most vigorously by the producers themselves. They are eager to see themselves this way as a reward or rationale for enduring the truer facts of their lives, because beneath this distorted and surface image there is a grittier reality.

Instead of 21, there is more often a cold BLT at the desk or in the cutting room or the rehearsal hall, gobbled down in spasms and flushed away by cardboard coffee—gallons of it in a producer's lifetime. For most, there are too many cigarettes, too little sleep, too much anxiety, and a pocketful of Rolaids. The money goes to the government, to the analyst, or to alimony.

On location, there are extremes of cold and heat and rain and jet noise which not only congeal your intestines, but cost money. (Things are always costing money.) Time is the other constant antagonist. Stingy and swift and unforgiving. There are mundane and repetitious burial mounds of paper and detail and endless flat stretches of life as barren and common as any citizen's, though I do believe these are always more painful to the producer, since the producer nearly always has higher expectations of himself than the average citizen does. Finally, failure is usually visible and the odds for success border on the frivolous.

Still—desire. If one has it, none of what I say will dissuade—nor do I mean to. Ironically, if one is good stuff, the negatives will no doubt stiffen desire. In my own early days—a beginner will hear the monotonous song many times—when somebody would say, "Let me give you some advice about this business, kid—get out of it," I would spur my own pony of desire from a gallop to a run.

A cupful more about glamour and riches: I grant that these are powerful engines of desire and I will not throw sand into their fuel tanks as motives and causes for success in a high percentage of the active and effective producers in television. It *is*, usually, more fun to dine at La Caravelle than at McDonald's. But, these are ends; a sterile harvest if not sown and nurtured by whatever talent you have or can develop through experience, hard work, and sacrifice.

The meanest and most disruptive people in this business are those who lack either talent or conviction. Because of its heavy gravitational pull of glamour, television is an industry which attracts Iagos irresistibly. Without legitimate talents of their own, they are forced to scheme to survive.

I do not by this mean that everyone has to be as talented as Reginald Rose or Quinn Martin or George Schaefer. Television needs thousands of people in a hundred categories—production, management, engineering, agentry, law, sales, research, advertising, promotion, clerical. It has thousands now who perform these tasks well, even creatively. Sadly, I do mean those human barnacles who add nothing to the voyage and who compound their uselessness by mostly insisting on riding deluxe.

Of course, I do know producers who get by on the thin soup of charm or nepotism or "knowing somebody," whose skills and concern are as debased as a losing parimutuel ticket, but, honestly, they would *still* be better off if they would learn their business! Too, they would have a better chance of staying in television after the charm has curdled or the father-in-law has croaked.

I know one "producer" who was totally without qualification, who was working in a minor job on a show and was thrust into the top spot by the star of the show who had taken a fancy to him. You will hear similar stories, but these remain exceptions, and the end result in the case I know about was sad and humiliating. When the star in question got over his fancy and fired the "producer," the producer got another job because of the first credit, but was soon let go when it was painfully apparent that he had no training or qualification to produce. From there, it was a steady decline for him, swept downward on a current of alcohol, until he was driven out of the business completely.

Earlier, I may have seemed to demean local station production. I do not, in fact, mean to in any way. All over the country there is good work being done by highly capable people. A television aspirant should take work in any local station he can. Here, because job categories are less clearly defined frequently, he will get a wider range of experience and an opportunity to observe every aspect of a broadcast operation.

As I have said, being a producer is the plum job in television production and the one to go for; but, in the early going, do not disdain any other job. It is impossible to get there or to stay there without previous experience in other jobs.

The beginning woman should take particular note. Certainly, I can understand her being wary of the traditional prejudices against women in television, as in other areas of our society, and therefore ready to resist anyone who suggests secretarial duties to her. This view is myopic. There is ample evidence from the past that typing and shorthand have been enslaving skills. However, if a secretarial position will give you a toehold in television or put you in a unique spot to learn, it is a fool's rebellion to reject it categorically. (Besides, today there are no "secretaries," only "assistants.")

At ABC, for example, my assistant has access to a total picture of the workings of network television: programming, sales, contracts, the evolutions of scripts and concepts, budgets, promotion and advertising, operations and engineering, plus a file of phone numbers and addresses to rival Rona Barrett's. Also, she has contact, on a first-name basis frequently, with a hundred professionals who would otherwise be inaccessible. If she is ambitious and does not learn or advance from the advantageous position she holds, the fault, after two years, is her own. If I let her stay or want her to stay against her will longer than two years, you know what I am. Pig or no, however, I am proud to say that former assistants of mine are now variously an associate director, an associate producer, a network programming executive, and a comedy writer. Another got married and Scarsdaled. Only one got trapped as a secretary. She loves it—and works for Arthur Penn.

As to other beginning jobs, I have mentioned my personal example of having broken in as a coffee boy. I also mentioned that I worked as a waiter in a saloon for a time. Not just any saloon, though. This was a show business saloon; otherwise, I would not have been interested.

This particular mug-house was nested in the back room of a neighborhood bar in a since-demolished brownstone at Fifty-Fourth Street and—what New Yorkers will always call it—Sixth Avenue.

This lovable and lamented gin-gym had been bank rolled by Marlon Brando, Wally Cox, Maureen Stapleton, and Judy Holliday. Among the regular patrons were these, plus agents, directors, producers, and other stars such as Richard (pre-Elizabeth) Burton, Jonathan Winters, Kim Stanley, Jason Robards, and playwright Tennessee Williams. I learned a lot in the back room and made a number of friends. Judy Holliday, that intelligent and tender lady, helped me by appearing in the pilot of a radio interview show which I tried to put together to emanate from the saloon. So did Maureen Stapleton. The program never sold, but I played the tapes for the producer of the "Tonight Show" when I was being interviewed for the talent job, and I know it had a part in his decision to hire me.

Other producers have started as network ushers (or pages, as they are called), in the mailroom, as tour guides, or as messengers or chauffeurs. Of course, not all producers begin so illustriously: Several have started as lawyers, accountants, or agents. What must be remembered is that no matter what mundane position comes along, welcome and seize the opportunity, since it will be widely coveted and hard to come by—even for a college graduate.

A few paragraphs earlier, I talked about not staying in a job for longer than two years. That may be extreme. But, in any job, especially the lowly job, the length of stay is a critical consideration. I was a coffee boy for six months. That seemed about right to me. It was long enough to demonstrate that I was reliable. It was long enough to observe fully the television operation around me. It was long enough to meet the people in higher positions. It was too long by five months, three weeks and six days to get to know my job.

How long to stay will vary with each situation, but an aspiring producer should set a timetable. Has he learned the job? Has he learned the job of the person he reports to—or others that he is in a position to observe? Is he being taken for granted in the position and overlooked for advancement? Whatever the honest answers to these questions may be, they are essential to an ability to make intelligent decisions about the length of stay. When one has fixed a timetable, he should stick to it—even if it means leaving the operation or temporarily losing income. People in this business live by their wits, not their pension plans. One gets another job.

Just as emphatically, one should not make the mistake of telling everybody else how to do his job. This is nearly always the mark of a graceless, twitching need to show off. Appreciation will come fast enough if you do your assigned job well. These days, that is a rare gift.

On the other hand, nothing is more flattering to a person, or more helpful to an understanding of how things work, than sincerely inquiring about his job. Find out from coworkers how they got their jobs and what their duties are. Why and how do they make decisions? Query them about their union or trade affiliations. Have them explain technical aspects. To be honestly and decently curious about other people is to make friends and nip enemies—and be remembered. Obviously, the advice is practical; more importantly, it is humane. The whole thing comes down, finally, to people.

Let me give some examples of successful people who follow this advice. When I was a very junior member (a talent coordinator) of the "Jack Paar Tonight Show" staff, I was assigned (a regular part of my job was to interview future guests) to Stanley Kramer. At once, he accorded me equal status and gave full answers to all my questions, knowing it was to his advantage to have Paar well-briefed. That way, both would come off well. (Beware the talk-show guest who says in these preinterviews, "Tell him to ask me anything.") But what impressed me even more about Kramer was his vigorous curiosity about my job! What hours did I work? How many people did I see a week? What access did I actually have to Paar? Who decided which and how guests got booked? Was there network interference with guest selection? What was my salary? How long had I been there? How and where did we find guests? How many people were on the staff? How was the show sold? And so on and so on.

Of course, I was deeply flattered, but I would like to believe, too, that Kramer, a deeply knowing film man, wanted to know a little something about television, and learned.

Garson Kanin and his wife, Ruth Gordon, are also big people with invigorating minds. Their curiosity and kindness extended even to inviting my wife and me to dinner in their home. You can imagine the glowing introduction I wrote and the positive interview I set up for them on the Paar show that night.

Bette Davis was rockier soil. When I arrived at her Plaza Hotel suite for her preinterview, she snapped, "What the hell do you want?"

"Ten million viewers and Jack Paar to like you," I said. "Maybe I can help."

Relenting, she gave a tangy interview and Paar had one of his best shows ever.

While I have warned you about not telling another person how to do his job, never miss the opportunity to do his job for him—to yourself. This internal game of second-guessing will sharpen your appreciation of the problems in that job and hone your decision-making abilities, without your having to endure the consequences of making mistakes. Perform this exercise honestly and seriously:

You are the "go-fer" (a person who goes for things) on a show. Nobody notices you, but you are in an excellent position to observe and second-guess the producer. A problem arises. What would you do? Decide something. Act it out in your head—even to framing your verbal responses. Pretend that it is really up to you to decide what must be done. Then, watch and listen carefully to what the real producer does. As you are able, follow through to observe what the results of his decision are. Was he successful or did his decision compound the problem?

Learn as much as you can about what went into his decision. There may have been factors, unknown to you, that dictated a different decision from the one you arrived at. There is also the possibility that he made an idiotic choice and that yours might just have been the right one, if you differed. Either way, you learn.

Three more essential points: (1) Ask for advice on how things are done, if you're not sure. (2) When you make a mistake, admit it. (3) Never blame someone else for your mistakes. Likewise, never reserve praise if others have shared in your success. Extending these simple, but scorned virtues will accelerate your growth as a person and as a professional.

About beginning jobs: One should try to find one in the area of television in which he is most interested. If one likes news and documentaries, he should try to hook on with one of these kinds of programs, rather than "Rhoda"—and vice versa. Television is pathological about pigeonholing people.

While I have been fortunate (and stubborn) about making crossovers, I know this phenomenon from personal experience. After I was fired by CBS from my job producing and writing the "Merv Griffin Show," I was very eager to avoid another high-pressure entertainment show until my wounds had healed. I decided, in fact, to cauterize the wounds by producing serious documentaries. I had several noble ideas and set out, as callow as Candide, to sell them. Agents and buyers reacted as though I had had a lobotomy.

"But you're a variety producer," one said. "What the hell you wanna do documentaries for?"

Another one said, "Sure, Bob, that's a swell idea. Now what about this talk show offer on the Coast—$2,500 a week, baby?"

"I've done a talk show," I said.

"Right," the agent smiled. "You're the best."

"I'd like you to sell my 'Great American Rivers' series."

"Schmuck—they buy rivers from the BBC."

For five months I persisted in trying to place seven different documentary concepts (still unproduced, still good) and television productions of a Joseph Papp play and of the American Ballet Theatre. Nobody would listen. Still, I was damned if I was going to take another talk or variety show, at least just then. (Unemployment is a fearless buzzard, pecking at the living body of principle, but saving your money when times are good can save your soul when they're bad.)

Finally, because they were trying to fuse show business techniques with a serious informational form, Bill Kobin, then programming vice-president of NET, and Al Perlmutter, the executive producer, hired me to work on the "Great American Dream Machine." The "Dream Machine" was an ambitious melange of everything from hard investigative reports to low-comedy black-outs, and I am proud of the work we did there. (Emmys two years in a row.) It remains one of the few television programs that is not a photographed radio show. Mostly, I am grateful to Kobin and Perlmutter for breaking the traditional rules and letting me out of my assigned caste. One ironic footnote: After "Dream Machine," I was able to sell a documentary series, but I had trouble getting variety entertainment assignments. "Oh, he does documentaries," it was said.

I have described Al Perlmutter as the executive producer. What is an executive producer? The job function varies depending on the circumstances. In Perlmutter's case, executive producer was akin to an editor-in-chief of a newspaper or magazine. He had the ultimate power to assign, edit, approve, reject, or cut stories out of the program. In his case, the job was defined and executed as an active and creative function. He was always there—"on the line" or "in the trenches" as TV folk never tire of saying. This is not always the case with executive producers. At Group W-Westinghouse, on the "Merv Griffin Show," we had an executive producer who played no creative role at all. I say this without fault to the man. He was not supposed to. His job was administrative—to make sure I brought the show in on budget and that Merv and his guests did not say dirty words on the air. He was also good at keeping visiting corporate firemen out of our way and answering high-level complaint mail.

An executive producer may also be the "packager," like Lee Rich of Lorimar Productions ("The Waltons") or Bud Yorkin and Norman Lear of Tandem Productions ("All in the Family," "Sanford and Son," "Maude"). These men are packagers as well as executive producers. Lee Rich does not produce, write, or direct. He is the pure packager. That is, he puts together a "package" of other talented people, under his sales, fiscal, administrative, and aesthetic supervision. I think it is fair to say that Rich, whose programs get high television marks for substance, begins with the perception of television as a business. Yorkin and Lear, on the other hand, are television creators, motivated by the content of their programs; the overwhelming financial success of their company is secondary.

Mostly, then, *executive producer* or *packager* means being one level removed from the working production, and being involved in administrative, managerial, corporate, fiscal, and selling responsibilities. The viewpoint is panoramic and strategic as opposed to close-in and tactical.

Occasionally, the title executive producer is meaningless—as in the case of a bloated star who demands the title; or when it is draped on the unworthy shoulders of a son-in-law who is principally occupied at the golf course. However, do not indict every star thusly. Lucille Ball and Dick Clark are executive producers who make vigorous and active contributions in this role.

Another kind of packager is the major studio or large corporate entity, which organizes and finances productions. Universal Studios is the packager of the "Six Million Dollar Man," among other programs. Warner Brothers packages "Harry O" and the "Streets of San Francisco." Viacom was the packager of the "Missiles of October."

When these big companies package, the "on-the-line" producer is frequently reduced to the role of salaried overseer, for the massa of an M-G-M or Fox or Paramount. Here, too, the layers become artichokian. There is the corporate upper management, then there are the sales vice-president, president or vice-president of production (or both), then there is the programming executive, then the creator or executive producer, and, above all of this, there is a similar hierarchy of network executives. Still, these large companies can play a valuable power role in getting your program on the air. They have more resources up front for developing a project, for assuming financial responsibility during production, and for reaping ancillary benefits beyond the network runs.

As you may have guessed by now, all of these titles resist precise description; they overlap and alter with the realities in various situations. Any and all of these depictions—packager, executive producer, producer—may also be referred to as the supplier.

In the case of small independents, the supplier, packager, executive producer, and producer may all be one person, as in the example of Dan Curtis when he was making "Dark Shadows," the Gothic soap opera. This, of course, is usually necessary in the early days of a company and saves a lot of overhead. Care must be taken, however, about holding onto every function too long, because the company will not grow beyond a certain point if you do. Once a program is successfully launched, an executive producer must let go of the daily responsibilities (and some of the profits) so that he will be free to develop and sell subsequent programming.

Not everything, of course, has been said about the producer in this chapter about the producer; moreover, everything to come in subsequent chapters is the producer's concern and will define more clearly who the producer must be and what he must know.

Chapter **2**
the staff: princes and attendant players

In television, the staff is essential. The jobs vary from the princely ones of director and writer to the lesser nobility of scenic and costume designers, musical director, choreographer, and lighting director, to the still lesser, but no less essential, work of associate producer, associate director, production supervisor, talent coordinator or casting person, production assistant, continuity person, assistant to, secretary, and, our old friend, the go-fer; nor does it end there.

An examination of the various work functions brings us to the line—most frequently called above-the-line and below-the-line. I do not know the derivation of these terms, but I can explain their working and practical definitions. Roughly, in the category above-the-line will be found those jobs and services which are creative. The people in this group, are usually called the staff. Below-the-line takes in those tasks and services that are mechanical or relate to hardware. People working below-the-line are referred to as the crew. You will get some arguments about these definitions, not the least of them from me. I know some people above-the-line who are as uncreative as a speech by Miss America, and crew members below-the-line who are poets in their crafts. No matter; the definitions are workable, as people in television use them.

THE DIRECTOR

The director should know everything the producer knows, plus a great deal more about "visual language" and technical equipment. Of course, the director will be less concerned with, though not unmindful of, administration and money. But his main responsibility will be creating the final look and sound of the program.

The director is responsible for shooting the show; that is, for planning and selecting the visual images that build one on another. He should, more than most do in fact, pay equally close attention to the sound of his program. It is the director's job to convey, through sight and sound selections, the meaning and tone of the material that comes before his cameras. His ability to master movement, composition, light, space, and to select angle, and to emphasize facial expression, body gesture, word, music, object, and locale will enhance or leave flat or destroy each fragile moment in the flow of time that is the nature of television. In sculpture, painting, the written word—there is a fixity of the perceived image and it is the perceiver who moves. In television (as in film, music, and dance), the perceiver, or viewer, tends to be static and the image is in motion.

The single word *director* covers, imprecisely, an anthology of assignments and forms which require varying aptitudes and talents. Just as everyone calling himself a writer cannot turn out *Hamlet,* so not every director is equal to every television task, or is asked to be. Television directorial assignments vary from the sublime to the ordinary. The sensitivity required of the directors of "The Glass Menagerie" (Anthony Harvey) or, in variety entertainment, the "Cher Show" (Art Fisher), are unnecessary and usually absent in the director of a local news program or panel discussion show.

Most often, the directors of the more mundane types of television programming never grow beyond their limited challenges and are not asked to. Most directors remain little more than foreman mechanics.

On the other hand, everything on television can be enhanced by a talented and imaginative director. Sports might seem a straightforward area, beyond a director's ability to improve. Not true. Sports directors, of course, do not get performances out of the people in their pictures, nor do they choose the settings. Still, the ABC directors who worked the Olympic Games in Munich elevated sports coverage to enlightening and aesthetic heights seldom realized by their entertainment counterparts. The rigors of this competition and the struggles for victory among the participants were made personal and vivid, and the home viewer's understanding was intensified while his emotions were deeply stirred. This applies to other sporting and live events. The utilization of close-ups, isolated cameras, instant replay, and slow motion by television is forcing major arenas to offer such techniques on closed-circuit systems and screens to spectators who are paying to watch the action in person.

Television programs are recorded in two basic techniques: film and videotape. While these disciplines overlap, there are significant differences in the techniques. Directors who are good in one can be bumbling incompetents in the other. Usually, it is harder to make the adjustment from film to tape—because of the multiple-camera technique in tape and the pressure of cutting a scene or show in real time in the pressure-cooker atmosphere of a control room.

As a general statement, I think it is fair to say, however, that those directors working in film television are out in front of their colleagues in tape on visual sophistication—or, if you will, artistry.

There are a number of reasons. First, the mechanical ones: Light passing through the body of the film stock creates distance in the projected image. What we get on film is not reality exactly reproduced, but an impression of reality. Aesthetic distance. For some reason, at least to my taste, this is more beautiful than the colder, more precise reproduction of reality captured by the electronic process. Simply, tape is more real, and, therefore, harder to manipulate or control to achieve beauty, mood, or distance. For instance, if you are in a studio shooting a scene against a set, the seams are more likely to show in tape than film. Another factor is color. Electronic color is more garish. Film paints more subtly. Other mechanical differences also persist. In studio situations, electronic television equipment requires massive air conditioning to prevent machine malfunction and to slake the heat of the extra lighting that electronic cameras need. This frequently creates a room tone that is loud and, even if it is only subconsciously perceived, distracting. As I have implied, tape demands more foot-candles of lighting than film does which impairs the mood of many programs. Also, since the lighting must work for many cameras in an electronic setup, instead of for one, as in most film setups, tape lighting is more generalized, flatter, and therefore less aesthetic. This creates an additional problem, especially for dramas or high-styled variety programs: With general lighting and multiple cameras, the microphone in tape—unless it is blatantly in the shot as it can be on talk shows or newscasts—has to work from farther away and with less freedom of movement than in film making. Thus, you get a "barrel" effect in electronic television sound.

Sometimes, of course, the fierce reality of tape or the electronic camera beats film for beauty and enjoyment, for instance, in the coverage of real events—space shots, sporting events, presidential inaugurals—or in those planned programs that are supposed to be happening as you see them—talk shows or game shows (all prerecorded). In these, film's distance becomes a disadvantage and the impression that what you are seeing is happening as you see it is lost.

There are studies which indicate audiences do not perceive any difference between film and tape. I question these data because they try to objectify what is subjective in perception. Of course, if you ask, "Is that film or tape?" not many will know for sure and most will not care; but people would know if the shows seemed more or less real, confined or cheap. I doubt that such responses as these are provoked or measured in the tests.

Film technology is sixty years old. Electronic cameras are twenty-five and their recording support system, tape, is a youngster of fifteen. Film equipment, always less cumbersome, has over the years been additionally refined and also made highly portable. Electronic equipment has, thus far, been bulky and more delicate to maintain, especially on location.

Editing and lighting techniques are also long-established in film and the craftsmen here have absorbed the mechanics of their medium and are more focused on artistic application of those skills. Electronic craftsmen in these same areas are for the most part a first generation who have come from the old country of engineering and have little feel for aesthetics. Some exhibit bad habits, instilled by the limitations of their equipment. Some may go through a whole program looking at oscilloscopes instead of at pictures.

Generally, film directors have more time and more control over their work than do their tape counterparts. In film, usually, there is only one camera, which is repeatedly reset for master, medium, close-up, reverse, or reaction shots. In tape, the director is working with multiple-camera coverage, so that he is required to see all of these various shots at the same time and edit his show as he shoots. This inhibits his blocking, his lighting, his camera movement and it rushes his editorial decisions. The process fragments his concentration.

Of course, multiple-camera setups get the edge when it comes to capturing the spontaneity of an event or the single, unrepeatable moment. There are times when film cameras are used in a multiple setup, but since each camera requires its own film stock, as opposed to electronic cameras which can all be fed onto one tape, this is a costly procedure. It is used primarily when it is impossible to retake a scene —such as in blowing up a bridge or burning a building—or in covering a live event such as "Woodstock."

Cost, as usual, is a determining factor. Multiple-electronic-camera coverage shoots a show faster and the tape is instantly replayable, as opposed to the slower and more costly film process of a single camera setup requiring more quantitative lighting setups and lab development of the stock. When shows have low budgets and quick, frequent airing—game shows, talk shows, soap operas, newscasts—tape is cheaper and more efficient. An exception, mostly because flexibility is required, is the use of 16mm film for location news and documentaries; here, aesthetics has a low priority.

I know all of this can and will change. Even in location news coverage, for instance, WABC-TV, WCBS-TV, and WNBC-TV in New York are now using the new lightweight, hand-held electronic cameras. KMOX-TV in St. Louis was the first to make the total transition from newsfilm to newselectronic. This will spread to all forms, since the electronic equipment is becoming more compact, flexible, and sturdy. And now, less obvious lighting is necessary for the new cameras to get an acceptable image. This will increase the use of electronic cameras for drama as well.

Along with the equipment refinements, a new generation of tape directors is emerging, directors who are more interested in aesthetics than in engineering. The same may be said for upcoming tape editors who also have new editing technology available to them. Electronic and tape technology will, in fact, eventually dominate, even aesthetically.

If directing is your goal, you should learn, of course, both film and tape techniques. New York and Los Angeles are best for film technology. It is more difficult to find formal training in electronic directing, since the equipment is so cumbersome and expensive. The places best equipped are the large state-owned universities.

Directing is a satisfying and creative occupation only if the show is challenging. Some of the best moments I have known have been in directing variety specials. On the other hand, I had no desire to direct the "Tonight Show" or the "Merv Griffin Show." The action in these formats comes with being the producer or writer. The directorial chore is as routine as that of the local news—even the network news. Imagine the boredom of directing the "Today Show"—and getting up at 4:00 A.M. to do it! But with a live event—a rock concert or a sports event or a musical show or drama—directing becomes the epicenter. This is especially true if the technique is electronic, and still more so if the show is airing live and one time only.

The director's specific duties will vary somewhat from show to show, depending on the content and circumstances of the shooting and upon his personality, and that of his star and producer. In film, the director works alongside or behind his camera. In electronic directing, he is in the control room, or control booth, whether in a studio or on location. In the control room, the director is seated at a long table, usually called a "console," flanked by associates whom we will come to. He faces a wall of television screens. Two large screens, centered toward the top of the wall, will be marked: on the left, "Preview"; on the right, "Program," or "Line." This latter "monitor," as television sets are called in our business, shows what is being sent out live or is being recorded on the tape. The line, or program, image is the shot the director is taking at the moment. On the preview monitor, the director will see the shot that he plans to take next. The juxtaposition of these two shots gives the director the opportunity to see side-by-side the cut or dissolve of the images he is connecting. If the program is in color, as they usually are these days, these two monitors will be color monitors.

Below these two large color monitors will be a row of smaller black and white monitors. These will be labeled, from left to right, "1," "2," "3," "4," "5," or "Film," "Slide," "On Air," or "Remote 1," "2," "3," and so on. On these monitors will be the images and angles being shot simultaneously by the various cameras.

"Film" is the monitor showing the director the images on film or tape inserts that have been previously recorded and that are to be "rolled in" to the show he is making. For instance, if on cameras 1, 2, and 3 the director is shooting an actor indoors in his living room and the next scene calls for that actor to be outdoors driving a car, chances are that the outdoor driving shot has already been recorded on film or tape; thus, the director would, for the living room scene, intercut cameras 1, 2, and 3, and then would call for the film monitor feed of the driving scene.

The "slide" monitor shows the director whatever slide or title card material he will be adding to his show. These may be superslides, that is, material to be superimposed over the output of the live cameras—perhaps the show's title or a guest's name—or these may be opaques—slides in which the content replaces the live camera pictures completely, as in the title slide.

The "remote" monitor is a feed which shows the director images from a camera positioned at a remote location. For instance, on New Year's Eve, Guy Lombardo is televised live from the Waldorf-Astoria Hotel Ballroom. This is the principle location for this program and the site for the location control room. During the course of the Lombardo show, the scene switches frequently to a camera that is located in Times Square, many blocks away from the Waldorf. In this case, on cameras 1, 2, 3, etc., the director will be getting the scenes in the ballroom. On his remote monitor, he will see the camera output from Times Square.

The "on air" monitor shows whatever the network or local station is putting out to home receivers at that moment. This monitor takes on importance when a show is live and the director needs to see the program feed preceding or intercutting with his, as he leaves for commercials and station breaks, or as he is coming back from them. (The on air monitor is also important when your own program, to be shown later, is hopelessly dull and you are desperate to watch something else.)

On top of each of these black and white monitors (on-air excepted) is a small red light which goes on when the director is taking that feed. In other words, if the director is taking camera 1, the little red light above the camera 1 monitor will light. When he goes to camera 3, the camera 3 monitor red light will come on and camera 1's will go out. If the director is supering the pictures of cameras 1 and 3, both monitor red lights will be on. These are called tally lights. Similar lights are on the cameras themselves so that the cameramen and performers (and nowadays, on-site spectators) know which camera is being taken.

The control room situation, with the feed of as many as nine different images all happening at once, requires a cool and confident personality to command it. Most of the good tape directors I know are high-energy, slightly neurotic individuals with very fast synapses and a Western Union vocabulary. They are the fighter pilot personalities of the television business.

I spoke earlier of the greater difficulty in making the transition from film to tape. Perhaps by now you can understand why. The tape director is bombarded by multiple images and has to make instant decisions as to which single image he will shoot. Many directors collapse or fail in this situation. Many good blocking (arranging actors and scenes) directors or directors who are good with actors will wisely share the electronic directorial chores with an experienced control room director. This happens frequently with comedies. For instance, directors Carl Reiner and Howard Morris, both excellent at inventing comedy ideas and staging, will call in an electronic director more used to the frenzy of a control room to cut, or "call," the actual taping.

Many times I have seen directors freeze in a control room. They will see only their preview or their program feed and forget their other pictures. Too often, directors simply cannot utilize all of the images available to them, and they will end up cutting the bulk of their show on only two cameras. The tape director must be able to see the output of these various monitors all at once. It is an excitement equal to *jai alai* to watch a really superb tape director—Marty Pasetta, Andy Sidaris, John Moffitt, Clark Jones—calling a live show with five cameras, film, slide, and remote feeds.

In a studio setup, the director can talk to the floor (the studio) on what is called the SA,—studio announce. He does this by activating a switch on the panel in front of him. Most control rooms are "blind," affording no direct vision of the studio or the stage from the control room. The director's only view is through his cameras and what his cameramen show him in their shots.

Since cameramen from show to show are hardly ever the same,

it is a good idea to tape up small cardboards with their first names just below the monitors for each of their cameras.

The electronic director talks to his cameramen over the PL—private line. This is a headset intercom system which allows two-way conversations between the director and the cameramen. All are interconnected so that each cameraman can hear what the director says to any one cameraman and vice versa. The director tells the cameramen the kinds of shots he wants, but the man who cuts those shots into the show sits next to the director in the control room; he is called the technical director. (Since the technical director, or TD, is below-the-line, I will discuss his job duties later.)

As I have said, a working television control room appears to be as frenzied as a Tokyo rush hour. When, however, the people involved are pros, the frenzy is more apparent than real. What seems a jumble of talk is actually controlled and coherent. The physical setup of a control room varies, but the principal players are always the same.

In the center, the director. Seated next to him, either left or right, is the technical director. Flanking the director on the other side is the associate director, AD. Next to the AD sits the production assistant, PA. Sitting next to the TD is the lighting director, LD. Sometimes, depending on the size and layout of the room, the LD sits on an elevated second tier behind the director. The LD has a separate PL so that he can communicate with the man at the lighting board who is actually making the board changes that the LD calls for. This lighting board person is in another location.

Next door to the control room is the audio room. Here sits the audio man. There is usually a double-glass window between them. The reason for the separation is obvious: The audio man must hear the sound of the program loud and clear, and the director must hear it muted on a speaker, the volume of which he can control), otherwise, he could not hear himself, his cameramen, AD, and TD. Despite the separation, the audio man should be considered part of the control room team. In a location-van control room, the principle of separating the audio man is maintained, but he is usually located just behind the control room, instead of adjacent to it; and, again, from his glass cubicle he has visual contact with the director.

These are the key control room people. The physical setup may vary, but the players are always the same. Of course, the producer, if he so desires, may also work from the control room. There may be a network supervisor as well and, inevitably, one person whom nobody knows and everybody assumes is there with someone else.

In the second-row tier, seated next to the LD, might also be, if one is being used, the iso director. Normally, the feeds of all cameras are being cut and then recorded on one videotape. (Actually, two tapes, since all programs are simultaneously recorded on two master videotapes as a precaution against damage or injury to one or the other. The recorded material is exactly the same on both of these videotapes.) In recent years, especially for live events, at which retakes are difficult or impossible to get, directors have come to rely heavily on iso reels, which require iso directors. Mechanically, an iso setup simply means that the output of more than one camera can be recorded at the same time. This is effected by having a third tape machine which records a separate, or isolated, series of pictures, thus *iso*. This is sometimes referred to as a slave machine. Isoing gives the director, later in editing, or postproduction as it is called in electronic television, the opportunity to make finer or smoother cuts in his show. It gives him a choice of shots; it also gives him an out in case his primary shot did not work. Isoing has become an especially popular and important part of sports coverage on television. While the director of a sports event is covering the main action, an iso director may be focusing on some specific star or detail, which is to be played back after the principal action is completed in what is called an instant replay. This may be further refined by using the slo-mo or freeze frame disc, which can create slow motion or suspended action frames.

Let us analyze an example of isoing with which I am very familiar: the ABC taping of "California Jam" for its late-night series, "In Concert." As a part of my responsibilities as vice-president, Late Night Programs, ABC Entertainment, I was in charge of that event. As it turned out, I was also the iso director.

"California Jam" was a huge enterprise with two hundred thousand rock fans on hand to hear eight groups—Rare Earth; Earth, Wind & Fire; Eagles; Seals & Crofts; Black Oak Arkansas; Black Sabbath; Deep Purple and Emerson; Lake & Palmer—play for over thirteen hours at the Ontario Motor Speedway, a facility located about forty miles east of Los Angeles. Covering such a visual spectacle—we also had sky divers, aerial balloons, and the Good Year blimp—was an immense directorial challenge for young Joshua White, an experienced "In Concert" director and veteran of "Woodstock."

An iso setup was clearly called for, if Josh hoped to capture the bands playing on stage as well as the simultaneous show that was going on in the crowd. In fact, the event was so large that we had ordered a second-unit tape setup that was completely independent of the control room. This second unit roamed the grounds of the Speedway, totally self-contained on a jeep—with its own director, camera, cameraman, and tape machine. This second unit went out early in the morning and we did not see it again until the end of the day. Iso, however, is not independent of the show's director. It works off the same equipment and records the same material that is being shot for the primary cut of the program.

For "California Jam," we, of course, worked in a mobile van, so that the control room was very cramped. Left to right in the front row (no room even for a PA) sat Eileen Carhart, the associate director; then the director, Josh White, in the middle; and on his right, Gerri Bucci, the TD. On a second tier behind these three were Vaughn Gaddey, the lighting director, and myself.

For this iso setup, an additional bank of tally lights had been added to the monitors across the bottom, so that everyone could know instantly which camera was being recorded on line, or program, by the tally light on top and which camera output was being recorded on iso, as indicated by the bottom tally light. When you are isoing, the iso shot appears on the preview color monitor and/or on its own small black and white monitor. The iso director's fundamental assignment is simply to call for the second best shot available.

The iso director is assigned a second TD, who is situated in another part of the van. Both, however, are on the director's PL, which requires the iso director to use the word *iso* for his every camera direction, so as not to be confused with the director's instructions. The director is the ultimate commander and may supercede the iso director's instructions. If the director takes over the iso commands—"Give me iso 2. Iso 3, etc."—the iso director must stay out of it until the director says, "Isos released" or "Release iso." So must the iso TD. The primary TD has now taken over iso. Furthermore, the iso director is never supposed to give camera directions or instructions to the cameramen. He can never call for reframing, zooms, pans, tilts, cranes-up or down. This remains the director's sole perogative.

Here's how it worked. Josh has Black Sabbath on stage, for instance; Ozzie Osborne is singing. Josh, in his cool, low-key manner, is calling his cameras to the shots and compositions and moves he wants, then giving his cuts. "Take 1—2 go in close on the lead guitar strings. 4—start tight over the drummer's shoulder on his hands—pull back, widen, crane-up for a cover shot of the stage and crowd. 3—hold Osborne. Start your move, 4. Take 4." (He, of course, called cameramen by name.)

As Josh is scanning the four black and white monitors and making his picture selections, so am I as the iso director. When he says, "Take 1," I look at monitors 2, 3, and 4 (plus the camera feed from the Good Year blimp), make my choice as to the best of these shots, and then I say, "Iso 3," or whatever it may be. In this case, Josh has cut into his master recording, identical on two videotapes, the picture on camera 1. I have cut in, on a completely different videotape, the output of camera 3. Two views of the same moment in time. Later, when Josh was editing, he had the choice of these two separate images.

The iso director, especially in a show such as "California Jam," has the added responsibility of looking hard for ambience or atmosphere or color shots, as they are called. These are peripheral moments away from the stage. For instance, during the taping of Seals and Crofts, while Josh was concentrating on their performance, he freed one camera for me to use to scan the audience. I spotted a girl in the crowd who was performing an intricate, delicate, nonstop, and spaced-out modern ballet. I isoed on her for virtually one whole song. Repeatedly, throughout the thirteen hours of "California Jam," I isoed on unusual or colorful little slices of life which were taking place in the audience.

For the performance, if I were isoing on camera 2, say, and Josh cut to 2, I would instantly have to go to another camera. It defeats the whole idea of isoing if the main reel and the iso reel both contain the same shot.

What an iso director must never do is cut the show, that is, call the shots. That job is the director's. Iso is second, and must serve that way. In a musical show, this means that the iso director should never cut on the beat of the music. The director will be doing that. If he misses, and the iso misses, too, he will have nothing later in postproduction to cut away to.

There is much to learn about being a good director. On the other hand, there is much that is either in you or not, an inherent talent. A director's sense of visual rhythm or pacing is best when it is part of his personality. Still, a lot can be acquired through training and experience. A knowledge of music (if you play an instrument or dance, so much the better) and a thorough study of great directors' work are helpful in improving directorial skills. A study of Alfred Hitchcock, for instance, will reveal that while almost nothing may be happening in a scene, he heightens suspense and mood simply by lighting—a human shadow thrown against a wall; or by sound—a creaking door, a hollow wind; or with music—or all in combination. In the *Psycho* shower murder scene, he achieves astonishing tension by cutting. There must be at least forty-seven cuts in this twenty-second scene.

Some basic techniques can be learned. The first I think—for television—is: Maximize close-ups. Television's frame is small compared to the stage or movie screen, so that the close-up becomes its quintessential visual tool. Of course, if you shoot an entire show in close-up, you will make a monotonous program and sacrifice the audience's sense of locale. Jack Webb created stunning visual impressions with his early television serial, "Dragnet," by a novel use of close-ups. The traditional movie formula for shooting and cutting a sequence has been first, a wide or establishing shot, then medium close-up, then close-up. Webb altered this formula to read: wide-shot, extreme close-up. The idea was revolutionary and the effect compelling.

Television's relatively small canvas works best for that which is intimate and worst for spectacle or panorama. I think in dance, for instance, television succeeds admirably with a single performer such as Fred Astaire, but it cannot touch the stage or large-screen movies for big production numbers. On film or stage, nothing escapes the viewer's forward and peripheral vision. In television, the figures in a production number are reduced to dots and all detail is lost. For me, the result is cold and unsatisfying. In shooting ballet for television, I have probably offended purists but, I think, enriched the experience of dance on television, by using the close-up frequently—for feet and faces—and by superimposing close-ups on wide shots of the dancing of the *corps de ballet.* When ballet is shot wide and straight-on, as on the stage, it is a complete loss on television. I also prefer television ballet which is shot on actual location rather than on stage. Given our conditioning to theatrical conventions, the senses will tolerate canvas scenery and bare spaces in stage presentations and call them castles or magic forests; seen in the glaring detail of television, these artifices look cruelly phony and banal. There is no possible emotional involvement or suspension of judgment. Television is too real.

A second technique: Fill your frame. It is impossible here to go into great detail about composition, but nothing is more boring visually than what we call a loose, or an empty, frame. (There are exceptions, of course. An entirely empty frame in black with one small figure in the lower corner in a pool of light can be very effective.) A medium close-up, straight-on, of a guitarist's hands and showing the guitar, with space around—maybe even a bored stagehand in the background—is flat and uninteresting. If you change the angle to run more acutely from the side or under or above, and tighten in so that one hand and sharp detail of the guitar jam the frame, you have a much more energetic shot. The same is true for faces. A head and shoulders medium shot never has the force of an extreme facial close-up. Of course, you must judge the mood of your content. An extreme facial close-up or series of them may be too exciting for what you want to say. These can also distort or be cruel.

Camera movement is essential to good direction. Static cameras are the gravest sin of all. Movement can be achieved in a number of ways. Say you have Sammy Davis singing. If you were there watching him in person, you would be viewing him from one angle and one shot, so to speak—from wherever you were sitting—though your eye would be in motion, going in and out for detail. If you held this one view of Davis on television, the results would visually nullify him as a performer. By trucking the camera (moving the base of it), panning, zooming in and out, cutting from one camera to another, supering shots, you can invigorate the visual impact and serve the spirit of Davis's energy. There are additional techniques: Angle is a powerful tool. Extremes of angle when overused may be annoying and amateurish. But acute angles can make impressive visual statements.

Detail: I search for it always. For instance, the bell of a trumpet or trombone, with light kicking off of it, if it fills the frame and I am on it out of focus and then slowly come into focus, can provide a marvelous abstract and surprise.

Speaking of detail, in a documentary I directed about the life of Theodore Roosevelt, I had the narrator, E. G. Marshall, walking slowly across the porch at Sagamore Hill where Teddy had accepted his party's nomination for president. As we panned with him, behind Marshall in the shot were the porch railing and trees. Marshall eventually ended by sitting on the railing at a point where he was backed by beautiful shrubs and flowers. It was an okay shot. But, then, my cameraman, Ted Churchill, saw the late afternoon sunlight fragmenting through the railing slats onto the porch floor, creating a strongly contrasting light and shadow geometric pattern. He suggested framing on this pattern, allowing Marshall's walking body shadow to come in and go through the frame, as he spoke the voice-over, then panning up to discover Marshall already seated against the flowers. It was a splendid way of seeing. "Good eye," I said, the ultimate compliment. The shot had aesthetic beauty and surprise. It evoked the romance and spirit of time past. It even suggested that the walking shadow might be Teddy Roosevelt himself. It had a firm and unexpected ending in the pan up to Marshall. Churchill had taken my okay shot and turned it into an emotional visualization.

Foreground: Wide or medium shots can be enriched by paying attention to something in the foreground. Foreground objects can also add depth perspective to a frame. If an actor is seated at a table and I am framing medium or wide, it will probably enhance the shot to include a piece of a wine or water glass or a bowl of flowers in recognizable, soft focus, in the foreground. If you are looking up to someone in a window and your next shot is that person's view of the scene below, it will strengthen your second shot if you include a piece of the window frame or a curtain gently blowing in the foreground.

This technique, of course, can become a cliché or confusing if you constantly have a leaf or branch or glass in the foreground—especially if it cannot be identified. But mostly, strong foreground pieces will add depth and vigor to the frame.

In a shot in which two people are talking to each other and where there is cutting back and forth between reverse shot close-ups of them, I try to include a piece of the shoulder or head of the one with his back to the camera. This will intensify the scene and relate the two figures more closely to each other. (A reverse shot is one that is a 180° angle difference from the preceding shot.) The usual method, which is more distant, is to isolate each individual face in close-up, back and forth, with total exclusion of the other person. Of course, shooting a scene this latter way may be what you want—to convey an emotional truth in the scene. As you surely realize by now, every rule has its opposite, if you know what you are doing.

Camera position: Particularly in a multicamera setup, it is extremely important where you place your cameras. You must arrange them to cover the basic needs of the whole scene, but place them in such a way that they will not end up in each other's shots. I see the simplest but most aggravating mistakes made in camera positioning. Three cameras side-by-side, for instance, or a recent example: The director was taping a dais setup for a celebrity comedy salute program. He had the stage area covered well. But, and he knew this ahead of time, he had no camera that could shoot the audience, where a lot of other celebrities would be seated, many of whom would be referred to during the program. When they were mentioned, the director distracted himself and his cameramen in their last-minute rushes to try to get these shots—almost always missing them—or getting there too late for the spontaneous reactions. Then, in the time it took to get the cameras aimed back at the stage area, moments there were missed. Also, he failed to light the audience sufficiently so that when he did get a shot there, the faces were in semidarkness.

Trying to keep tape cameras out of each other's shots tends to make tape shows, dramas especially, more static than film shows. That is why on "In Concert," where energy of shooting is more important than formality, I freed our directors to include cameras in the shots of other cameras. Even in tape drama, however, this added challenge need not hinder good coverage. You can get a reverse shot by hiding one camera in a shadowy spot of the scenery or by making it a part of a painting or a window. Advance, coordinated planning with your scenic designer can be most effective here. With film technique, of course, reverse shots are never a problem since you change setups for each angle.

For film, continuity problems become major: Was the actor's

hand up or down when you cut the last shot? What plane of angle was his head in? Did the actress have the drink, cigarette, etc., in her hand, or was it on the table—and if in her hand, which hand? When the actor turned around, did he turn left or right? When the couple walked out of the frame, did they leave frame left or right? This cut and reset technique in film requires a keenly observant person—usually called the script girl or continuity person—to watch for these details as well as for changes in dialogue and to keep the director so informed. I have seen these incongruities cut together by film editors in their spare time, just for fun. The results are funny—if they are not by accident in your film.

Camera left and camera right stand for left and right direction from the point of view behind the camera, facing the object being photographed. The language is used for both electronic and film cameras. Stage left and stage right are left and right direction from the point of view of the object being photographed and facing the camera. Thus, camera left is the same position as stage right and camera right is the same position as stage left. Stage left and stage right are also used as precise terms for both electronic and film cameras. Upstage describes areas away from the camera; downstage describes areas near the camera.

Camera left and camera right, though logical, tend to confound even seasoned pros who forget about it or get confused by it when they are shooting a film. Jerry Lewis, for instance, marks the back of his camera with green tape on the left and red tape on the right; thus, it becomes camera green and camera red, rather than left and right. He finds this easier to comprehend and remember. Why is it important?

Film is like a contiguous series of panels of cartoons, each frame a new panel:

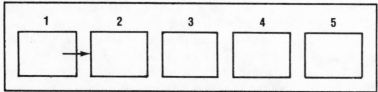

If a person walks out of the first frame right, as indicated by the arrow, how logically should he enter frame two—left or right? The correct answer is left. This is called camera direction. If a car leaves frame right, in the next frame the car must enter left to give the viewer the sense that the car is continuing in the same direction. Otherwise, the effect is that the car has miraculously turned on itself and is now headed in the opposite direction.

Seeing the frame—the whole frame: I am always astonished by

experienced directors who do not see the whole frame. Recently, I was watching a director get ready to shoot a large, outdoor musical number that he had spent over an hour blocking and rehearsing. I felt sure, all through rehearsal, that he had seen in the background what I was seeing and assumed that he would deal with it when he was ready for a take. But now, he was in the control room, ready to tape, and there in his frame—I stopped him. The scene involved twenty or so children in folk costumes and several of them had left their modern coats draped over a retaining wall that was prominent in the shot. The coats were very apparent and distracting, but the director had been so intent on the action of his scene that he had been made completely blind to them.

This happens frequently. I have been guilty of it myself many times. Once I started shooting a scene in Thomas Jefferson's dining room in Monticello—and there, vividly in my shot, totally out of place, stood an aluminum step ladder left by one of the gaffers who had been using it to set lights.

Coats, scripts, coffee cups, cigar butts in ashtrays, microphone boom shadows, crew shadows, shadows of cue cards turning, a yawning stagehand, copulating dogs—these visual gremlins are always turning up where they absolutely do not belong. Or how about the self-winding wrist watch on a cowboy star—or worse, on the Indian chief in a nineteenth-century Western? Or tire tracks or jet trails in a medieval knight's story? Or, as I actually saw once, an immense vaccination scar on the arm of Helen of Troy as she reached up to embrace her lover, Paris.

Watch the frame! Look at it first for the central subject or action, but then train your eye to be vigilant for any wayward foreigner—a cable, a car seen through the window of a scene in *Moby Dick,* a beer can in the Garden of Eden. For myself, I start on the central object of the frame, then take my eyes in a continuing series of circular scans around the entire frame—every frame. With electronic setups, remember you can see the images all at once. In film, only the camera operator is seeing the frame as he looks through the lens or view finder. If you are directing film, never be shy or lazy about looking through the lens before you begin shooting. Also, I check the final frame when I have yelled "Cut."

Cutting: As a basic technique for getting from one shot to another, use the cut. A cut is simply a quick change from one point of view to another without overlap. It is the one you should use most often, in tape and in film. For film, of course, the cut is a step in postproduction or editing; it is only in the electronic technique that you can build your shots as you go. But you can save yourself time and problems in film if you will preplan how you want to handle sequences when you get to postproduction. A simple tip in controlled, stop situations (in tape also): Always let your shot run a few seconds before you call for "Action" and always let the camera keep rolling for a few seconds after the action has stopped before you call "Cut." This will give you room for dissolves if you decide later to use them.

Dissolve is another technique for going from shot to shot. In a dissolve, the image of the shot you are on mingles with the image of the shot you are coming to. The two shots overlap. Dissolves are good for showing the passage of time, or a complete change of scene; for going in and out of flash backs; or for evoking a romantic mood, such as their use in slow love songs, or in slow motion montages of lovers.

Other ways to change shots are through the use of a pan, a tilt, or a natural wipe. A pan is a lateral or horizontal movement of the camera. A tilt is the vertical movement. You could pan off a performer onto a detail of scenery or tilt up to the sky or down to the grass, for instance, and these could be matched in the incoming shots. Even here, one must at last either cut or dissolve. A natural wipe is the technique of blocking out the content of the frame with some natural object. A star, for instance, could be walking along in the clear, when, suddenly, a wall comes into the frame between the star and the camera, and thus wipes the star from the frame. Or say that the star is facing the camera and a bus comes along between him and the camera. This, too, would wipe him from the frame. This bus wipe is a favorite of directors who want to show you that they are in London. There it is, the old red double-decker moving between camera and star. There are, as opposed to natural wipes, optical wipes in film and board wipes in electronic shooting. The optical wipe is made by effects achieved in a laboratory or animation house, one frame at a time, which cause the star or central object to be wiped from the frame. These can have geometric configuration and/or color or abstract designs. Board wipes are made electronically and can be inserted as the show is being recorded. They, too, can be vertical or horizontal in geometric shapes and colors and abstractions. The board is the control board where the wipe buttons are located. More on the mechanics of this later.

Another way to change shots—and it has enormous finality to it —is the fade to black or the fade up from black. This technique is nearly always used only to show the definite beginning or ending of a scene. It is also called fade in and fade out.

Finally, as a discipline, you must learn to check your work. In a taped situation, especially in dramas, I play the scene back instantly to check it. If I find flaws or performances I am not happy with, I can reshoot the scene immediately. In film, there is nothing to do visually until I see the dailies, or the rushes. But I make certain that I do. These are my best opportunities to see if I am getting the coverage I need, or if there are mistakes I need to correct, or crew or casting changes that I have to make. Dailies, or rushes, are the developed and printed film of each day's shooting. Rushes because they are rushed out of the lab in a one-light print (more on this later); dailies because they are printed and you look at them daily. (An old film joke: The Pharoah says of the baby Moses, "Madame, that is the ugliest baby I have ever seen." Moses's mother replies, "Gee, I can't understand it—he looked great in the rushes.")

As for checking audio, in tape, I am able to hear it as I view the tape, since the sound is recorded simultaneously with the video. In film, where sound is recorded on a separate quarter-inch machine, I always check the sound man to see if he is happy with a take. If he has any reservations at all, I stop and listen to the sound take myself. I did not do this once, to my regret. I was shooting a complicated documentary scene, involving six generations and seventy-five members of one family. I did have enough control over the situation to ask for a retake, if I had thought one was necessary. I asked the sound man after the initial take if it was okay with him. He hesitated and said, "Well, it's okay. A little wind." I went ahead. When I got the film and sound back to New York and listened—*a little wind!* It sounded more like a hurricane—and much of the take was totally unusable.

I always assure my sound man that he has an absolute right to stop a take if he is not happy with what he is hearing. Otherwise, he is cheating me and himself and everybody is wasting time. On their own, sound men sometimes feel inferior next to the director and the cameraman, and many will be reluctant to interfere unless they have absolute confidence that that is the director's wish. Cameramen get so intent on picture that they seldom think of sound problems. I make sure that the sound man knows I welcome his stepping in. If it is a new sound man I am working with, I take the time to listen to a few of his takes even if he assures me that they are all right.

Techniques and disciplines: When you have mastered them and have learned the logic behind them, do not be afraid to break them. As a case in point, I remember not too many years ago, technicians were telling me I could not aim electronic cameras into lights. The image of the light would burn into the camera's tube and ruin it, they said. I did not believe it. On several occasions I had seen the cameras accidentally shoot into the lights. When they had, I saw that the effect was beautiful and that Columbus's ships did not fall off the edge of the earth. Finally, after failing at persuasion, I ordered the cameramen, taking full responsibility upon myself, to shoot into the lights during a musical number. Blasphemy! But fantastic and beautiful. And by now, alas, a cliché.

THE WRITER

The writer is a special angel or in league with the devil, depending on your view. The writer is prophet or colicky infant. But either way, the writer is to be indulged, spoiled, cultivated—especially if he is a comedy writer, since there are never more than fifty good ones on earth at any one time. Everything begins with words on a page. Good scripts make good shows. Max Gordon, the famous Broadway producer, was listening one day as his staff rhapsodized about a new production. "We have the best stars," they said, "the most marvelous scenery, the finest director, the best press campaign and ads, a superb conductor, New York's favorite theatre"—Gordon, quiet through all of this, finally interrupted, "Gentlemen, that's nice, but I only want to know one thing—who's gonna write the jokes?" You must pray for good writers as fervently as for salvation.

THE ASSOCIATE PRODUCER

The associate producer should complement the strongest abilities of the producer. If the producer is strong on business and negotiating, but illiterate with script and tactless with talent, then the associate producer should be capable in reverse. The functions of the associate producer therefore vary, depending on the talents and personality of the producer. They will also be affected by the nature of the show and the size of the staff.

In my own case, since—as I view myself—my strengths are mostly creative, I have always sought associate producers with experience and ability in business and below-the-line matters. If I preferred working with the cast, director, and writers, as I always have, I would assign the associate producer the tasks of keeping the budget, negotiating contracts, setting schedules, arranging logistics and locations.

In those instances, however, when the staff was large enough to include a production manager to take care of these activities, I would seek an associate producer who was creative and could contribute to the main business of the program. For instance, talent bookings and interviews were the highest priorities of the "Merv Griffin Show," so I hired first Tom O'Malley and then Bob Murphy (we used to call it the Irish Seat) as associate producer, since they had proven strengths in these areas. Murphy, in fact, is currently producing the "Merv Griffin Show" and does an excellent job.

"Candid Camera" was another show that lived solely by its constantly inventive wits, so again, I opted for a strong creative associate. This time I hired Bill Anderson, a writer and producer, who was good at coming up with ideas for sequences.

However, it is common enough to be able to state as a definition that the associate producer is mostly concerned with administrative and financial considerations. He should know equipment and union regulations, production services houses and facilities, and costs—of everything. For dramatic shows or variety shows which use rotating performers, an associate producer should also be familiar with agents and the existing talent pool. Last, and most difficult, the associate producer is frequently the hatchet man when the producer wants to remain Mr. Nice Guy.

CASTING DIRECTOR OR TALENT COORDINATOR

In dramatic shows, the function is usually referred to as casting director; for variety or talk shows, the job is called talent coordinator. Since I broke in in this capacity, I have a special fondness for this job.

Here, of course, the essential quality is love of talent and a keen sense for spotting it. A casting director's life is a constant round of television viewing and movie-going, plus attendance at all the plays in his area. In New York, it is obligatory for a casting director to cover not only Broadway, but Off and Off-Off Broadway, as well as summer stock. The really good casting directors will also regularly drop in to monitor classes at the major acting schools. The same is true for casting directors in Hollywood. At least once a year they also try to get to London to see all the shows there. They have very close relationships with talent agents and usually develop strong friendships among actors, actresses, and directors; and they are fountains of showbiz gossip. Finally, in my experience, casting directors are, quintessentially—fans.

Talent coordinators will work the same beats as casting directors, but in addition will cover nightclubs, coffee houses, club dates, and concerts. When I was a talent coordinator I augmented these rounds by holding weekly open auditions for anyone who wanted to make an appointment. The yield from these was low relative to the number of people who came in, but out of the open auditions I did find Tom O'Horgan, Leslie Uggums, Nancy Kovacks, Lainie Kazan, Stiller and Meara, Stanley Myron Handleman, and Burt Convy. (I saw but rejected Peter, Paul, and Mary. Ugh.)

Later, when I was producing, I insisted that the talent coordinators continue this ritual of holding open auditions. They let Flip Wilson slip by. The report said, "A so-so comic who does a tasteless female impression." (What we saw is what we didn't get.) For months, Renee Taylor, whom I had discovered for the "Jack Paar Tonight Show," kept telling me her husband, Joe Bologna, was a funny man. I would always nod and think how touching (but misdirected) this new bride's loyalty was. "Not old Joe, the dutiful husband, who hangs around backstage, unassuming and smiling sheepishly," I thought. Then—there he was in *Made for Each Other*—a movie star and very funny.

The misses are depressing, but the successes are better than any other high. I will never forget the first time I booked the Smothers Brothers for the "Jack Paar Tonight Show." During the afternoon rehearsal, other members of the staff had watched them work and had run to Jack to report that Shanks was fashioning a bomb for that night's show.

Paar called me into his office and told me to cancel them. I protested and said that they were funny and would be a big hit—I'd stake my job on it. I did, in fact, threaten to quit if they were canceled, and I further insisted that they had to come over to the panel after they finished their number. As a compromise, Paar sent me to get the Brothers and bring them into the office. This was unique. Paar never saw the talent prior to meeting them on the show.

"Shanks tells me—you—you fellas are—fu—funny," Paar said, when they had been introduced. "I—I never met funny folksingers."

"We're—uh—ethnic singers," Tommy Smothers said. I had told the boys on the walk from the studio to the office that they were headed for a sudden death audition.

"What's the difference, pal?" Paar asked.

"We sing higher," Tommy said. Not George Bernard Shaw, maybe, but the line and Tommy's innocent manner and halting presentation made Paar laugh.

Paar turned to me and said, "You're right, kid. That's enough. See you on the show, fellas."

The Smothers Brothers were a smash.

So was Woody Allen. His first routine—good God, how nervous and faltering he was then—was built around the notion that in Sweden, since there was such sexual freedom, all the taboos had to do with food. Suspicious-looking types lurched out of doorways at street corners to sell you dirty postcards of a ham and cheese sandwich or—a leg of lamb. Swear words were—artichoke or bacon, lettuce, and tomato—and the ugliest—smorgasbord.

With Bob Newhart, I drew credit for discovery—and I took it— but he was really found by my wife. After bringing home a stack of records and audiotapes, I had rebelled, for that night anyway, at listening to any of them. "I'm sick of it," I remember saying. "I'm overentertained!" When I had gone to sleep, Ann put one of the audiotapes on the machine. The next morning she said, "There's one guy you'd better listen to. He's very funny. Especially the submarine monologue." On the tape were all of the now classic Newhart phone routines.

As talent coordinator for a talk show, you must not only find talented people, but one must also work with them in shaping the on-air interviews. (The talent and the host seldom or never meet before the show goes on the air.) This requires a long preinterview to develop leads and elicit anecdotes. You always write the introduction. I never knew I could write comedy until I had the assignment thrust upon me by this situation.

My first one-liner came in an introduction of Errol Flynn, in the twilight of his career. Flynn had just returned to New York from the mountains of Cuba where it was reported he had fought side-by-side with Fidel Castro. Flynn was, of course, a notorious womanizer who at the time was making naughty news with his Lolita, Beverly Aadlands. I wrote, "Here he is, folks, welcome him please, direct from Cuba, where he's been fighting *in* a Castro, Errol Flynn." Another was —for Jack E. Leonard, the insult comic, "You all know Jack E.—the original hoof and big mouth disease." And my favorite—"Here they are, folks, Jayne Mansfield."

THE PRODUCTION ASSISTANT

There are two kinds of production assistants. The show PA and the staff PA. Often, the staff PA is a high-level go-fer, who is usually female and usually has clerical duties. The show PA has precise duties and more prestige. During taping, the show PA normally sits in the control room next to the AD. This PA, in tape, assumes some of the functions of the script or continuity person in film. The PA follows script for continuity, consistency, and for dialogue. The PA keeps two timings going: cumulative, or overall, running time of the show, and segment time, that is, the length of each item or segment. The PA will time items during rehearsals. If the show is live and must come in on time, it is the PA who back times the show so everyone knows exactly how much time is left in the program. The PA is responsible for getting lyrics for songs and for logging all musical numbers for music clearance. If there are script changes during rehearsal, the PA is responsible for noting these and for making sure that one of the secretaries types the changes. The PA will be responsible for publishing scripts, schedules, call sheets, and show and rehearsal run-downs or routines. In tape shows the PA will usually notify the talent as to rehearsal and tape times. In many instances the PA will be a below-the-line function, but when possible, I always prefer to have this person on the staff. In small, low-budget productions, the PA will also be responsible for cue cards and, on the road, for arranging transportation and hotel accommodations.

I think the tasks of the musical director, scenic designer, and choreographer—frequently above-the-line functions—are clear from their job titles, as are the duties of the secretaries—oops, assistants. The go-fer, as we have learned, goes for things—and, as a rule, reads everybody else's mail. Even so, be nice to him or her, since in a year or two he or she will probably be producing the show.

BELOW THE LINE

In tape, the principal below-the-line jobs are (excluding musical director and scenic designer) the associate director; the technical director; the lighting director; the stage manager; the production manager, or unit manager; all the personnel of props, electric, and cameras; and stagehands.

THE ASSOCIATE DIRECTOR

In tape, the associate director sits next to the director. His principal task here is to keep telling the director what is coming up. That is, if there is script or there has been camera rehearsal, the associate director will tell the director what the next planned shot is and on which camera. In musical numbers, the AD will give advance notice of the same planned shots and add information about the instrumentation or the singer. The AD will also keep track of segment times and cumulative times. He will remind the director what lighting effects had been planned. Too, the AD is on a second PL with what is called telecine (this is where the film and slide projectors are located often on another floor or even in another building) with the video man and the tape machine operators. It is the AD who calls for roll tape or stop tape, changes in the intensity or color of the picture, and with telecine gives the cues to roll film and slides. He will tell the director how much time to commercial break, or how much time coming out of commercial break.

In film, this job is called first assistant director. The first assistant director is a combination stage manager, PA, and associate director.

In tape, if the director is on the floor or stage and wants camera shot changes, the AD will effect them. The AD keeps footage counts and exact notes on script and where things are in the tapes. This is vital for later use in postproduction. The AD will frequently supervise the actual editing of the show. He is responsible for communicating the director's instructions to the camera crew and for union hours, keeping track of meal and coffee breaks and overtime, along with the production manager.

THE TECHNICAL DIRECTOR

In tape (there is no TD for film), it is the technical director who executes what the director calls for. He sits before a complex board of buttons and levers which regulate the shots and effects that the director calls for. He physically controls the cut of a show. A heavy-fingered one can be a disaster. An alert and talented one can save a mediocre director. The crew for cameras and video report to him.

THE LIGHTING DIRECTOR

He is responsible for making the basic lighting plan or design. During the show, on tape, he sits in the control room and talks on a separate PL to the lighting board man and cues the lighting changes as they are required. In film, the director of photography usually designs the lighting along with a lighting director.

THE STAGE MANAGER

This is a key player in tape shows. He has no exact equivalent in film, the closest one being the assistant director. The stage manager—on most shows there are two, one out front and another backstage—makes sure that everything on the stage runs as it is supposed to. He is responsible for getting the talent to the stage and to the right place on the stage. He orders scenery changes. He cues talent when to start and when to get off. The stage manager is connected to the AD by a PL and takes instructions from him as the AD gets them from the director.

THE PRODUCTION MANAGER

The master sergeant of television, he is responsible for scheduling, ordering equipment and facilities, estimating and keeping the budget, observing union rules and regulations, conducting surveys of locations and liaisoning between show and network or station below-the-line. He issues and receives signed contracts and okays payment of invoices. He orders transportation, gives out per diem cash on the road, arranges hotel rooms, hands out petty cash, sees to catering, and is absolutely indispensable. As a breed, they are the best and nicest people I know in television.

THE CAMERAMAN

They are the people who actually operate the cameras. In electronic shooting, they have lagged behind the film cameramen in terms of aesthetics, although this is beginning to change. In film, the cameraman is in a critical position. During actual shooting, he is the only one who can see the image as it is being recorded. In film, usually, there is a hierarchy of people in this area. First, there is the DP, or director of photography. Then, there is first cameraman and second cameraman, and finally the operator. The DP is among the most creative positions in the industry. The DP is responsible for lighting and setting up the camera to get what the director has asked for in a scene. In low-budget films, the assistant cameraman is responsible—this is for film only—for loading magazines, following focus, setting exposures, and servicing and maintaining the camera in good working condition. In high budget, these duties are divided among several people.

OTHER FUNCTIONS

While the functions are the same in film and tape, there are title differences in certain job categories. In tape, the mover of scenery is called a stagehand. In film, he is a grip. The foreman is called the key grip. His assistant is called the best boy. In tape, the men who work with the lights are called lighting men or electricians. In film, these men are known as gaffers. The foreman is called the head gaffer.

I have not yet defined for tape the video man. His job is to keep the video pictures stable and in correct color. He has almost nothing to do with the show (he can instruct the lighting man to give more or less light) except to watch his scopes and keep correcting video. He gets upset when people come on shows dressed in white.

As in combat or in sports, so is it in show production, that intense and deep relationships develop among the members of a production team. I have had rich and memorable experiences working with members of a staff and crew. On one show we had our own softball team and the LD was the manager. He took me out of a game once! Even so, as often as I could, I would request and demand key members to be with me as I went from production to production.

Occasionally, I have run into a lazy, bitter, or negative crew member. This can be poisonous, especially if such a crew member is working on stage where the talent can see him and be brought down or inhibited by him. Never hesitate to fire or replace such a crewman. On the other hand, go out of your way to take care of and be considerate of the good ones. They are precious and can be the making of you and your show.

Despite their having caused me frequent and painful poker losses and death-defying hangovers, despite their constant demands for overtime pay and lunch breaks, despite his having pulled me out of that softball game (you know who you are, Karl Vitale), I have respected the vast majority of my crews and staffs and have the best affection for them.

Chapter **3**
networks: history and structure

Tread cautiously through this chapter on networks, since you are, remember, being led by a paid hand, who likewise will be as wary as Cain of "Kung Fu" is walking on rice paper. But, so admonished, let us begin.

First, there is geography, and first there is New York geography. When you are there in the City, among them and looking up, especially in the fall or spring when the wind is high and soft as flannel and the air is clean and the light is irredescent and their tops, like all great peaks, seem not to be anchored to the earth at all, but to float as freely as the balloon when a child forgets what wonder rides at the other end of the string and lets it go, or in winter when the sun in the city does not so much set as abdicate at half-after-four in the afternoon and down the sides of these pinnacles with their waffle-gridwalls comes pouring the silver syrup of their flourescent lighting, it is then possible, truly possible, to believe that these formations, these fabrications, these manufactures, these scrapers of the sky, are the topless towers of nature. Ice Age geological phenomena. You forget that humans made them—or that inside such a wonder they have just picked up the option on "The Price Is Right."

In three of these phallic boasts along a short stretch of the road named The Avenue of the Americas (but always called Sixth Avenue), the people who run and control the nation's commercial networks do their business. The network road runs from Forty-ninth Street to Fifty-fourth Street, from 30 Rockefeller Plaza (between Forty-ninth and Fiftieth Streets) where stands the oldest network building, NBC's; on to 51 West Fifty-second Street, where stands the most successful, home of CBS; and on north to 1330 Avenue of the Americas (between Fifty-third and Fifty-fourth Streets), home of the upstart and the youngest, ABC—the only one that honestly admits its Sixth Avenue location.

These are waggishly nicknamed in order, "30 Rock" for NBC,

"Black Rock" for CBS—its headquarters is a graceful tower in black granite—and "Hard Rock" for ABC—because of its affinity for contemporary music and its history of difficulty in getting established. The only name that gets much use is "Black Rock," to the utter dismay of CBS, which is most painfully conscious of its image.

It has always amazed me how businesses in New York City cluster. Department stores on Fifth Avenue, art galleries on Madison Avenue, diamond stores on Canal Street or Forty-seventh Street, lighting fixtures on the Bowery, "sporting" ladies on Eighth Avenue, and so on. I suppose it has to do with New York's tradition as a walking city. Certainly, it is convenient, and the phenomenon extends in broadcasting beyond the herding of the three networks. Along this same stretch of Sixth Avenue are also the Corporation for Public Broadcasting, the Public Broadcasting Service; 20th Century Fox; M-G-M; the giant talent agency, William Morris; Time-Life Films, Inc.; the A. C. Nielsen Company; various smaller packagers; syndicators and agencies. Nearby are Warner Brothers, Columbia Pictures, and International Creative Management.

Blame the networks, if you will, on Guglielmo Marconi, an Italian engineer, who in 1894, at age twenty, transmitted radio signals for the first known time. Radio signals are defined as radio waves of different frequencies that are electromagnetic radiations traveling through air at the speed of light (186,000† miles per second).

As early as 1864, a Scottish physicist named James Clark Maxwell forecast the existence of these radio waves, a theory that was successfully demonstrated by the German physicist, Heinrich Rudolph Herz in 1887, made practical by Marconi, and enhanced by Lee DeForest's vacuum tube.

The first application of this new medium, then called wireless, was for ship-to-shore and ship-to-ship communications. The term *radio* first came into use around 1912 when the United States Navy adapted the term. *Broadcast* was also a word that originated with the navy.

There is dispute as to whose was the first voice to be heard on radio. My favorite contender is Nathan B. Stubblefield of Murray, Kentucky, who is said to have spoken to a neighbor, Rainey T. Wells, in 1892, as follows:

"Hello, Rainey."

Despite a certain flatness in the content of the message on this historic occasion, and despite a lack of confirming evidence (Marconi was two years off), my heart remains with Stubblefield. And the thought certainly makes driving through Murray, Kentucky, more exciting. Rainey's reaction to the electronic wonder is lost, though it may be assumed that he had no other station to turn to. There Stubblefield had us; the competition, ever since, has been fierce.

By 1910, Enrico Caruso had sung on the air, and by 1915, trans-Atlantic voice communication was a fact. The first American radio station is generally conceded to be KDKA in Pittsburgh, although WBZ (now in Boston), then in Springfield, Massachusetts, was granted the first regular broadcast license on September 15, 1921. KDKA is the only station east of the Mississippi River whose call letters start with a K rather than a W. FCC regulations state that all stations east of the Mississippi begin with a W and those west of the Mississippi with a K. Why KDKA is an exception in the east and WBAP, WFAA, and WRR in Dallas in the west—unless it is because of their historic status—I do not know.

In those early days, broadcasting was about as orderly as a Rolling Stones concert. Station signals overlapped, content was homegrown and amateurish, and broadcast schedules were whimsical. Too many people were in the act. In 1924, there were 1,400 "stations," a figure that, fortunately, had fallen off to 620 by 1926. 1926 was a key year —the year of the network.

There had been experiments in the networking of special programs on the radio. New York City and Schenectady were tied together in 1921 to broadcast the Dempsey-Carpentier fight. New York and Boston were joined for a football game in 1923. President Coolidge's State of the Union message to Congress was broadcast in six cities in that same year. But serious and stable network operations began in 1926 with the formation of the National Broadcasting Company. This service was inaugurated with a four-hour broadcast on the evening of November 15, 1926—along with the first remote—from the Grand Ballroom of the old Waldorf-Astoria Hotel at Thirty-fourth Street and Fifth Avenue.

A thousand black-tie guests were on hand for the occasion and twenty-five stations in twenty-one cities carried the broadcast to, one guesses, most of the four-million radio-equipped homes in the country. Mary Garden was introduced by Milton Cross, and sang "Annie Laurie" and "My Little Gray Home in the West," thus becoming the first network performer. There were five orchestras that night, a brass band, soloists from the Metropolitan Opera, a light opera company performance, and the comedians Will Rogers, and Weber and Fields.

The National Broadcasting Company was the child of David Sarnoff, a Russian-Jewish immigrant who grew up poor on New York's Lower East Side. By way of a historic footnote, David Sarnoff was the radio operator on duty for the Marconi Company in 1912 when a CQD signal (now we call it SOS) came in from a distressed ocean liner—the *S.S. Titanic.*

As early as 1916, when he was twenty-five years old, Sarnoff was writing a letter to his superiors at the Marconi Wireless Telegraph Company urging the creation of a "radio music box," and by 1922 was further urging the creation of a radio network; or, as he called it, "a national program service." By then, Sarnoff was general manager of the recently formed Radio Corporation of America—RCA—which had bought the Marconi Company's patent rights. RCA was owned by General Electric and A.T.&T.

Sarnoff's 1922 proposal for a radio network was set forth in a report he submitted to the chairman of General Electric. It is interesting to note his idealism about broadcasting as well as his prescience about its eventual scope.

> Broadcasting requires a job of entertaining, informing, and educating the nation and should, therefore, be distinctly regarded as a public service. . . . When the novelty of radio will have worn off and the public is no longer interested in the means by which it is able to receive but rather, in the substance and quality of what is received, I think that the task of reasonably meeting the public's expectations and desires will be far greater than any so far tackled by any newspaper, theatre, opera or other public information or entertainment agency. The newspaper, after all, caters to a limited list of subscribers. The theatre presents its productions to a literal handful of people, but the broadcasting stations will ultimately be required to entertain a nation.

Sarnoff was not alone in hoping for a high moral role for radio, though the then secretary of commerce, Herbert Hoover, feared the worst when he said, "It is inconceivable that we should allow so great a possibility for service, for news, for entertainment, for education, and for vital commercial purposes to be drowned in advertising chatter."

It was not until late in 1925 that the vision expressed in David Sarnoff's report could become a reality. Until then, there had been confusion and legal combat between RCA and A.T.&T. over broadcast rights and patents. Finally, in December of that year, the great corporate storms subsided—A.T.&T. sold out its broadcast interests to RCA which got the New York City station WEAF (now WNBC); for its part, A.T.&T. was granted the exclusive rights to manufacture, lease, and sell broadcast transmitters.

Originally, RCA owned only 30 per cent of NBC, with Westinghouse Electric owning 20 per cent and General Electric owning 50 per cent. It was not until January 1, 1930, that RCA acquired the GE and Westinghouse portions of NBC and became the sole owner, which it still remains. GE and Westinghouse got satisfactions similar to those for A.T.&T. in the earlier solution.

NBC's first studios were in the A.T.&T. Building on lower Broadway, though in less than a year the network had moved uptown to 711 Fifth Avenue. In 1933, NBC moved to its present location in Rockefeller Center, which soon became popularly known as Radio City. In those high-minded days, NBC had a symphony orchestra of its own, conducted by Arturo Toscanini. They performed in the fabled Studio 8-H, which still exists. Toscanini, a notorious Malaprop, once scolded an erring messenger by saying, "The next time I send an idiot, I'll go myself!"

In the beginning, NBC provided a single broadcast service, but network radio became so popular that in less than a year's time, the company launched a second, separate network service. These two networks were identified as the Red Network and the Blue Network —colors used by NBC engineers—to trace the separate network coverages on national maps. Also in the early months, there was a Pacific Coast network, since consistent coast-to-coast broadcasting did not begin until 1929. (The first Atlantic-to-Pacific connection took place on New Year's Day, 1927, when NBC carried the Rose Bowl game from Pasadena.)

Until electrical transcriptions—recordings—came into use, all programs were broadcast live—twice. Once for the nation from the East to the Rockies, and a second time, because of the considerable time difference, for the Pacific Coast. "Once more for the Coast" became a popular slang expression of the thirties and forties.

I will never forget lying in bed as a little boy in Lebanon, Indiana, listening to those identifying NBC chimes and the stentorian voice of André Baruch or Ben Grauer, "This is NBC, the National Broadcasting Company. And now, from Radio City in New York . . ." I was transfixed. Staring at my radio set and promising in prayer to my God, Philo T. Farnsworth, that I would make the pilgrimage to New York City and do His work. And I have always had a special fondness for NBC, since it was there that I had my first big-time professional broadcast job.

It has been my experience, having worked at all three networks, that NBC is the most impersonal in character—the grayest—the most corporate, albeit the least self-conscious. Perhaps this is conditioned by the fact that NBC has always been a wholly owned subsidiary of RCA, a corporate-non-show-biz giant; thus NBC has been tempered in its broadcast single-mindedness. This probably is reinforced by NBC's home—the RCA Building, a dark gray, eighty-story slab of limestone; an Art Deco behemoth in which NBC shares space with Rockefellers, other corporations, banks, firms, and a self-contained small town of shops and stores, which moderate against television obsession.

In my years at NBC I never met David Sarnoff, Robert Sarnoff, Robert Kintner, Walter Scott, or David Adams, who were at the time the power hierarchy. I never even had them pointed out to me, and I doubt that many NBC employees could have identified them by sight. (One of the Mrs. Robert Sarnoffs did come to our studio one holiday time to wish us a Merry Christmas. I enjoyed introducing her to W. H. Auden and Santa Claus who were sharing the bill on that particular day.)

My sense memories of NBC physically—and I hear things have not changed very much—always put me in mind of old-money rich people who think nothing of wearing clothes that are out of style, and rumpled. The wall paintings are hung indifferently and the quality is uneven. The furniture is somebody's grandparents'. The hallways could be in warehouses and windows are scarce. By the time I had left, the corridor walls had been covered in sheets of linoleum. There never seemed to be enough light.

I worked from a bunker 9 by 10 feet with a 7½-foot ceiling, and no windows. Paar and Griffin each had a 9-by-12 cubicle with an 8-foot ceiling and no windows, though each did have a drape covering one wall that seemed to intimate a window.

To my knowledge, NBC carried its black list actively into the early sixties. (Maybe the other networks did also. I am not sure.) All guests for shows had to be submitted in advance. I have knuckled under as often as the next fellow in broadcasting, but I do pride myself for hacking away at this particular oppression and I will now publically thank myself for restoring Max Eastman, Zero Mostel, Judy Holliday, Jack Gilford, Phil Leeds, and Eve Merriam to NBC air. I further thank Jack Paar and Merv Griffin for their courage in this regard. For me, it was easy. I was a beginner with little to lose, but Paar and Griffin had careers and fortunes at stake and, lest we forget, the black list was no joke.

I found that out in 1962 when I submitted, among others, the name of a bit player from England who was then appearing in a Broadway show. I had been told he was witty, probably good guest material. A memo came down from the legal department asking where this person had been in 1938. I handed it on to Jean Meegan, one of my talent coordinators, who had interviewed the Englishman. Jean, an ex-AP reporter, could be as tough as George Patton and as funny as Groucho Marx; she scribbled across the bottom of the memo, "His Nanny was pushing him in a pram through Hyde Park." I thought the comment probably true, so I initialed it, "FYI, B.S." (B.S. is not a judgment; those are my initials. FYI means "for your information"), and sent it back to the legal department. The legal department,

like Queen Victoria, said, "We are not amused." I was hotly summoned to the head lawyer's office—he had windows—and was
severely reprimanded for my frivolous attitude concerning this "company policy." Nobody called it the black list. Though I undermined it when I could, thereafter I stopped treating the black list
lightly.

Another case involved a distinguished New Yorker who had
written an interesting, amusing autobiography. He seemed safer for
our program than Grandma Moses. I did not even bother to submit
his name for clearance. When his name appeared on our advance
booking sheet, however, again I was summoned. No one was eager
to specify the man's sin, but I persisted. Finally I was told—and sworn
to confidence in the matter—that twenty-one years earlier, this man
had accused James Forrestal (by then long dead) on a "Town Hall of
the Air" radio broadcast of having at one time represented the giant
German industrial firm, Krupp, in the United States.

I was dumfounded. All I could say was, "Well, did he?" "That's
hardly the point," I was told sharply. I was too stunned to probe
further, though I did insist on the booking on the narrow ground that
it was likely to cause more trouble to cancel the man than to play the
date. It is an argument I have used often and never insincerely. We
in the networks frequently make unnecessary conflagrations by rubbing two or more Vice-Presidents together. The man played the date
and the Richter Scale was none the wiser.

Perhaps, in this instance, it was not the point whether this man's
charge against Forrestal was true or not—I believe there was later
evidence to substantiate the accusation. In any case, at the time of the
charge, Forrestal was alive and could have responded. The truly appalling point for me was that apparently somebody was keeping very
strict and thorough records of what everybody said on NBC's air. Did
they, I wonder, have in their files, "Hello, Rainey"?

Another thing about NBC I could never understand. Why did
David Sarnoff, chairman of the board of RCA, one of the most prestigious and powerful men in the world, insist on always being called
General? And Brigadier General at that! I don't know for a fact, but
I am satisfied with the answer that Harry Golden gave me. He said
that in czarist Russia (perhaps it is still true in Soviet Russia?) no Jew
could hold officer rank in the Russian Army; and so, in America,
Sarnoff would naturally and especially be proud of being not just an
officer, but a general. I like that. It has Rosebud the sled in it. (Incidentally, Sarnoff earned the rank of brigadier general in World War II,
serving on General Dwight Eisenhower's staff.)

Despite its warts, NBC remains a place I feel affection for. Not just for the stars and the slightly cockeyed show staff people I knew then, but for the really corporate people. Among them was Herb Schlosser, now president of NBC Television. In those days he and I argued over furniture:

"What do you mean you want two lamps in your office?"

"Yeah, and I want hundred watt bulbs in both of them." According-ing to industry talk—which is torrential and endless—NBC is, under Schlosser's leadership, shedding much of its former torpor. The men-tal vests are off and they are bustling like ambitious poor boys.

If NBC gave me a few headaches, sixteen of its people also gave blood to my wife when she needed transfusions following an opera-tion. (As a minor insight about the perilous existence of broadcast people, at least thirty people tried to give blood, but could not qualify since they themselves were so depleted in some way or other.)

With it all, I have never quite lost the hayseed thrill of entering the RCA Building and taking the middle-bank elevators up to NBC.

Two forces worked to diminish NBC's singular dominance of network programming. One was the Federal Communications Com-mission, which made NBC divest its Blue Network, which became ABC. The other force was William S. Paley, progenitor of CBS.

CBS grew out of an effort by George Coats, a New York pro-moter, and Arthur Judson, manager of the Philadelphia Symphony and the New York Philharmonic Symphony, who in 1926 formed something called the Judson Radio Program Corporation. Their main intention was to fight ASCAP, the American Society of Composers, Authors, and Publishers, which to this day collects fees on music performances. Coats and Judson further tried to interest NBC in an artists' bureau which would control and manage talent and which was to be headed by Judson. NBC rejected this idea, so Judson and Coats decided to form their own network. Along with Edward Ervin, an associate of Judson's and an investor in the new company, they organ-ized the United Independent Broadcasters on January 27, 1927. They contracted with sixteen stations to buy ten hours a week from each station at $50 an hour. When they tried to resell this $8,000 worth of time to advertisers, there were few takers.

Fortunately for Coats, Louis Sterling of the Columbia Phono-graph Co., alarmed by rumors that RCA was to merge with the Victor Talking Machine Co. (the rumors were true), bought all ten hours. In a twofold plan, he hoped to resell the time and to plug his company in the network identifications as the Columbia Phonograph Broadcast-ing System. To get this name change, the record company paid Coats and Judson $163,000.

The Columbia Phonograph Broadcasting System lost $100,000

the first month, and Columbia Phonograph wanted out. They had a thirty-day cancellation clause in their contract and they exercised it fast. Judson then approached Dr. Leon Levy, owner of his Philadelphia network-affiliated station WCAU, who got Philadelphia millionaire Jerome H. Louchheim to buy the ailing network. Louchheim hired Major J. Andrew White as president, the same Major White who had done the blow-by-blow description of the Dempsey-Carpentier fight on the first network broadcast between New York City and Schenectady. No matter. Soon, Louchheim also wanted out. Losses were mounting steadily. But, as they say, it's an ill wind that blows no man some cigar smoke.

One of the network's few sponsors was the Congress Cigar Co. of Philadelphia. Congress had been advertising its La Palina Smoker on CBS—the network name had been shortened to CBS when Louchheim bought it—and sales had gone from four hundred thousand cigars to one-million a day in six months. The man behind this was the scion of the Congress-owning family and advertising manager of the company—twenty-six-year-old William S. Paley, who was absolutely convinced of the enormous potential profitability of the network. He persuaded his father and other relatives to back him, and he purchased CBS. He moved to New York City and completely reorganized the company, then housed in the Paramount Building on Times Square. There were sixteen employees. Paley's considerable talents extended to hiring first-rate people and bringing off complicated but shrewd financial deals. He also established the talent bureau—Columbia Artists' Management—which NBC had rejected (it was dropped in 1941 when the FCC questioned the propriety of CBS both managing and hiring talent), and later (1939) bought the Columbia Phonograph Company, now Columbia Records, the most successful of all recording companies.

By 1928, CBS had grown to fifty-three affiliated stations, had purchased its own New York station, and had moved to new headquarters at 485 Madison Avenue, which was to be its corporate home for the next thirty-six years. By 1930, CBS was grossing over $7.5 million and was surely a success, but little more than a cold in the nose for NBC, which was grossing over $22 million a year. NBC continued to dominate broadcasting until after World War II; but through all the earlier years, CBS was an aggressive and innovative second and ready to take first place, given a break or two.

One break Paley himself engineered; another was thrust into his corporate lap by the FCC. In May 1941, the FCC determined that no single organization should own or control more than one broadcasting network, and declared in its "Report on Chain Broadcasting" that it would issue no license to any station that was so affiliated. This decision forced RCA to divest itself of one or the other of its two NBC Blue and Red Networks. RCA lopped off, by organizing a subsidiary, the assets and operations of the Blue Network, which in January 1942 became the Blue Network Company, Inc.

In October 1943, RCA sold the Blue Network Company for $8 million to Edward J. Noble; a multimillionaire businessman (the Life Saver Company) and philanthropist who had also held posts in the federal government. The company's name was changed to the American Broadcasting Company. This gave CBS an enormous boost toward becoming number one; but it remained for Paley to whip it in.

CBS (Paley, really) has a philosophy. The philosophy is that the structure of programming success is built on a foundation of "stars." Though he early built a news department and went through his own Toscanini phase, Paley's belief that entertainment stars are the force for attracting audiences and thus, advertisers, plus his certain gift for discovering and building these performers, finally thrust CBS into its dominant position.

Bing Crosby, Kate Smith, the Mills Brothers, and Frank Sinatra were early CBS successes—but most established stars eluded Paley. The turning point came in 1948 when Paley wooed Jack Benny, radio's number one star, from NBC by offering to buy Benny's corporation, thus giving Benny a huge capital gains profit on the sale. Paley also wooed Benny personally, whereas General Sarnoff had never bothered to meet Benny. It was a broadcast first and a master stroke. Paley also stole Red Skelton, Amos 'n' Andy, Edgar Bergen & Charlie McCarthy, and Ozzie & Harriet. CBS has been first almost ever since.

Broadcast journalism became a significant and respectable enterprise with the outbreak of World War II, and CBS led the way in this area, mostly on the smoke-clouded, hunched shoulders of Edward R. Murrow, that good man in a bad time. To this day, I think, there has never been Murrow's equal in broadcast journalism, nor a staff to match that one assembled by Murrow and Fred Friendly during CBS's journalistic heyday. Eric Sevareid, Walter Cronkite, David Schoenbrun, Charles Collingswood, among others; not to mention the producers, directors, and writers schooled there. They were the best and are, I think, responsible for burnishing the true bright image that CBS so cherishes. Certainly, it was not the "Beverly Hillbillies" nor James Aubrey nor Clive Davis and other such CBS embarrassments.

Today, all three networks have solid and talented news personnel in depth. It was not always so. In the early days, broadcasting thought nothing of stealing news from the local papers and embellishing the stories on the air. Once, a local station's voice spoke glowingly of the visit to its town of a foreign potentate named Meti Nelots. Next day, the local newspaper—with unrestrained glee—was able to point out that it had invented the potentate, Meti Nelots—which spelled backward is Stolen Item. This and similar shameful abuses (not to mention the economic threat posed to print press by radio) led to a press-radio war and, in 1934, to the formation of the Press Radio Bureau, which provided stations with their own source of news. This was eventually replaced by the resumption and extension of service to radio by the national wire services, and finally by the independent news-gathering staffs and departments that networks and local stations have developed.

For my taste, CBS has the handsomest headquarters of the three networks. This work of art by the late Eero Saarinen, in black polaroid glass and black granite, is on Sixth Avenue, with its official or address entrance located on Fifty-second Street, and listed with pure graphic forethought as 51W52. There is nothing to identify the business inside, except discreetly emblazoned CBSs over the bronze doors. William Paley leaves to McDonald's and Holiday Inns the corporate shout. In fact, all three networks—considering their business, or perhaps because of it—are remarkably restrained in the presentation of their corporate faces.

According to those who know, this consciousness of low-key good taste reaches obsessive proportions at CBS. Until very recently, no one working in "Black Rock" could alter the interior decoration of his or her office or work area by even so much as a spouse's photograph, without permission, which was given stingily. Again, until only recently, women could not wear slacks or pants suits and men—still, I think—are expected to wear dark suits rather than sports coats and slacks. CBS stationery has a dot which, when held to the light, indicates to a secretary where she should begin a letter. The CBS pages (ushers) wear uniforms and are inspected prior to the studio audiences being allowed in. Large wallboards with photographs, names, and job titles of all key CBS executives are placed prominently in each studio or department so that underlings will not err about recognizing VIPs, quite unlike NBC's policy of executive anonymity. Paintings at "Black Rock" are chosen and hung with the care of a serious collector. (Paley is chairman of the board of directors and a founder of the Museum of Modern Art, half a block away on Fifty-third Street.) The furniture is updated Bauhaus, all clean lines, metal, and leather, and sometimes molded plastic and color-coordinated fabric. Walls are painted museum white, washable glossy enamel, or done in charcoal gray imitation flannel cloth. Certainly, there is no lack of glass at CBS. At NBC, the windows that are are windows that open, while the CBS windows—floor-to-ceiling—are permanently sealed. All of their weather is of their own making. We at ABC are also sealed in by hectares of glass and view Manhattan at its best—from a distance.

Until his retirement in 1973, Dr. (a Ph.D. in statistics from Ohio State) Frank Stanton was regarded as the chief keeper of these corporate cosmetics, among other valuable and powerful services rendered to the company. President since 1946, Stanton came to CBS in 1935 as a twenty-seven-year-old, $55-a-week worker in the three-man research department. He had been spotted a year earlier when CBS, always keen for research, had commissioned Ohio State, among other universities, to provide it with audience and sales research data. Over the years, Stanton became an eloquent and forthright spokesman—a statesman—for CBS, indeed, for the entire broadcast industry.

My own impressions of CBS were earned during my years there as producer, first of "Candid Camera" (Allen Funt was hurt that CBS never hung a photograph of him among its stars in the foyer of the Programming Department floor), then of the "Merv Griffin Show."

True to its philosophy of comforting stars, CBS treated my stars —and me—wonderfully. Most of our meetings were held in restaurants—21, Le Mistral, Brussels, the Ground Floor, Pearl's, the Forum, and, in California, Chasen's and Scandia. All the executives I dealt with were very knowing about food and wine and could always be counted on for information about the nature of a restaurant's national, historic, or cultural background. There was a lot of this conversational foreplay from CBS executives and nearly always it was quite sophisticated—from one executive, the philosophy of educational broadcasting, even. In fact, the preliminaries were often better than the main bout, which might have to do, say, with the counterprogramming of Tiny Tim's wedding. Actually, I nearly always felt these men were embarrassed by the crass minerals of the true mine they worked in. (I understand this is not true about the current Program Department leadership.)

The CBS programming executives were tirelessly polite, low-key, and charming, even when we all knew that matters were tough between us or even disastrous. I never felt strong-armed at CBS. Certainly, there was no quibbling about furniture. They only winced once—about Broadway's Cort Theatre.

Merv Griffin and I were convinced that a major contribution to the show's success during the Westinghouse days was our studio—the Little Theatre, an ex-legitimate house on West Forty-fourth Street, next door to Sardi's, between Broadway and Eighth Avenue. When it came time to make the move to CBS, we insisted on continuing to tape in a theatre setting. The Little Theatre was unavailable to us, since

Westinghouse had a hold on it and would be using it for its new "David Frost Show."

I scouted other Broadway theatres and finally settled on the Cort on Forty-eighth Street between Sixth and Seventh Avenues. At first, CBS balked, but then—Mr. Paley himself made the final decision, I am told—plunked down $2 million in rent for two years and another $1 million to convert the theatre for television use.

It did not seem to help. Fourteen months later I was gone and Merv had left the Cort to tape the shows in a studio in Television City in Hollywood. By March 1972, Merv was gone. (Now, of course, Merv is back on, in syndication through Metromedia, and is taping his shows—where?—in a converted Hollywood legit house called the Hollywood Palace.)

Bob Wood, the good and gregarious president of CBS Television, still grimaces when reminded of the Cort. On the other hand, I am always warmly greeted by the executives of the Shubert Organization, which owns the Cort, a cordiality that must stem in part from the handsome profit they made on the Cort Theatre's rental.

As further evidence of the serious nurturing of stars at CBS, on opening night of the "Merv Griffin Show," the network flew in twenty-five or more newspaper television editors to attend the program and followed the telecast with an expensive supper party in the ballroom of the Americana Hotel. Also in attendance that night was one Mrs. Lillian Miller.

Mrs. Miller, as she is called (though she never married) came to minor celebrity status during the days when Steve Allen was hosting the "Tonight Show" and she was sitting in the studio audience for every telecast. Jack Paar inherited Mrs. Miller when he took over the "Tonight" chores and spoiled her occasionally by chatting with her on the air and by taking her, all-expenses-paid, on one of our show trips to California. By the time Mrs. Miller got around to sitting on Merv's aisle, she had become the Golda Meir of studio audiences.

Before Merv's show went on CBS, the network hired Mrs. Miller to star in a series of clever on-air promos, which were themed to the idea that she had seen them all—talk show hosts—and judged Merv to be the best of the lot. CBS paid Mrs. Miller handsomely for these commercials and for the opening-night party had purchased her a new dress, a corsage, and an afternoon at the hairdresser. Even so, at the party, Mrs. Miller was out of sorts. She strode up to the CBS executive I was talking to and, without so much as a by-your-leave, started scolding him, "I shoulda had a limo," she said. "Merv and Treacher (Arthur) had limos. Woody and Hedy had limos (Woody Allen and Hedy Lammar were opening-show guests). I had to walk here from the theatre. It's four blocks. It don't look right." I was amused—and slightly annoyed. But the CBS executive smiled politely, nodded and disappeared. He had gone to arrange it, and later, Mrs. Miller went home by limousine.

The true depth of Mrs. Miller's ingratitude became known the next day. During that year Merv and Johnny Carson were both taping in New York City and at the same hour, 6:30 P.M. With the flush of opening night behind her, and despite the CBS commercials and the limo, Mrs. Miller chose to sit in the Carson audience. I knew then, without waiting for Nielsen, that our show was in trouble.

Another example of CBS's care for its stars came during the course of our troubled ratings. Bob Wood had to talk to Merv about what could be done to perk up the numbers. Some months earlier, Wood had heard Merv say that one of his favorite restaurants was Anthony's Pier 4, so Wood called Merv, made a lunch date, and took him to Anthony's Pier 4. What's so special about that? Anthony's Pier 4 is in Boston and Wood flew Merv up in one of the company planes.

While CBS never interfered with the guests for the "Merv Griffin Show," there were those, obviously, they would have preferred I did not book. Still, they made no scene about the bookings of Tom Smothers—then recently fired by CBS and involved in a multimillion dollar litigation with that network—or maverick FCC Commissioner Nicholas Johnson, who was forever scolding the networks. Of course, they did try to suggest. They would, for instance, show me complicated charts, minute-by-minute ratings graphs of shows, meant to prove audience tune-out when certain guests came on. As often as not, these tune-out guests were the so-called big names. They gave me data that indicated certain of our regulars from the Westinghouse show were actually hated. I tried to point out that Merv's image was nice (all talk show hosts are) and that it was good show business to balance this by a few villains, or the whole show would turn into tapioca. Through it all, CBS's motives were simply to maximize the show's ratings to stay number 1.

One classic night—one of the few nights we were number 1—Abbie Hoffman came on the show in a buckskin jacket. After he sat down, he took the jacket off and revealed a shirt made out of an American flag. At the time, 1969–70, this use of the flag was illegal in several states and political feelings in the country were white-hot. While I had skirted the tempest of CBS's ire on a number of occasions, I knew this time for sure I was in the hurricane of the Eye.

There was fevered talk of not airing the show at all. Again, I pointed out that this would only call extra attention to the incident and make it more important than it was. I also tried to point out that no one had seemed upset when Roy Rogers and Dale Evans had dressed up in spangly versions of the flag a few weeks before; this proved to be a feathery argument.

Finally, to its credit, CBS aired the show, though Hoffman himself was electronically edited out. You could hear him but you couldn't see him. This television phantasmagoria was explained to an otherwise bemused audience by Bob Wood in three on-air appearances; one in the beginning, one in the middle, and one at the end of the program.

The next day, rather than the raging censure I was expecting, Wood phoned and said, "Hey, Bob, let's not do that anymore, hunh? I hate the way I look on camera."

(Going back to NBC for a moment—the care and feeding of stars is not so uniformly attended to, but for years has been sustained zealously by David Tebet, the warm-hearted vice-president of talent relations. There is one story that defines Dave's exuberance. Tom Sarnoff, then head of NBC on the West Coast, was taking over delivery of his son's paper route during one week while the youngster was sick. A minor crisis occurred when Mr. Sarnoff misplaced the list of customers' names. Hearing about it, one NBC executive cracked, "I hope it didn't get put in the pouch to New York, or Dave Tebet's sent them all flowers by now." For at least ten years after I left NBC, I nevertheless got a warm New Year's telegram from the network—from Dave Tebet.)

The end came for me at CBS in August 1970, and it was no surprise. The show's ratings were low and various writers, talent coordinators, directors, and the announcement of Arthur Treacher's "retirement" as the show's side-kick announcer, had all preceded me to the tumbrel and the scaffolding. Already there had been affiliate station defections, and more were threatened for the fall, if CBS didn't "do something." I was the next "something" they could do, and I knew it. I would have done the same, in order to buy time to hold the late night line-up together. There was money to be made in late-night and they would have to keep Griffin going until a new program idea could be devised.

For me, it is not the fact of being fired or cancelled that matters, for that is the nature of television, but only the manner in which it is done. In this case, Merv himself was the first to tell me, of course, which, rightfully so, he had insisted on doing—and I will tell you about that. But, immediately afterward, Irwin Segelstein, now president of Columbia Records, then a high-level Programming Department vice-president, spoke to me. He thanked me warmly for my efforts, explained CBS's position and assured me that there was nothing personal in the decision. Its necessity was regretted. Not bad. As for style, I liked my CBS execution.

I know, too, at ABC there is great and sincere attention paid to the feelings of people, as well as to their practical circumstances, when these unpleasant scenes become necessary. When Jack Paar's return to television as one of the rotating elements in the first year of "Wide World of Entertainment" failed to capture a sufficient share of the late-night audience, he resigned gracefully. But with equal grace, Martin Starger, then president of ABC Entertainment—the entity responsible for programming the ABC Network—made a visit to Paar to thank him and express his regrets. If this does not seem so surprising, consider it in the context of a world in which such grace is rare.

All of this is a detour, I realize, this business of getting fired or firing someone yourself. But it is important since it is sure to come up in every television career.

I was fired by Allen Funt, which is about as singular an experience as shaking hands with a presidential candidate, while I was in the hospital recovering from an emergency appendectomy. Well, not actually. In truth, his agent called me at the hospital and asked me what my plans were when I got out.

He said, "I think you better have some, Keed—away from "Candid Camera." It's just a gut feeling I have."

"Yeah, I know," I said, "I've got one myself."

The real ending came my third day back on the job when Allen's accountant (later on, he came to a tragic end when he committed suicide, after having been charged with embezzlement of Allen's funds), who had been assigned the task, came into my office and delivered the news officially. So be it.

You may think I am crazy, but I am fond of and fascinated by Allen Funt to this day. He is intelligent, amusing, creative, complicated—and damned fine company—away from his office. Despite the fact that "Candid Camera" was the number one show in the Nielsen ratings when all this happened, Allen was right to give me the ax. We were in constant disagreement about how the show should be done, and our personal temperaments were as far apart as Baffin Bay and Tierra Del Fuego. This is debilitating to a show and to the staff. Since one of us had to go, the choice was clear. Sometime later, Allen told me, "You should have quit, kid. Lyndon Johnson didn't have to fire Bobby Kennedy when they fought. He resigned." Actually, I had never thought of Allen and myself in that light, but the comparison was flattering, I thought, and I let it stand.

Maybe you think I am soft for not holding a grudge against Allen —the truth is I always believe I am to blame when things go wrong (see "Protestant Guilt")—but think again. Beyond my personal regard for him, there is a tough business consideration involved here. Ours is a small business and the creators are few. Bridges are not for burning lightly in television. Allen was later a frequent and always reliable guest on the "Merv Griffin Show" and gave me a number of entertaining programs. Among my "Wide World of Entertainment" programs for ABC, Allen's "Candid Camera" retrospective was one of the highest-rated ever. All else being equal, we will do business in the future. Especially when they are talented, I admire uncommon individualists and, certainly, Allen is that, and they are rare.

It was different with Merv. A few months earlier it had been my responsibility to fire the show's director. Over the years, my wife and I had been friends with the director and his wife, so we felt the news had to be broken away from the office and with care. We invited them to our home for dinner. Ann, my wife, went all out with a veal cordon bleu. After dinner and after the firing business was out of the way, the four of us began joking that this had been a very civilized way to get the boot, but to beware in the future of veal cordon bleu. It became synonymous with the Mafia kiss on the cheek or the black hand. The next day Merv asked me how the director had taken the news. "Okay," I said, "good humor and stiff upper lip." I told Merv about our joke with the veal cordon bleu.

Then it was my turn. My wife and I were to begin a one-week European vacation the next day. For me, a vacation and one week. Ann was going to Denmark to shoot a film and would be gone several weeks. I had warned her that the vacation might be the occasion for my dismissal, since I had observed over the years that vacations, holidays, illnesses, and such seem to be salutary times for executions, since the "corpse" won't be around to haunt anyone.

Just prior to our regular late-afternoon staff meeting to go over that night's show, Merv's secretary came into my office and said, "Merv would like to see you—alone." "Alone" went off like a radical's bomb. When I walked into the office, Merv said, "Bob—" and couldn't go on.

"Veal cordon bleu—right?" I said.

He nodded and laughed. "I couldn't do any more. Stations are dropping us. It's not your fault, you know that. I did all I could."

I knew all of it was true. "I know. It's okay. It'll buy you time."

On the telecast that night, Merv gave me a warm and fulsome farewell. The money settlement was equally fair and generous. And that pretty much was that. For eight years, off and on, we had been working together, and both of our careers had advanced because of it. Neither had been the worse for it financially. From the night in January 1962 when Merv had had enough faith in me to produce his first talk-show experience (the first guest was an unknown singer named Aretha Franklin), and I had had to shove him physically back on stage when he had come bounding off in a panic during the first commercial break saying, "I can't do this kind of show—I'm terrible!" up to this final, frustrating yellow-hot August night in 1970, we had been good professional and personal friends (and still are). Do not doubt it—the ending hurt; but I believe we both handled it with grace and had done our equal best over the course.

That, for anyone interested, especially younger people in the business who have yet to know the experience, is the point of all of this. When it does happen, remember that it is not terminal and that bitterness is poor soil for new growth. I had not chosen the security of tenure jobs, but the high-risk profession of television, with its compensating kick of having to live by my wits and of earning more money than I probably deserve. Television is a high-wire profession and there is seldom a net.

One last thing. It will help you to get a good and gutsy spouse. When I called my wife and said, "Guess what's for dinner tonight?" there was a pause; then she said, with real happiness, "Veal cordon blue—that's *terrific!* Now you can stay longer in Europe!"

It is time to tell you something about ABC. What is the name of that bird which defies the laws of aerodynamics by flying anyway? That is how it has been with ABC's success, which is large. Until coming to work there in the fall of 1972, I had no idea of the immense struggle that lay behind ABC's emergence as a full-service, fully competitive national network.

As we have seen, ABC was a spin-off of NBC and did not become an independent network until October 1943. At its beginning, the network had 715 employees, owned two radio stations fully and half of a third, and had 168 affiliated stations. Not bad, except that NBC and CBS were so much better off as to represent almost a difference in kind rather than in degree. They were running powerfully, and with at least a sixteen-year headstart. Catching up has been an ABC reality ever since.

Not only was ABC behind as a radio network, but the whole broadcasting industry in 1943 was on the threshold of a technological revolution which would alter the entire weaponry of the contest—not to mention the sociology of the nation. Had ABC emerged in a time when radio was to last as the dominant technology for another decade at least, the network would surely have had a more realistic chance at narrowing the gap between it and NBC and CBS. But television's time had nearly come.

As early as 1915, Marconi, relying on existing scientific work rather than visionary hunches, was predicting "visible telephone." By 1923, the Russian-born American physicist, Vladimir Zworykin, had applied for a patent on his iconoscope camera tube and by 1927 a television program had been transmitted by wire from Washington,

D.C., to New York City. In the 1930s television firsts were as frequent as rumors on Wall Street.

From the start, NBC, through its electronic parent RCA, and CBS, through its CBS Laboratories under the guidance of Dr. Peter Goldmark (father of the 33 1/3 rpm phonograph record), were key centers of television development. NBC was on the air by April 30, 1939, and in its first year broadcast 601 hours of television programming.

Various competing systems of transmission were imitating the earlier birth confusions of radio, however, and the FCC in the spring of 1940 withheld approval of the various technical approaches until its industry-wide committee could recommend uniform standards. The committee fixed on the 525-line scan and the 30-frame-per-second standards that are still in use. Though World War II turned this FCC drag on television's development into a brake, the idling giant began to move swiftly in 1945 when the war ended.

For everyone, of course, the obstacles were formidable—in technology, production, organization, marketing, and distribution. To overcome them, television companies would require enormous sums of capital. Between 1947 and 1951, when it finally showed a profit, NBC lost $18 million on operations alone. William Paley has said about CBS, "We went into the hole $55 million before income from television started to catch up to output." Still, NBC and CBS were positioned for orderly endurance. ABC was positioned like a serial hero—faced with peril at the end of each episode, only to be saved at the beginning of the next.

The fact that ABC has not simply survived this shift in the broadcasting industry, but has achieved a success, will pass for a miracle. Let us see how it happened and in what context.

In 1945, when the FCC allocated thirteen VHF channels for commercial television's use, there were only 16,500 television sets in America, mostly in the Northeast, and the channel allocation was reduced to twelve when the FCC took back one channel and assigned it to landmobile and two-way radio. The Commission further specified that 170, 190, or 220 miles of separation was required—depending on the part of the country—between stations transmitting on the same channel among these twelve. Given the large number of requests to build television stations, it was soon apparent that the twelve channels were simply not enough to feed pictures to the American multitude.

The situation by 1948 brought forth the FCC's "freeze" order, as it is called. The Commission stopped granting construction permits and licenses for additional television stations, to prevent overlapping signals and deteriorating service. The "freeze" froze ABC most of all.

Given their enormous head-starts, NBC and CBS had signed as affiliates of their respective television networks nearly all of the potentially plum stations in the country. ABC took the hindmost.

Take, as an example, a city large enough to support profitably at least three television stations. At the start in such a city, there would be a first station and this would go to NBC or CBS, depending on a number of variables (most often a historic link, since most television stations were begun by interests which owned radio stations). For certain, the next station would go to NBC or CBS, whichever had not gotten the first station. Then, just when it was possible for a third to compete, which could be expected to sign with ABC (already behind), down came the "freeze." This situation lasted for four years, in which time NBC and CBS, grazing in near-monopoly preserves, feasted on entrenchment of viewing habits and accumulation of capital.

Furthermore, there were—and are—a lot of markets, even granted a television channel allocation, that simply could not support three television stations. In nearly every such instance, the network shut out has been ABC. Even today ABC must compete with roughly thirty to forty fewer stations in its line-up.

The FCC lifted the freeze in April 1952. The new allocations called for an adjusted V position on the spectrum and for the addition of seventy UHF (ultrahigh frequency) channels, but even as these latter stations came on the air, their effectiveness was impaired. It took years for viewers in sizable numbers to buy receivers equipped with UHF channel selectors and, even today—you know it from your own experience—people do not turn to these channels (14 to 83) with the same thoughtless ease or habit as they do to the VHF channels, 2 to 13.

The accumulated effects of these historic, technical, and economic forces become the mountain against which ABC's difficulties must be measured and its triumphs given extra praise. If CBS and NBC were climbing the Matterhorn in their adaptation to television, ABC was climbing Mount Everest—with one leg missing and an arm tied behind its back.

While there was something in television called the American Broadcasting Company as early as August 1948, when it began a regular program schedule through its New York station, WJZ-TV (now WABC-TV), ABC needed millions of dollars in capital to avoid becoming a banana republic network, or indeed, to survive at all. Going public in May 1948 provided ABC with the money to open stations by the fall of 1949 in Chicago, Detroit, Los Angeles, and San Francisco; and to build network facilities in New York and Hollywood. But, to become a major network, ABC desperately needed additional millions.

Around this same time, on another front in the entertainment industry, Paramount Pictures was being ordered to dismember itself. In 1950, at the conclusion of an eleven-year antitrust action brought by the Justice Department, Paramount and the other major film companies were forced to consent to a rule that decreed, A motion picture company could not make and own pictures and also own and control theatres in which they were exhibited.

Faced with this ruling, Paramount decided to amputate its theatre division, which became the independent company, United Paramount Theatres, Inc. This new company was further required to reduce its theatre holdings from 1,298 houses to 651. It was clear that while the new company had great short-term assets, its future ability to generate profits and pursue growth was severely diminished. Also, for those paying attention, you could feel the first tremors of television shaking the established movie industry and depleting the audiences it had so long taken for granted.

One man paying very careful attention to all of this was the president of United Paramount Theatres, Leonard H. Goldenson. Goldenson, raised in a small town in Pennsylvania and graduated from Harvard and the Harvard Law School, had joined the parent company, Paramount Pictures, in 1933. He had advanced rapidly in the company from his start in the Legal Department, through various jobs of ever-increasing responsibility, until his appointment as vice-president of Paramount, before becoming president of United Paramount.

Goldenson realized that his new company was being launched in a period between two great eras in entertainment, one dying and one struggling to be born. Rather than resist television, Goldenson decided to join it. He did not have far to look for a way in. There was ABC.

Negotiations for a merger of United Paramount and ABC were begun by Goldenson in 1951 and the merger was consummated, with the required FCC blessing, in 1953. Leonard H. Goldenson was named president of the newly formed company and Edward Noble was named chairman of the Finance Committee. They called the new organization ABC-Paramount. ABC had survived a cliff-hanger on its journey up the mountain. To be sure, there would be others in the future, but for the time being, there was guarded optimism.

Even with the boost from the merger, ABC was a distant third in the network race with NBC and CBS. Industry wise-guys dubbed it "the push-cart network," "fourth in a three-network race," and said they knew how to end the Korean War: "Make it an ABC series and it would be over in thirteen weeks."

ABC had to scratch for everything—programs, sales, equipment, facilities. For more than a decade, the network's executive offices had no more aesthetics or sense of permanence than a store-front election campaign headquarters, and they were located in the distinctly parvenu province of Manhattan's Upper West Side. (ABC maintains a complex of offices and facilities—constantly being upgraded—in this West Side neighborhood still, though the nearby Lincoln Center cultural compound has invigorated the area. CBS's Production Center in New York, superbly equipped, is located on Fifty-eighth Street between Tenth and Eleventh Avenues, in a setting of urban alienation fit for an Edward Hopper painting. NBC has a first-rate major studio setup in the dreary depths of Brooklyn, in addition to its facilities in the RCA Building.)

Except for 1960, the ABC Television Network lost money every year in the 1950s and 1960s—other divisions provided the profits to keep the company alive—and it seemed again to be moving toward the precipice. I have heard Mr. Goldenson describe the difficulties of these early years. Apparently, there was a period when meeting the network payroll each week meant flying a satchelful of cash cross-country from the successful ABC-owned station in Los Angeles, KABC-TV.

Then, adding to its chronic historic problems, ABC was to face another technological avalanche—color television. The network would need over $50 million to make the conversion to color. It had no choice; NBC and CBS were going all out.

Dr. Peter Goldmark of CBS had been experimenting with color television in the thirties and on August 27, 1940, color television pictures were beamed—for the first time, it is thought—from the CBS transmitter atop the Chrysler Building to the network's Madison Avenue headquarters half a mile away.

In 1946, engineers from the NBC parent, RCA, were publicly demonstrating all-electronic, color television pictures; in 1947 they were demonstrating "compatible color" television—color pictures which can be received in black-and-white as well as in color. Compatible color was an enormous breakthrough for promoting the stable and flexible growth of color television in a relatively short time. By 1972, 50 per cent of the television sets Americans owned were color.

In a color-only system, black-and-white sets and recording and transmission equipment systems would have been instantly obsolete and the transition to color would have been disruptive, erratic, and painfully expensive for everyone. This was not so readily apparent as it might seem.

In 1946, the year before RCA was to have demonstrated its compatible color system, CBS petitioned for acceptance of the standards of its color-only system by the industry at large. The FCC opened hearings and RCA fought the CBS petition, reasoning that the industry would be better off waiting for its all-electronic (CBS's system also employed a mechanical disc), compatible color system which would soon be perfected.

In 1947, the FCC ruled that color television technology was not yet acceptable for commercial application, but this was only a retard sign and not an ending. The FCC launched new hearings on color television in September 1949. The interested parties were CBS, RCA, and something called Color Television, Inc. A month later, the FCC ruled that the CBS system would become the industry standard. RCA went to court to undo what it considered the FCC's mischief, and in May 1951 the Supreme Court upheld the FCC decision. On June 25, 1951, CBS broadcast the first commercial color television program via its New York station. The nation had eleven million black-and-white receivers and zero color sets.

Other snags developed. Color set manufacturing was curtailed by the Korean War and was stopped cold when the various set manufacturers rejected the CBS system. CBS suspended color-casting and its own set manufacturing operation, through a subsidiary called Hytron, which was eventually to lose over 40 million CBS dollars.

Then, on December 17, 1953, the FCC, in a reversal of its earlier ruling, approved the RCA all-electronic, compatible color system and authorized NBC to go ahead with color broadcasting. Enter the Peacock. It started with "Kukla, Fran, and Ollie" and, a scant twelve years later, NBC was hailing itself as the first "full-color network."

ABC, confronted once more with a sheer-face ascent up the money mountain to convert to color television, hoped to repeat its earlier success with survival-by-merger. At a later date, Howard Hughes flirted with ABC, but in 1965, I.T.&T. started a courtship in earnest and was valuing the company at 400 million dollars.

It has been reported by Les Brown, in his good book, *Television, the Business behind the Box,* that during the two years in which I.T.&T. was seeking to acquire ABC, the network lapsed into "partial paralysis . . . morale was low . . . there was a loss of faith in ABC's ability to compete," and that when the merger was frustrated by the U.S. Justice Department's grave reservations about its propriety, which finally caused I.T.&T. to break off its courtship and withdraw its proposal, "the entire company [ABC] was in a state of shock."

Leonard Goldenson had been quoted in *Business Week* (August 18, 1973) as saying, "In retrospect, the collapse of the deal was a good thing. It made us realize that we would have to make it alone, so we rolled up our sleeves and went to work."

Goldenson solved the financial dilemma with a $50 million sale of convertible debentures and with loans against the company's considerable real estate holdings; for the network itself, Goldenson finally found an effective leader in Elton Rule. Elton Rule is tall with California coloring and has a Jack Kennedy kind of winner's good looks, style, and reserve. From the assumption of his leadership role in 1968, Rule, former head of KABC-TV in Los Angeles and well schooled in station and sales areas, stimulated the officer corps (many new men were brought in), lifted morale, revitalized programming, modernized equipment and facilities, made money, and began to win for ABC.

A quantum jump took place in ABC's fortunes as Goldenson and Rule began the orderly execution of a plan that called for measured and steady growth—winning by inches, rather than blowing hot on the dice and hoping for a lucky roll. In addition to its patient and intelligent pursuit of its internal plan, ABC got a break when the FCC brought forth its Prime Access Rule (see Chapter 4). This curtailed network programming by seven half hours a week, which allowed ABC to drop the really bad shows in its schedule and to use its fewer development dollars than NBC and CBS in greater concentration. Furthermore, with fewer advertising minutes available in network prime time, sponsors flocked to ABC in record numbers and paid record prices. (Ironically, this allowed NBC and CBS to charge more also. They had always been held down by the threat of sponsors going to ABC at the cheaper rate.)

The Sports Department became pre-eminent and "Monday Night Football" was innovative as well as successful. Made-for-TV movies were not invented by ABC, but ABC was the first to make them work, and the competition was scooped in the acquisition of important theatrical films. The staple entertainment forms improved. Specials and "ABC Theatre" challenged and occasionally embarrassed NBC and CBS with prestige programs. ABC News, with Howard K. Smith and Harry Reasoner and with "Close-up" documentaries on a regular basis, came of age. Daytime and children's programming closed neck-and-neck with the other networks, late night grew by over 60 per cent in two years, and, in January 1975, ABC introduced "AM America," which was superceded by "Good Morning, America" in November 1975, to compete with "Today" and the "CBS Morning News." By 1973, ABC won a basketful of Emmys and other important awards, in number almost equal to CBS and far more than NBC. ABC was and is still third, but now a respected third of three and definitely on the same track and lap as the front-runners.

What of those things I have described about the other networks? At ABC the atmosphere is looser and there is a sharper sense of irony and humor, of confident consciousness about what we are doing than elsewhere. (Rule has a trenchant wit, as do many down the line.) It strikes me that fear is not an instrument of reign and that candor is encouraged. Certainly, I have had ideas shot down at ABC, but never because I could not get a hearing. Best of all for me, there is considerable freedom to succeed or fail; I like the responsibility of that in either direction.

The Sixth Avenue ABC headquarters in New York (since 1966) is no monument such as 30 Rockefeller Plaza nor is it the spike of art that is 51W52. In fact, the rented building is a prosaic modern tower, but it is light years away from the former rooming-house quarters and it is well-maintained, clean, functional, and modern with lots of light. The walls are mostly white and the furniture is like CBS's. There is good use of space. Wall art in the public areas runs from splendid contemporaries to a couple that look like framed Christmas wrapping paper. You are permitted to personalize your office. The ABC cafeteria beats the competition hands down and is the best bargain since the five cent Staten Island Ferry. I sense the same conservative suit code for men, especially in the upper reaches, but this is no inhibition for me since I have been accused of going to the beach with my attache case, wearing a shirt and tie, and I believe I can better express myself through my head than by wearing a love chain and studded dungaree suit.

I have not said anything about Hollywood and, since most of the entertainment shows are produced there, it is very important. All three networks have vast amounts of money invested in West Coast manpower, offices, facilities, and equipment. As physically concentrated as the three networks are in New York, so in California are they spread out. NBC is in Burbank, CBS is in Hollywood, and ABC is divided, with its executive offices in Century City (cheek-to-cheek with Beverly Hills) and its production facilities near downtown Los Angeles.

CBS's West Coast video complex is called Television City. (The former Republic Studios in Studio City are owned by CBS under the name Cinema Center. Shows produced on film are made there.) Television City was built in 1962, is roughly four stories high, but sprawling, and it contains four large studios, some smaller ones, electrical and carpentry shops, rehearsal halls, support, tape, and telecine facilities—and an office area which is comfortable if not as intense in decor nor as worshipful of image as "Black Rock." There *is* a helicopter pad on top to accommodate visiting New York VIPs who ferry straight from and to LAX, the Los Angeles International Airport.

From outside, Television City looks like a tractor factory. It is located at the intersection of Fairfax Avenue and Beverly Boulevard in a predominantly lower-middle-class Jewish neighborhood (there is an incredibly good delicatessen nearby), and its next door neighbor to the south is the famous Farmers' Market.

There is a vast parking area for workers and visitors and a cordoned-off section of it for stars and executives. The pecking order is easy to keep track of by reading the paint-stenciled names of executives on assigned parking places. The closer a parking place is to the office door, the bigger is the man who has it. This social phenomenon applies at West Coast NBC and ABC as well and is taken very seriously by the participants. There is hardly a graver network sin, especially if he is above you, than parking your car in the preserve of a "net-topper," as *Variety* calls network high-level executives. Several spots stand empty much of the time. These are reserved for the high commanders in New York; though they may be three thousand miles away, their California stalls remain chaste.

NBC does business from a set of stucco buildings that looks like an airport Wiley Post might have used, in a forgettable section of Burbank north of the Hollywood Hills. It has wonderful studio facilities, but the same kind of absent-minded office decor, though not so dowdy, as "30 Rock." Like its counterparts, NBC Burbank has a studio gate with uniformed security guards and your name must be on a list at the gate to pass into this electronic holy city.

ABC's production center near downtown Los Angeles, in a time-abandoned part of town that appears to be peopled with refugees from novels by Nathanael West and John Steinbeck, is the former movie studio lot of Vitagraph, established there in 1912. (ABC took it over in 1949). Gloria Swanson, Norma and Constance Talmadge, and Mabel Norman began their movie careers there. John Barrymore, Mary Pickford, the Gish sisters, and Wallace Beery made pictures there. (ABC also has studios at 1313 Vine Street and at the Hollywood Palace, also on Vine.) This center at Prospect and Talmadge has one first-rate large studio, several smaller ones, and all the expected support facilities. Equipment there has traditionally lagged behind NBC and CBS, but is catching up. However, the ABC executive offices in Century City win the prize for sumptuous digs.

Century City is a modernistic urban center that sprang up large in little more than a decade on the former back lot of the 20th Century Fox Film Corporation. We have Elizabeth Taylor and Richard Burton to thank for it. The enormous overruns in cost on *Cleopatra* had put Fox so into financial jeopardy that it had to sell its real estate to keep from folding. (Eventually, all the movie companies had to reduce their landed domains.) Plunked down anywhere in America, except in the few largest cities, Century City would be an important and impressive "downtown" of itself.

In the midst of Century City is a Fellini-fantasy of a building in white stone called the ABC Entertainment Center. The Entertainment Center contains a legitimate theatre, two movie houses, several restaurants and stores, a Playboy Club, four heroic levels, acres of concrete plazas, expressionistic escalators, an underground connection to the Century Plaza Hotel across the boulevard it fronts on—"The Avenue of the Stars"—and a four-tier underground parking garage that is a menace to those in delicate balance. The ABC executive offices in the Entertainment Center are ultraplush and the kind you would like to have those snotty kids back home who said you would never amount to anything see you in. "Take that, Wanda Jean!"

How are the networks structured? I will not go into a description of the nontelevision departments and divisions and groups or into specific detail as to names and job titles and functions. (All of this is complicated enough to warrant a separate book—which should, when it is published, be in loose-leaf form, since organizational tables and especially names change so frequently.) Instead, I will try to construct a simplified model of a network's program department structure close enough to all three to be helpful in understanding any single one.

Before we get to that, however, keep in mind that all three companies have far-reaching enterprises beyond network television programming. All three own and operate (or are permitted to) five VHF television stations, two UHFs, seven AM and five FM radio stations in major cities. CBS has a wholly owned record company, publishing house (Holt, Rinehart and Winston), a film company, Steinway Pianos, Creative Playthings, the Fender Guitar Company, and much else. ABC has a wholly owned record company, several other labels, movie theatres, a movie company, five outdoor scenic attractions including Silver Springs, Florida, magazines, and a pure-water bottling company. NBC is part of the vast RCA constellation that includes beyond its many electronic divisions, a record company, a publishing house (Random House), frozen foods, real estate, and the Hertz Rental Company. I think, if I am not mistaken, they also own a piece of Disney on Parade. All three do or have invested in Broadway; CBS grossed over $30 million on its piece of *My Fair Lady*.

As an entertainment program maker, your first and most frequent stop at a network will be the Program Department. Sports and News are separate divisions or departments shaped along similar organizational lines, and will have either presidents or senior vice-presidents of their own who report directly to a president or presidents.

Our simple model:

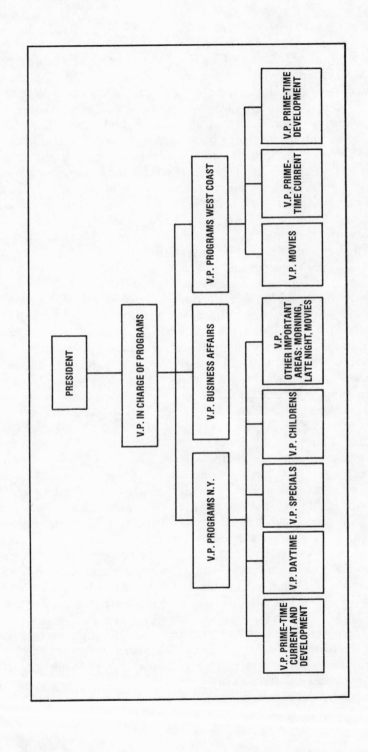

A reminder—none of the networks is set up precisely like this, but the model does demonstrate the relative hierarchy in all three. It shows clearly the important posts and the important areas of programming. Keep in mind also that this model relates to the Program Department only and does not show the extremely important higher (corporate, group, division) and lateral areas such as Sales, Network Operations, Planning, Standards and Practices, Research, Affiliates, Operations and Engineering, Press Relations, or Advertising and Promotion.

Top-level officers are located in New York City, although I expect there will be further migration west in the next few years. For certain, the final program decisions are made and the schedules are set in New York. On the other hand, most of the heavyweight program sellers and makers and talents and facilities are on the West Coast. This continental division is especially satisfying for the airlines and for those on both coasts who desire a change of time zone and life style.

Heads of Daytime, Children's, Specials, and other areas such as ABC's Late Night and Early Morning programming run their departments from New York, with other executives in these areas on the West Coast.

But, because Prime-time is so important to a network's power and prestige (it is almost the only time the financial-influentials watch television, except for weekend sports), and because the major suppliers are there, the top network Prime-time executives in California usually hold greater power than those Prime-time vice-presidents on the same level in New York.

As I have said, under each of the vice-presidents in our model, there is a further table of organization. These lesser posts are charged with carrying out the front-line operations and grittier details—the farther down in the chart, the more menial the tasks. These at the first descent may be still more vice-presidents; if not, directors; under these will be managers, supervisors, program executives and/or coordinators. Assistants-to and secretaries ornament the chart from top to bottom.

Usually, anyone from the program executive level up is empowered to receive a program submission, though at the lower levels, this power is strictly negative—they can say no if they are cool to an idea. They cannot say yes. Instead, if they like an idea, they pass it up the chain of command in the form of a recommendation. Many yeses can begin at the director level and yes power increases as you move up. Still, there are all kinds of yeses. Even a president is circumscribed in his power to say singly a really big yes—putting a program into the prime-time schedule, for instance. This is usually legislated in committee by a group that may be called the Program Board which consists of one or more presidents, the chairman of the Board of the company, and the highest layer of program vice-presidents—plus vice-presidents of Sales, Research, Affiliates, Business Affairs, Standards and Practices.

All three networks' Programming Departments have Departments of Business Affairs. While the programmers are involved with creative aspects, from first submission to final on-air, the Business Affairs people negotiate the deals, write the contracts, and keep tabs on the budgets and costs after programmers have decided which shows and talents they want. Business Affairs can veto or curtail programmers' actions. Mostly, they try to facilitate.

For a program maker or seller, it is important to know and to cultivate the power players in Business Affairs. First, for obvious reasons, these people structure the deals and control the money. But the more political and seasoned program suppliers know there is a subtler reason, and the phenomenon behind it is at work in all of the other areas. Everybody in the network, whether he is in the Program Department or not, is in the Program Department in his heart. Wake the cleaning lady at 4:00 A.M. and she will tell you what to put in the schedule at 8:00 P.M. Saturday night or who to cast in the leads in a made-for-T.V. movie.

And why not? Programs are what a network is essentially about, where the action is and the excitement and the glory. So—the closer network people get to programming in their allied or service areas, and the more powerful they are, the more enthusiastically will they try to exert programming influence. Thus, in turn, when a program maker or seller can influence any one of these powerful people in the other departments of a network, he has given himself potential allies, inside lobbyists for persuading programmers to decide his way; he knows further that these nonprogram people will be flattered by the attention and friendship, by the heady clime of rubbing with the program creators and sellers. I have seen any number of savvy sellers pitch an idea to the Program Department and then bank shot their way off Sales, Business Affairs, Research, and other cushions to angle a commitment.

Knowing that everybody around wants to do the programmer's job, and feels infinitely more qualified, induces anxiety, if not dementia, in an uncertain programmer—and Lord knows there are plenty of these. Even a confident programmer must spend time protecting his flanks. The programmer is visible and vulnerable. The repository of all the network's hopes—and fears. Other areas deal in more apparently concrete considerations.

Business Affairs, for example, when you are good at it, is specific in columns of dollars and cents and legal language and construction with a long history of precedent to guide you. Deals can be creative, yes, but usually troublesome only in ways that can be blamed on the programmers:

"I didn't pick that cost-unconscious producer or a star who comes late to the set; or the boring script. I didn't decide to shoot on location where it has been raining for four days." The other departments have equally sheltering certitudes to lean on. Sales: "I sell ratings." Research: "I say this will work—if you do it right." Affiliates: "My station guys love me. I can clear anything—if you give me the product." Standards: "There is almost nothing I won't allow—if your taste and tone are acceptable." All right—enter the programmer—Candide in a Cardin suit: "Of course it'll work!" (It's fragile as a soufflé.) "It'll be fantastic!" (As lacking in science as falling in love.) "It can't miss!" (Despite my experience, my showmanship, my care to be sure to get endorsement from the committee—who in the hell ever knows finally, 100 per cent, whether a show is going to work or not?)

When a show does work, of course, everybody can lay claim to a piece of the victory; when it fails, everyone points to the programmer: "How do you expect us to negotiate, sell, clear, forecast, or accept—that garbage you concocted!" But—and keep it confidential —all of this is what makes being a programmer so much gut-wrenching, pulse-pounding fun.

If you doubt that program jobs are the network center ring or that programmers are vulnerable or that workers in other areas want to be or can be persuaded to become programmers, consider the evidence at the top level in all three networks. You will find men who have come up through Sales, Research, Planning, Business Affairs (and station management). There is not a single showman-by-trade or even one who has survived internally all the way upward through the programming ranks.

Every television show is at least indirectly affected by the Planning, Research, Sales, and Affiliates areas of a network, even though direct contact may not be there. One cannot avoid Business Affairs or the department that watches over standards. (This latter department is variously known officially as the Continuity Acceptance Department or the Broadcast Standards and Practices Department. People in it are more commonly called the censors.) For most program makers, this department is usually the most frictious. Though it can be scoffed at, ridiculed, cajoled, negotiated with, and often persuaded, it cannot be ignored or ultimately defied.

Because of their vulnerability to government regulation, adherence to a self-regulating industry code (the NAB—National Association of Broadcasters—Code) and their responsibility to their stations and to a widely disparate audience, dominated by the mores and standards of the broad middle class who are, along with their children, the largest consumers of television, networks are extremely sensitive in the area of standards and give great autonomy and veto power to their Standards and Practices Departments.

Assessing the heterogeneous tastes and moral attitudes of the nation is nearly as futile a task as arresting dust in a shaft of sunlight, and I do not envy the censors their duties, nor do I think on the whole they have been ridiculous or mercurial in pursuit of them. Given its power to influence, and the pervasive and passive use of television by masses of people—some homes leave a set on almost constantly—and the democratic nature of the society, the majority views of which television will follow rather than seek to lead, it seems obvious to me that there must be more discretion in content and tone in television than in other entertainment forms that require assertive or individual choice.

I believe in these other media—cabarets, books, magazines, plays, films, and concerts—there should be no state or external intervention. One seldom selects exposure to these as carelessly (for one thing, they cost money), or without some advance knowledge of content via word of mouth or critics, or without a heightened expectation of more revealing and unvarnished truths about life. Nor is their impact so widespread or cumulative. Why not the same standard for television, then? "People can turn it off if they're offended," you can argue. True, but they do not want to turn it off. Television is used mostly as a stroking distraction from the truth of an indifferent and silent universe and the harsh realities just out of sight and sound range of the box. Television is a massage, a "there, there," a need, an addiction, a psychic fortress—a friend. Appalling? Perhaps; but, in such a way, do I, in one sense, understand Marshall McLuhan's thesis that the medium itself is the message more than the individual content of any single show. People, like it or not, do not want to turn television off and that is why they are so deeply offended when they are turned off by it. And, of course, "Turn it off, if you're offended" is absolute heresy to those of us making television. Our mission is to enlarge the audience, not to shrink it.

Where does this leave us? With a cave-in acceptance of total electronic oatmeal? Of course not. But it does give you a reality base from which to fight for a television that does not hide societal truths, exclude responsible if unpopular points of view, ignore realities or distort the use of language's power to provide understanding, emphasis, or honest emotion. I have fought for this kind of television all my television life—though by steps or reason, I hope, and not by hurling puerile hand grenades.

We have, in fact, come a long way from the deletion of Jack Paar's innocuous joke about a water closet and the "scandal" of Petula Clark touching Harry Belafonte, and the harsh retribution demanded for adulteress, atheist, criminal, Indian, or honest questioner.

I credit television with stimulating the civil rights movements of blacks and women, of shortening America's participation in the Vietnam War, of hastening the fall of Senator Joseph McCarthy and President Richard Nixon—without shredding the social fabric—with confronting all of the conventional wisdom regarding our cherished myths and fattened assumptions, and with refining the tastes and broadening the experiential attitudes of millions of Americans who would otherwise never be touched.

Frequently, I thought Dick Cavett was winning the first half and losing the game in his implacable stands against the censor. Sure, he was very clever in these postshow sessions and could make mincemeat out of the logic of the censor's position, but nearly always over the deletion of a word, a phrase, or a paragraph, when he had already won the prize by opening the entire program to formerly taboo and controversial subjects and guests. (Dear Richard, if freedom cracked the Liberty Bell, enlightened compromise bound up the states.)

I believe George Carlin, whom I admire and was the first to put on television, is climbing the wrong cross by crusading for his banished "seven words," rather than taking justifiable pride in the greater effectiveness of his biting and enlightening monologues about the hypocrisy and injustice in our social and political mores.

On the other hand, by quoting the Bible, Shakespeare, and the Constitution, Senator Sam Ervin did more on television to save and enlighten the nation than a hundred comics or dramatists who feel suppressed if they cannot say dirty words, do genitalia jokes, or cut someone's nose off with a switch blade in extreme bloody close-up and pretend that it passes for *Hamlet*.

As for enforcement of standards and practices, industry folk knowledge has it that NBC is the freest, CBS slightly right of center (Norman Lear excepted), and ABC the most conservative. These distinctions in my experience at all three networks are moot. Significantly unmeasurable. All three networks have similar policy guidelines and adhere to the same industry and government codes.

I do feel that NBC lets Johnny Carson "get away" with a great deal. Nothing that he shouldn't, mind you; just more than others. Carson raises an interesting point. There is a direct correlation be-

tween success and censorship. There is nothing like a plus 35 per cent
share of the viewing audience to keep the scissors away.

It is not so much network policies that vary as the individuals who
interpret. Not only do the public's tastes and opinions vary, but the
individuals who are responsible for trying to interpret those riptides,
and the network standards, are also subject to their own psychological
warps as well (which are frequently revealed by the cuts they ask for),
so that great absurdities and high comic moments do occur in your
dealings with Standards and Practices at all three networks.

And curious negotiations: More than once I have found myself
confronted with sweet grandmotherly-type censors or angels fresh
from the convent or young men straight from Boy Scout camp, saying
such things as 'clitoral orgasm' can stay, and 'oral sex'—the doctor is
saying those—but 'clap' and 'mouth on genitals' have to come out."
Or, "I'll give you the knife in the throat, but the girl in the bra and
panties who sounds like she's coming has to go." It seems I am always
the one blushing in these sessions.

On what bases do the censors make their decisions? There is
always the nervous look over the shoulder at what the FCC is thinking
and there are two sources of industry guidance. One is the NAB
Code, established in 1948; the other is each network's own standards
and practices policy book. These policies for all three networks
evolved from the NBC program code which became a formal document in 1934. There have been revisions in all three to respond to
changing times and problems, but the original NBC code is still
instructive and reflective of basic network philosophy.

The NBC code calls for positive program treatment concerning
religion, race, marriage, and the home. It calls for the maintenance of
high moral standards, respect for the law, and good taste, with particular concern in children's programs. It declares for standards of accuracy, impartiality, and freedom from sensationalism in news broadcasts. It lists products and services not acceptable for advertising and
calls for truth in advertising claims. It establishes rules governing
game shows and prize contests or offers of premiums. It sets forth rules
for what—and how—goods and services may be traded for mentions
on shows.

Standards and Practices Departments record and file all program
submissions, read all scripts, monitor all filmings and tapings, and
screen all final shows. They can demand changes all along the line.
Every network contract has a paragraph stating that all other provisions are subject to a network's Standards and Practices Department's
acceptance of the program.

How do you deal with Standards and Practices—the censors?

First, I think, by respecting the job they have to do, and them as people—or, at least, in being smart enough to seem to. No one, including a censor, responds reasonably or openly when you are exhibiting your contempt for his very existence. If you are abusive, he will harden his own position in the current test—has the unquestioned power to enforce it—and will be laying for you in future situations.

Next, certify your own motives. As a television pro, you will know rather much what goes and what does not. When you are testing the boundaries—and you must in all areas but violence—weigh the honest personal convictions behind your arguments. If you judge the content in question as being necessary for solid moral and intellectual reasons, fight for it. Even if you judge the material to be cut as harmless and inoffensive except to very uptight people, fight for that. But if you yourself are cynically defending material that is unconsciously designed to titillate, exploit, or gratuitously shock audiences, get off the censor's back.

Next, argue in the specific context or tone of the seemingly offensive material, rather than a head-on literal defense of each X-word, Y-opinion, or Z-action.

There are two categories of external forces that cause me more fear in the area of censorship than any network Standards and Practices Department.

Since the activist movements of the late 1960s, everybody has learned to use the techniques of demonstration and group pressure to influence events and institutions. Abbie Hoffman becomes professor to parents of West Virginia who protest their children's textbooks. Jerry Rubin is mentor to hard hats and gay liberationists. Stokely Carmichael is mimicked by white mothers in South Boston. And, our former vice-president, Spiro Agnew, taught everybody to hit on television. Everybody is offended. I am not afraid of that. What I do fear is network overreaction to the pressures of the offended and, thus, a further gelding of programs so as to appease proseletizing and propagandizing special subaudiences. Television has to offend somebody sometime, or there can be no redeeming programs at all.

A greater danger even than these visible pressure groups comes from the "old boy" or "we're in the same club, you know," groups who never picket, demonstrate, or get up angry petitions to broadcasters or the FCC. These folk do it quietly over lunch or on the telephone or at the golf course. Large corporations, professional groups with clout, government and political officials are the culprits here.

In the early 1970s, the three commercial networks appeared to be in danger of decline and perhaps even eventual extinction. The ban on cigarette advertising—a $170 million revenue source for the networks—coupled with a recession in the overall economy dealt a heavy and immediate economic blow to the networks. New technology in the form of video cartridges and cassettes, cable and pay TV, which were being touted highly and hotly, threatened the ability of the networks to maintain programming sources, copyright of their material, and to avoid fragmentation of their audiences.

The White House was hitting them hard and was exerting enormous pressure on them to soften their news and turn in their integrity. The pressures were real and potentially lethal. The White House threatened station licenses and condoned license challenges; spoke of banning program reruns, an economic necessity for a network; and sought to exploit traditional grassroots suspicions of New York "Eastern Elitists," by trying to turn affiliated stations against their networks.

On April 14, 1972, John Mitchell's Justice Department filed a series of civil antitrust suits against all three networks. Justice said the suits were not aimed at news, public affairs, documentaries, and sports programs—only entertainment programs. Lovely. This is like a man with a gun saying, "I am not aiming at your feet, your hands, your legs, or your arms—just at your heart." Entertainment programs are the economic life source of a network, and revenues from these frequently pay to sustain all the other programming.

The White House pressures sank in Judge Sirica's courtroom. The FCC has made license challenging more difficult for the challengers. Cigarette advertising has been more than replaced by aggressive Sales Departments and increasing sponsor appetite for television advertising. The public preferred its "free television" and rejected costly home cartridge and cassette equipment and that industry died aborning.

True, the Justice Department refiled its civil antitrust suits against the networks in December 1974, again only against entertainment programming, but most of the charges are woefully anachronistic and ignorant of what is required in the marshaling of resources to generate quality programming. I cannot possibly see these dangerous suits being won by the government.

Among the charges in the suits is the allegation that the networks deny advertisers and independent suppliers the right to air time. And what kind of programs are these "shut outs" going to bring us? Their past performances are a frightening forecast. And the FCC Prime-time Access Rule as an outlet for independents has not spawned distinguished programs, which was its intent, but rather a spate of discredited network retreads: game shows, game shows, game shows. Bitter new wine in old bottles.

As much as the networks rely chiefly on staple popular forms of entertainment, much of it admittedly banal, they can in their consolidation of resources afford a steady supply of fine dramas, documentaries, and variety specials, as well as sustaining far-flung Sports, News, and Public Affairs Departments. They and they alone can afford the staggering costs of live coverage of such events as moon shots, political conventions, and congressional hearings.

Who will give us all this if the networks fall? Single units in the industry? Individual stations, producers, advertisers? These industry fragments are right now the largest drags on network boldness and innovation in programming.

And will such a piecemealed television industry be strong enough, if even concerned enough, to counter government policies that may be ruinous; or dare tell the truth about an administration or other powerful public institution, rather than be forced, out of weakness, to simply show their cosmetized faces, eyelids fluttering innocently behind lying press releases?

Think twice before unmaking the networks. Yes, of course, they need public criticism and all of their procedures should be public business. But, they or the nation do not need, in fact, cannot permit, dismemberment.

For our national safety, we absolutely cannot dispense with networks. They must be big in order to countervail the other big and potentially dangerous sources of power in our country. Only networks can generate the intensity of light we need to reveal those who prosper in the dark.

Enough about networks, except for this final personal thought. For all their faults—and they have many—and for all my private wars against them, it is in the end, for me, as Robert Frost said, "a lover's quarrel."

syndication

Networking means that a program plays simultaneously on all stations which are affiliated with the network, on the same day and at the same hour—at least in theory. There are refinements. All network programs emanate, or are fed, from New York City and are transmitted on long lines—underground cables and/or microwave relays. This keeps the long lines all feeding in one direction—east to west—and establishes a one-way national flow at a standard price. Currently, this is a twenty-four hour service for which each network pays $11.5 million a year. The system is owned and operated by American Telephone and Telegraph.

It is possible to feed programs from Los Angeles or other points of origination and this is frequently done, especially in news and sports coverage. But it requires ordering up special long lines—at considerable additional cost. Most regularly scheduled programs, therefore, even those produced in Hollywood, are flown to New York City for origination of airing.

How then can "The Waltons," for instance, air at 8:00 P.M. in New York, and also at 8:00 P.M. in Los Angeles, which is three hours earlier than New York time? It works like this: At 8:00 P.M. in the Eastern Time Zone, "The Waltons" plays and is simultaneously telecast to the entire country. In the Central Time Zone, where, in this case, it is 7:00 P.M., the program airs concurrent with its Eastern Time Zone airing. This is typical. The entirety of network programming airs one hour earlier in the Central Time Zone, so that prime-time there runs from 6:00 P.M. to 10:00 P.M. instead of from 7:00 P.M. to 11:00 P.M. This has not been an inconvenience for the Midwest, since traditionally this time difference has been in accord with the general sociology of the area.

"The Waltons" continues to be fed "down the network" or "down the line," as we say. In the Rocky Mountain and Pacific Time Zones, the affiliated stations are picking up the program, which they do not air, but rather videotape for telecast at the appropriate hour in their zones. In Los Angeles, for instance, "The Waltons" comes down the line at 5:00 P.M., is videotape recorded by the local CBS affiliated station, and then is telecast at 8:00 P.M., local Los Angeles time.

Often, the network affiliated station will tape programs and hold them for telecast at a later hour or date. When this is done, it is called a DB, or delayed broadcast. Networks and network national advertisers do not like DBs because they adversely affect potential audience and ratings. For instance, our Dallas affiliate on ABC did not carry "In Concert" on Friday night at its regular time, because they had a successful movie package playing on Friday night. They DB'd "In Concert" to a later time. This diminished the national rating because the Dallas audience is smaller than it would have been if the show had been carried at the normal time.

There is another way besides networking to distribute television programs—syndication. In syndication, the programs are sold separately to each station, and these stations air them according to their own scheduling needs. There are no network affiliation contracts and no set number of stations or compatability of stations required for syndication. For example, a syndicated program might air on twenty stations or two hundred; it might air at 8:00 A.M. on the NBC affiliate in Miami, at 4:30 P.M. on the CBS affiliate in San Francisco, at midnight on the ABC affiliate in Seattle, and at various other times—and days—on independent stations in New York, Chicago, or Los Angeles.

As we have learned, network distribution is accomplished by transmitting programs one time via cables and microwave. This requires only two copies of a program. Syndicated programs are distributed by a process called bicycling. Bicycling shows means sending them to individual stations manually; that is, through the mails or by rail or air express. This system, naturally, requires many more prints or copies of a program. Gang printing is what this is called.

For example, when the "Mike Douglas Show" has been videotape recorded, it is then dubbed (copied) and sent by air express to local stations. The major-market stations air the show exactly one week after taping. For some curious reason, this is called zero delay. Smaller markets play the show later.

Indianapolis, for example, as a major market, would air Douglas on zero delay, then would bicycle the print, perhaps to Fort Wayne, for a single delay, meaning two weeks after taping. This same print would keep following a designated bicycle route for perhaps as long as six weeks before it would be returned to the Westinghouse Tape

Center in Pittsburgh. The last station to air it would probably simply return the tape through the mails.

Syndication lacks the immediacy and the prestige of network airing, but it does constitute an important and valuable programming alternative. With the extension of UHF stations and cable systems, syndication will, I believe, become an increasingly fertile field of program supply.

Syndicated programs air in what is called either station time or local time, as opposed to network time. The usual hours of station time are from morning sign-on (6:00 or 6:30 A.M.), until the networks open (at 7:00 A.M. with "Good Morning, America," "Today," and "CBS Morning News"). Again, syndicated programs are aired from 9:00 A.M. until 10:00 A.M., when network daytime programs generally begin. (ABC does not open until 11:30 A.M.). The networks then feed programs until 4:30 P.M., when the local stations take over again until 8:00 P.M., with the exception of network news for half an hour at 7:00 P.M. (All of these are Eastern Time.) The stations take over again at 11:00 P.M. and either keep the time until sign-off or until they join ABC's "Wide World of Entertainment," NBC's "Tonight Show," or CBS's "Late Movie." With all three networks feeding expanded sports coverage, the local affiliated stations have fewer and fewer weekend hours available to them for their own programming. Of course, all of this applies only to those stations which are affiliated with one of the networks. Independent stations have only station time.

Traditionally, syndicated programs had been mostly old movies bought in packages from the major Hollywood studios or television series which had completed successful runs on network. "I Love Lucy" is the classic example of this latter category. This series went off CBS in June 1957, but, as I am sure you know, is still running in scores of markets—sometimes twice a day and even on competing stations.

The success of "I Love Lucy" in syndication has had enormous influence on the television industry and probably has done much to stifle innovation and topicality in television. First, it proved that reruns can attract and hold audiences. This is simple to see: Each half hour or hour taken up by a rerun displaces a program newly made. "Lucy," furthermore, increased the dependency of the industry on film, since film has been so much easier to handle, mail, store, and air. (This has been slowly changing.) As packagers foresaw the golden egg of syndication profits, they avoided new forms, topical content, and boldness, so that their shows would be safe and salable, ten, fifteen, or twenty years hence. Furthermore, they were reluctant to produce live shows, since these would have no rerun value at all.

In the past, the majority of these series in syndication—called off-network reruns—were owned in partnership by the packager and the network which had originally aired the series. It was, to be sure, a shotgun marriage, imposed on the packager by the network. Each of the three networks had a division specifically set up to handle syndication: NBC Enterprises, CBS Enterprises, and ABC Films. These divisions were for domestic U.S. syndication only. Other divisions were established to sell programs on a world-wide basis.

You have probably seen examples in the form of clips on talk or variety shows of these American programs as they are dubbed in foreign languages. There is Lorne Greene as Ben Cartwright speaking Japanese as he rides around the Ponderosa, or Raymond Burr as Perry Mason, cracking the case in hoch Deutsch or fluent Italian. Within our frames of reference, these clips are funny. The shows, however, are taken quite seriously by the audiences they are dubbed for and are intensely popular around the world. In fact, they have so threatened to dominate international television that local governments have been forced to impose quotas on American programs.

As you can imagine, all of this was and is an enormous profit center for a television series and for the people or company which own one. For instance, "Bonanza," true to its name, was once airing in seventy countries at the same time.

Of course, packagers were not happy to have the network as partner in a program's syndication, but there seemed no alternative. A project would probably be worthless in the international market without the original network airing, so it seemed sensible to have 50 per cent of something rather than 100 per cent of nothing. Not everyone was so resigned, but we will come to that story.

In the early days, very few programs were made specifically for syndication. A few exercise shows, such as "Jack LaLanne" and some children's shows were the exceptions, and one additional form that I am surprised no one ever copied. A program called "Romper Room" is on in many markets, but is locally produced in each market. The originator of this program franchises each local station to use his format and logo, but otherwise the hostess and children are from the local area.

So profitable and popular were the off-network reruns that even networks began airing them—mostly in morning daytime—and this effectively foreclosed new production designed for syndication. Soon there were fewer and fewer program suppliers as networks came more and more to dominate. Certainly, local stations did not object. They were relieved of the responsibility both of producing new programs and of buying costly shows. While throwing up their corporate hands and blaming the networks, they were throwing the blame back to the networks while reaping the profits.

However, in 1970, the Federal Communications Commission, under persuasive pressure from some broadcasters and packagers, passed what came to be known as the Prime-Time Access Rule.

The fight for the rule had lasted twelve years in various forms. It was strenuously opposed by the networks, major suppliers, and most of the stations; it was advocated by Don McGannon, president of Group W-Westinghouse Broadcasting, and an acknowledged industry leader. By virtue of Group W's five television stations in key markets (Philadelphia, Pittsburgh, Baltimore, Boston, and San Francisco), it is the most powerful station group outside of the networks. A station group is simply a company that owns a group of stations. Seven television stations is the maximum number allowed under the law to any one company (provided two are VHF). Among such groups are all three networks. Their stations are called network O and O's, which stands for "owned and operated." Other major group companies are Capitol Cities, Taft, Corinthian, Storer, Kaiser, and Doubleday.

McGannon's station group had been enormously successful as an independent source of programming prior to the Access Rule with its early and continuing hit, the "Mike Douglas Show," and a series of monthly specials, produced specifically or acquired exclusively for Group W. The "Merv Griffin Show" added impressively to this success. (At one point it was making over $10 million a year in profit.) These were innovations and McGannon had others to his credit. Group W had dropped cigarette advertising eight months before the law required it, and had led the industry in producing made-for-television movies. Group W dealt the final blow to network radio (later revitalized by ABC) when it dropped its network affiliations on seven radio stations and set up its own world-wide news reporting operation. Two of McGannon's radio stations were the first in the country to go "all news, all the time." Constantly, McGannon was a burr under the saddle of broadcast thinking, reminding a generally unmindful industry of its responsibilities through the sponsorship of numerous industry meetings and symposia, public service advertisements, and statesmanlike comments before congressional committees. The first time I met McGannon, I was working at Bob Banner Associates and he called, inviting us to a lunch. The sole purpose of the lunch was to discuss television philosophically. Among pros, such thoughtful meetings are rarer than rain on the Sahara.

All of this had won McGannon and Westinghouse respect, but few friends. Now, heresy of heresies, McGannon was wanting to change the system! The McGannon argument, before the FCC, contended that the three networks monopolized prime-time, those hours between 7:00 and 11:00 P.M., when most people watch television. He further contended that broadcasters and syndicators were thus foreclosed from these maximum audience and profit potentials. As a result, they could not generate quality programming at budgets competitive with the networks and major studio suppliers. It followed that the "public interest, convenience, and necessity" were not being served.

McGannon argued further that the networks had narrowed the production sources by relying on a small group of Hollywood majors who ground out basically the same programs year after year. To him, local stations were remiss in fulfilling their public trusts through their dependence on this system. The local stations did not feel remiss! They were delighted with the system and recoiled from the idea of making their own programs on their own money. But McGannon was relentless and, finally he prevailed. The FCC voted yes for the Prime-Time Access Rule.

Under this rule, the three networks would be allowed to program only three hours of prime-time every night of the week. Local stations would thus now be responsible for filling the additional hour. As a means of "uplifting" the quality of this hour, an underlying FCC motivation all along, the Commission further ruled that local stations would not fill the hour with off-network syndicated reruns. Goodby to "I Love Lucy" in prime-time. Nor were old movies allowed in this time. The programs must be "newly made." The rule was applied to the top fifty population markets, but this made it effective for the whole country, since it would be unprofitable for the networks to offer programs which did not play in these huge areas.

At the same time, the Commission ruled, networks would have to divest themselves of wholly owned syndication operations; nor could they enter into partnerships with suppliers in the ownership of programs. ABC Films was spun off as an independent company now called Worldvision. CBS Enterprises became Viacom and NBC Enterprises sold off its assets to various companies. The networks could, if they wanted, continue to produce their own shows; but they could not enter into partnership agreements with independent packagers.

Opponents of the Access Rule, among them the chairman of the FCC, Dean Burch, declared that you could not "legislate" "do-good" programming. They forecast a spread of the "wasteland" as a result of the rule. Unhappily, these doom-sayers were right.

Beyond McGannon's own group, very few stations took up the challenge to produce their own programs. (The rule was modified to exempt network news at 7:00 P.M., Monday through Friday, and further modified to allow the networks to recapture 7:00 to 8:00 P.M. on Sunday night.) Group W-Westinghouse Broadcasting did produce and offer to other stations a number of new programs. All were dismal failures—whether from low quality or industry spite remains a moot point. For the most part, in any case, local stations quickly turned to outside suppliers to fill the time. All right, still not so bad, since one intention of the ruling was to expand the pool of program suppliers.

Did young, talented innovative producers—previously shut out —rush through this creative floodgate? Yes. Most were drowned in the tide of business as usual. Occasionally, some good programs floated through, but for the most part, the rule spawned trash. What were the new programs? Remakes (in newly made version, to be sure) of all the exhausted and abandoned old formats ever devised. We got the "New Adventures of Lassie," "Police Surgeon," and a flotsam of game shows from "Let's Make a Deal" to "Beat the Clock."

Ironically, the Access Rule also *increased* the number of commercials in this half hour! The network code of practices calls for only three minutes of commercials in each prime-time half hour. Local stations are permitted to have as many as six commercials per half hour and, of course, that is what most of them programmed in the access half hour.

Too bad. The rule was well-intended and public-minded. Because it did not absolutely dictate quality programming (a difficult and perhaps unconstitutional thing to do), but rather trusted to individual stations to be responsible, the effect was to heap additional television abuse on the viewers.

Like it or not, the Access Rule appears to have opened up more time for syndicated programs. Let us examine the ways they are made and marketed.

As I told you, all of the majors—Fox, Warner's, Universal, M-G-M—have syndication divisions. They will probably not be interested in any new program ideas you bring to them, however. Theirs are mostly grind operations to sell their movie product and off-network programs. They do not produce or finance new productions. Worldvision and Viacom, basically syndication companies, are interested in financing new projects, both for initial network airing and/or syndication. They do not buy very much, except from well-established producers and by acquisition, that is, programs that are already made.

The next best place to sell a new program is to station groups, such as Westinghouse and Metromedia, the most assertive and imaginative syndicators.

There are smaller independent syndicators—Jack Rhodes in Los

Angeles, Len Firestone in New York—but these do not have the resources to finance new productions and mostly are hired by others to do the selling, marketing, and the mechanical work of distribution.

Mainly, though, the half-hour or hour film show has been too costly to compete in syndication. Thus, prime access for the most part has promulgated bulk and inexpensive programming. This explains the resounding success of game shows in prime access syndication. These programs can be and are produced on tape, five half-hour episodes at a time, all made in a single day. This cuts costs and reduces both the number of decisions a local station programmer has to make and the slots he has to fill. If he opts for "To Tell the Truth" or "I've Got a Secret" across-the-board (in a strip, we call it), he has filled every 7:30 P.M. Monday through Friday slot at one stroke. Local station programmers love strip shows and the more time these shows fill, the better. Airing "Merv Griffin" or "Mike Douglas," a local station fills 7½ hours of air time a week with minimum fuss, staff, and cost, and it gets a network quality product which it could not hope to match locally, even granting the desire. Individual programs (one shots) are extremely difficult to sell.

Since it is unlikely that you have a "Bewitched" or "Room 222" to your credit yet and ready for off-network syndication, let us confine ourselves to the study of products newly made for syndication. This may be your best opportunity to become a packager.

Because programs, aside from budget, are made rather much the same for network or syndication, the chief distinction comes in the marketing. There are three principle ways in which syndicated programs are marketed.

First, there is the program newly made for syndication and sold for cash to individual stations. Such a program is usually costly to produce and requires a good-sized company to underwrite it financially. In most cases, such a program requires its own production facility and national sales organization to achieve success.

Such a program and setup would be the "Mike Douglas Show," which is packaged by Group W-Westinghouse Broadcasting. Douglas tapes his show in the Philadelphia station which is owned by Westinghouse. The "Douglas Show" is the most successful newly made syndicated program of all time.

As I have reported, Westinghouse owns five television stations and when the Douglas show first began back in 1960, one of these was in Cleveland. (NBC had forced Westinghouse to take the Cleveland station in exchange for the Philadelphia station in order for Westinghouse to get NBC affiliations back in the early days of television. The court later ruled against NBC in a suit brought by Westinghouse and the network was forced to return the larger and more profitable Philadelphia station to Group W.) Douglas began as a local Cleveland program. When it showed strength in this market the program was aired on all five of the Westinghouse stations, from Boston to San Francisco. With the cost of show production now shared among five major markets, the program became instantly profitable within the Westinghouse family of stations.

With a story to tell about its success in five markets, diverse and geographically spread across the country, Westinghouse set up its own syndication organization and sent salesmen around the country to sell the program in other markets. All of the salesmen had actual tapes in hand for local station programmers to screen.

Westinghouse offered the show on a cash basis and provided each local station not only with an attractive program with name guests, but also a coordinated local promotion campaign backed up by a national advertising budget. The programs were "slugged" with eighteen blank minutes of commercial time, which the local stations could sell either to national spot or local advertisers. The show was offered in five ninety-minute programs a week, or in five one-hour versions. Additionally, Westinghouse had another division which represented local stations in getting national spot sales advertisers and, of course, a lot of these were encouraged to buy into the "Mike Douglas Show." Westinghouse, at its videotape dubbing center in Pittsburgh, also made the tape copies of the show and supplied these to the local stations. Again, the locals had only to throw the switch and mail the tape, after they had aired it, on to the next town.

The "Mike Douglas Show," now fifteen years old, is telecast on more than two hundred stations in the United States and Canada. The amount of cash which a local station must pay for the "Mike Douglas Show" is first predicated on the size of the market and next on how soon after taping the station airs the program. Following its initial contract-period run, the program's pricing would be negotiated up or down, according to its ratings performance.

I do not know what the "Douglas Show" brings in, but I do know that Douglas himself is paid $2 million a year (plus some percentage probably), and that the show costs (exclusive of sales, advertising, tape dubbing, and mailing) about $85,000 a week for five ninety-minute programs. When I was producing the "Merv Griffin Show" for Westinghouse, Channel 5 in New York was paying $11,000 a week for five shows.

To get local stations to put out this kind of hard cash for a program requires a very strong product with a good track record. As you can see, it also requires a complex national administrative and sales force. Not many local stations are willing to pay green dollars for new, untested programs, nor are many production organizations equipped or motivated to make such programs. All of this has given birth in syndication to barter programs.

Barter shows are like barter is—the exchange of one desirable thing for another. Most often, a barter program is made by a producer on behalf of an advertiser, who, at minimum cost, is seeking maximum identification and promotion with a program or personality. A prime example would be the "Galloping Gourmet." This program was underwritten in its production costs by Young & Rubicam, a major international advertising agency. Y & R, as it is familiarly known, represents various food and household clients who felt they needed a specific programming vehicle for advertising their products, a vehicle which would be aimed at a high-level, special-interest, receptive audience. Encouraged by the success of Julia Childs's "French Chef, Y & R undertook the "Galloping Gourmet."

The "Galloping Gourmet" satisfied many specific Y & R requirements. The whole show is about food. As extras, the host, Graham Kerr, appears at point-of-sales (supermarkets) in promotions ranging from life-size cutouts of himself to stick-on labels reading "as seen on the 'Galloping Gourmet,' " thus giving the product the respectability of an expert endorsement. An identifiable personality was available for in-person appearances at sales conventions and food industry conferences.

In order to cut costs of production, the half-hour strip was taped in Canada (a savings of up to 50 per cent in production costs), two or three per day. Further, since a beef Wellington is a beef Wellington is a beef Wellington, the program can play forever.

But how is it bartered? All right. Here is another show with which I am very familiar, since I conceived it. The program is "American Life Style," a series of half-hour specials which star E. G. Marshall. Each half hour is an on-site tour of a great American home, conducted by Marshall who also gives a chatty biography of the person who lived there—F.D.R.'s Hyde Park, William Randolph Hearst's San Simeon, Thomas Jefferson's Monticello, and so on.

I had had this idea for a great homes series, all researched and written in detailed presentation, lying in the drawer for ten years before it became a reality.

As a known television packager, I, among others, was queried by the advertising agency, Vansant, Dugdale of Baltimore, on behalf of their client, the Bassett Furniture Company. For years, Bassett had used print and spot television advertising without much prestige, visibility, or satisfaction. Trade names in the furniture business, I learned, are traditionally hard to establish. People, it seems, buy a dresser, chair, sofa, or bed by genre rather than by name. Bassett and Vansant, Dugdale decided that Bassett needed its own television program in order to establish the Bassett name, not only with consumers, but also with furniture retailers.

"We want a prestige barter show for Bassett," Henry Otto said, in the initial phone conversation. Otto had been designated by the agency to find a show and a packager/producer. "Got any ideas?"

I had not thought about my great homes idea for years, but instantly, at the mention of a furniture company, it came to mind.

"I do, Henry," I said, "as a matter of fact. I think it's just what you need."

Henry responded favorably and we arranged a meeting. Thus began a series of meetings that resulted in actual production.

Bassett would underwrite the costs of the programs and of their distribution. Our company, my wife's and mine, Comco Productions, Inc., would make the shows and retain the majority ownership. Showcorporation and Vansant, Dugdale would syndicate them. During the term of the contract license, Bassett retailers would have the right to show the programs in their communities, off-television, to schools, service, and fraternal organizations. E. G. Marshall, as host, would not do Bassett commercials, but would appear twice a year at the spring and fall furniture shows.

We had to change the title of the program, since at about the same time Sears launched a series of commercials using the theme "Great American Homes" for a line of house paints it was selling. (You must have all show titles cleared and registered by a title registry service.) Bassett's commercials, designed for the program, used the theme, "Bassett lets you choose your life style," to get across the point that Bassett offers a varied line of furniture designs and styles. The agency recommended that we call the series "American Life Style," as a tie-in. We agreed.

For its investment, Bassett got an opening and closing billboard identification in the show—". . . is brought to you by Bassett, the world's largest manufacturer of fine furniture for every room in your home, and by the more than twenty thousand Bassett dealers throughout the country"; and ". . . has been brought to you by, etc., etc." These opening and closing voice-over announcements are accompanied by the Bassett logo supered over the picture. (A logo is a trademark or visual signature.) Within the show Bassett got two one-minute commercials out of the four available. The other two minutes contained black leader to be filled later.

At this point, Showcorporation and Vansant, Dugdale took the programs around to local stations and said, "All right, here is a network quality series which we will give you. In the barter you get two minutes to sell." As an additional fillip, Bassett persuaded several of its retail furniture dealers to buy these two minutes of commercials in their individual markets, which made each half hour then totally visible for furniture and for Bassett. Some of these dealers had never used television to advertise, which pleased the local station since it represented new business. Vansant, Dugdale further provided kits of feature stories on E. G. Marshall, the series, the famous Americans, and cuts for newspaper ads and listings.

Some stations, negotiating toughly, would say, "Fine, that's all very nice and we want the show, but only with an extra commercial minute to sell." So, an additional minute would be carved out of the program, occasionally by brutal amputation when left to the local station surgeon. (In later programs, we designed a minute specifically for this cut purpose—a minute that was without music or effects and which usually contained a talk piece by Marshall that went into more depth about the famous American than was really essential to the program.) Finally, the series was placed in 150 markets.

Bassett got what it wanted: A prestige series (it won numerous awards) with which it was highly identified, and at a price, even with production and distribution costs, that gave it a lower CPM (cost per thousand) than buying scatter minutes in network prime-time. "American Life Style" has since been taken over by the patronage of the United States Fidelity and Guaranty Insurance Company of Baltimore. In addition to its television runs, USF & G is making maximum use of the series in schools and organizations.

But I have ignored one of the primary motivations of advertisers to seek syndication programming. In radio and in the early days of television, sponsors always sought and got the identification they wanted with their program: the "Colgate Comedy Hour," the "United States Steel Hour," "Kraft Theatre," and so on. When television production costs skyrocketed, no single company or product could bear the costs of a series. (Occasionally, you will see major companies sponsoring specials or a limited series of specials—"General Electric Theatre.") Multiple sponsorship of network shows became the norm. This gave birth to what is called commercial clutter. This means that your commercial is lumped in with the commercials of a lot of other companies. Thus bombarded, a consumer is less likely to remember any one commercial message. Things got worse in 1970–71, when advertisers began to buy fewer and fewer full minutes, so high had the prices zoomed. The networks then were forced to sell 30s, that is, thirty-second commercials, instead of 60s. This, of course, produced a quantum jump in clutter, and further pushed advertisers toward syndication for identification of their product through barter, or right-out buy.

In the second year of the Prime-Time Access Rule, Chevrolet took a novel approach. They produced five different half-hour syndicated programs to cover prime access Monday through Friday, among them, "Stand Up and Cheer," the "Wacky World of Jonathan Winters," and the "Golddiggers." In addition to subsidizing the program costs, Chevrolet went into the top local stations they wanted and simply bought the time, at the stations' going rates for commercials in the desired half hour. They did this in the top fifty markets; in smaller markets, they distributed the programs on a barter basis. So, direct buy is the third, and most effective, form of syndicating a program.

There is also one additional off-network form of distributing a program which should be noted: forming your own network for a single occasion. This has been done frequently by advertisers and usually through a company called the Hughes Sports Network. This company was formed to put together a network of stations on a one-time basis for major, live sporting events—such as the "Indy 500."

Some advertisers, wanting to launch a new product all at once all over the country, or having only seasonal marketing requirements, have used Hughes for variety or drama of a special nature. The most notable example is Fabergé, who used the Hughes Network four times a year for its variety entertainment specials. Such a network is a moveable feast. It changes with each program and each client's needs. It may be made up of various network affiliates and independent stations and, again, may be twenty stations or two hundred. The Hughes Network, like networking generally, does provide an advertiser with day-and-date airing, to which he can key all of his promotion and print advertising and get ample inventory to stores.

Why not just go the regular network route? Some programs, even fully sponsored, cannot find a home on the network schedule. In 1973–74, for instance, ABC turned down forty fully sponsored ideas for specials because they were not compatible with their other programming requirements; and in 1975–76, CBS cut its specials by 10 per cent. Remember, we are dealing with a fixed amount of hours and time in the network schedules. Not everything fits.

An additional stimulation for advertisers to use Hughes and other forms of distributing their programs has to do with content and control. Networks are reluctant to allow advertisers much influence in the content of a program; on the other hand, advertisers are not always eager or willing to be identified with the content of some network shows. Syndication and personal networking are alternatives.

If you are a performer or packager, always subject to your relative negotiating strength, here are some points you should try to get for yourself in syndication deals.

In the case of our first example—where a show is being sold for cash to local stations—if you are Mike Douglas, or the person who suggested or conceived a "Mike Douglas Show," you are entitled to the best salary and profit participation you can get. This should apply, however, just to doing the show and to its airing in, say, fifty markets. If the show sells in more than fifty markets, you should get a per market override.

For example, one syndicated game-show host gets $1,250 for five programs, which can for that price air in fifty markets. Beyond these fifty gross markets, the host gets $35 per market for any of the top fifty markets, $25 per market for the next fifty markets, and $10 per market for any markets beyond these. The packager can run each program twice in each market without additional payment. If a show plays more than twice in a market, the host gets additional payment. He also gets a percentage (of gross profits, subject to negotiation—always try to get percentage of gross) if the show is sold in other countries.

An override may also be in gross percentage of sales. If WNEW-TV paid $11,000 a week for Griffin, he perhaps got 5 per cent of that figure for the New York market alone.

In barter or outright buy situations, you will get only the original production monies and fees agreed upon; of course, with the reservation that if the show is sold to stations for cash, instead of being given away, you are entitled to an agreed-upon compensation. Here—in barter or buy shows—the idea is to retain as much ownership of the programs as possible so that you profit from their subsequent and future use. This would include additional domestic runs, world-wide use, or use in ancillary forms—books, records, plays, movies, cassettes —even T-shirts.

Chapter **5**
advertising agencies and sponsors

"Nothing is for nothing," it has been truthfully if inelegantly said, and certainly this pungent expression applies to "free" television, which, of course, is not free at all. While there is no direct payment by viewers in the United States for the programs they watch on television, they are expected to pay for the programs, ultimately, by purchasing the products and services which are advertised in the commercial messages. Program makers are supposed to devise and produce shows that will attract mass audiences without unduly offending these audiences or too deeply moving them emotionally. Such ruffling, it is thought, will interfere with their ability to receive, recall, and respond to the commercial messages. This programming reality is the unwritten, unspoken *gemeinschaft* among all professional members of the television fraternity.

Even those who should know better have a tendency to respond to this reality with indignation and swollen self-righteousness. They begin to cast stones—at the sponsor and the advertising agencies. Ridiculous. Commercial television is paid for by advertisements and programmed by networks and stations which are usually publicly owned and always meant to be profit-making organizations. These networks and stations must seek the widest possible mass audiences whose levels of taste vary and whose intellectual appetites are frequently base. Television will not get better until all or most of the foregoing changes. The *Daily News* outsells the *Times;* there are more McDonalds than Luteces; and, in our architecture, there is more that is wrong than Frank Lloyd Wright.

I think we should have an elitist national service as a companion to the three commercial networks. Until one is established in this country—where tastes and decisions are dictated as they are with our museums, symphonies, and our opera and ballet companies—any changes in programming will be more apparent than real. Ripples, not tides.

So, if you mean to work in commercial television, do not blame the advertising agencies or the sponsors. They are only components in a complex system. Concentrate rather on their roles as they may affect you as a program maker, and how you should function in relationship to them. Consider also the very real possibility that you may one day work for an advertising agency.

Advertising agencies are not so much in television programming or such "really closh frens wish Carol Burndette un Walsher Conkrite," as a drunken account executive, whom I have not been able to avoid in a mid-Manhattan bar and who has missed his train to Connecticut, is likely to try to tell me; but they are in it—as representatives of the corporate Sforzas and Medicis.

As advisors and decision makers about where and how to spend their clients' monies, advertising agencies exert forceful influence on television programming, though today this influence is circumscribed and not commensurate with the nearly $2 billion they spend annually for advertising on the three commercial networks. (This amount is spent for time and programs; it does not include costs of production for the commercials themselves.)

Radio started airing commercials in 1925. In those early days and in the beginning of television, advertising agencies, and sometimes the sponsors, directly controlled much of the time and produced many of the programs carried in the schedules. To wit, the "Colgate Comedy Hour," the "Kraft Music Hall," "Armstrong Circle Theatre," the "U.S. Steel Hour," "Lux Presents Hollywood," the "Dinah Shore Chevy Show." They exercised veto power over all programs, other than news and sports which were autonomous or at least more distantly influenced. Since the mid-1960s, however, the networks themselves have insisted on or have had thrust upon them dominance in the control, production, and scheduling of programs.

Currently, no regularly scheduled programs or time periods are owned or produced by one advertising agency or single sponsor. Seldom are these programs even fully sponsored or supported by one advertiser. Procter and Gamble, Bristol-Myers, General Foods, and other major purchasers do come down with considerable weight in certain daytime situations and Coca-Cola, in the 1974–75 season, for instance, did have full sponsorship of "Kojak" and "Barnaby Jones" in prime-time. Even so, Coke neither produced nor controlled these programs. Persuasion with regard to program content was the only force available to them.

An advertiser's power to control or affect programming is reaction rather than action. When presented with a program idea or schedule not to his liking, the advertiser can refuse to buy in. An advertiser, already committed to a program, can and frequently does, pull out his message if he does not like the script, or if the star should make page one of the *News* for moral turpitude. (On this point, it is difficult to imagine what situation might not make the star more salable than repellent, however.) Pulling out or pulling your commercial usually means that an advertiser will be entitled to a make good. The network makes good the commercial by running it in another comparable minute. Or, *in extremis,* sometimes a network will rebate in full or in part if a commercial does not run, runs without video or audio, is cut in too late, is up cut (cut before it finished), or if one or more affiliated stations does any of these things. No network likes to rebate; when there is acknowledged trouble, each would prefer to make good. But a big advertiser can threaten to take his big dollar across the street, i.e., to another network, if he is not listened to. But finally, advertisers are to regularly scheduled television what the Queen of England is to the British Commonwealth.

Why do agencies and sponsors accept this modest role when they have such money to muscle around—the money that makes the whole system work? It began, I suppose, in the early sixties (Remember Newton Minow's "The Vast Wasteland"?*) when strong pressures from government and citizens' groups attacked the low quality of advertiser-dominated television and reckoned that the networks should bear full responsibility for the kinds of programs they transmitted. This coincided roughly with rocketing program costs, which few individual advertisers could sustain.

The networks also played a part. With increasing sophistication they realized that individual shows, though fully sponsored, could pull down the shows on either side of them or be incompatible with these shows, not only in gross numbers but in audience differences. Thus were born program flow, block booking, and counterprogramming.

Program flow means that the audience that watches one program will flow into the program that follows. ABC Monday night clearly illustrates a design for program flow. "Cash & Cable" is meant to grab the male audience that would then flow into the obviously male-appeal "Monday Night Football." CBS Monday night is designed as a female-appeal, full-comedy menu to achieve flow from its super lead-off hit, "Rhoda." A network attempts to achieve this flow in all parts of the broadcast day. Flow strategy is most effective when a programmer is working around a clear hit. A network can attempt program flow from another network's hit. A strategy of CBS for instance might

---

*Newton Minow, a Chicago attorney, served as chairman of the Federal Communications Commission and depicted American television in a stinging address as "a vast wasteland."

be to put two situation comedies in the Friday night hour following NBC's hit comedies, "Sanford and Son" and "Chico and the Man," in the hope that the large NBC audience would flow to still more comedy on CBS.

Block booking is an extension of program flow. You schedule, or book, a block of compatible programs.

Counterprogramming means designing a schedule to offer programs that are different from (counter to) the programs available in the same time periods on the other networks. A clear example of counterprogramming is Wednesday night (autumn 1975) from 8:00 P.M. to 9:00 P.M.: ABC with two half-hour situation comedies ("When Things Were Rotten" and "That's My Mama"), CBS with musical/variety ("Tony Orlando and Dawn"), NBC with family drama ("Little House on the Prairie").

Counterprogramming as a strategy disappears completely on Wednesday night at 10:00 P.M.: ABC with "Starsky & Hutch," law-and-order action/adventure; CBS with "Kate McShane," law-and-order action/adventure; NBC with "Petrocelli," law-and-order action/adventure.

Frequently, program flow and counterprogramming turn out to be as scientifically precise as a tout on a race horse from your mailman. Nevertheless, these notions of programming are viewed as golden tablets of faith by the industry and are, in fact, more valid than not.

Where were we? Oh yes, the advertisers got out of programming and the networks got in—"Kinda like us taking over for the French in Vietnam," one jaundiced TV hand has said. In any case, there are additional reasons that make the moneybound agencies submit to network programming dominance while continuing to spend their $2 billion.

Advertisers must use television on whatever terms they can get it, for television is the most potent merchandising vehicle ever devised. Despite your battered senses, there are only a fixed and preciously small number of desirable commercial minutes—six network commercial minutes in a single network prime-time hour, or eighteen minutes in that same hour for all three networks (per half hour in other parts of the day). If it seems at least twice as many, it is because, since 1970, the networks have been selling thirty-second commercials instead of sixties. Most advertisers simply could no longer afford to buy sixty seconds; at the time, this upped the Gelusil intake, but the resourceful advertisers adapted and learned to sell as effectively in thirty-seconds as in sixty. Since there are usually more than enough sponsors competing to fill these limited number of "availabilities," as the commercial minutes are called, the advertisers are caught between a rock and hard place. Their decision is not so much whether to buy the time or not, because they like the program or not, but rather at what bearable price and delivery efficiency—before they are shut out completely. As one agency man said once, "Bad television is better than no television."

Moreover, the advertising agencies and sponsors know that everyone plays it safe. The networks and program makers are not going to come up with shows that are too esoteric or far-out; that is, no shows that are very different from those the agencies or sponsors themselves would produce, in pursuit of mass audience.

Everyone understands. Even with specials—good drama, for instance—you will more likely get marbleized Tennessee Williams and Arthur Miller than Bertold Brecht, George Bernard Shaw, or, God forbid, a serious new playwright. A truly noteworthy exception to this rule is the "ABC Theatre" which has presented new works such as "Pueblo," the "Missles of October," and work from Joseph Papp and the Negro Ensemble Company.

In fact, if a particular program fails or is embarrassing or controversial, the agencies or sponsors can always blame the network or producing company or team or star, which they could not so readily do with more direct involvement. (In turn, of course, a great many programmers sit sunning themselves next to their swimming pools and blame the agencies and sponsors for "what we have to put on.")

Finally, it is not the function of an advertising agency or sponsor to produce programs. To do so would place them in potential conflict-of-interest situations, since they might put their clients or products in such a television program to sustain its success, or simply on a whim, rather than objectively determining if such a show is truly the most efficient outlet for selling.

Nowadays, most network advertising dollars for regularly scheduled programs go toward the purchase of isolated network minutes; that is, as we now see most often, thirty-second commercial messages which are inserted into the programming. These messages are called participating spots, and they are not particularly identifiable with the shows. Usually they must run cheek-by-jowl with the messages of other sponsors' advertisements. (To keep your soap from washing up against your competitor's soap, however, there is a provision called product protection. Product protection means that you are promised a minimum time separation between your brand and their brand of a same product.) Participations are usually part of what is called a scatter plan. This means that an advertiser will scatter the same message in many shows and times and different networks. The scatter plan strategy looks to accomplish with volume what might be missed with intensity. It is Machine Gun Kelly as opposed to William Tell or, more simply, not putting all your eggs in one basket. Given the economics and vagaries of present-day television, scattering is a sound way to reach the maximum audience at the most efficient cost; moreover, for the fainthearted, it is a hell of a lot smaller risk than betting on one show that might be a disaster.

Spot sales are those commercial times bought by national advertisers in local stations (not network), usually in many markets and frequently at the same time, but not necessarily. By the same time I mean 8:00 P.M. in New York, 8:00 P.M. in Seattle, and so on. Local spots are commercials bought by advertisers, mostly in a single or in their local market.

Of course, a big advertiser can still sponsor, say, "Streets of San Francisco" for a whole season (even with participating minutes) and, yes, the sponsor's salesmen can still go on the road talking about our show. There are additional promotional advantages, too. But, even though he may get larger numbers, the advertiser nowadays gets very little identification with the show or the star, Karl Malden, and he certainly will not be allowed to dictate content, time, or day of the series in the schedule.

The mention of Karl Malden brings to mind a new advertising strategy. Malden, as the very visible star portraying a clearly defined detective in a hit series, was hired as a spokeman by American Express Traveller's Cheques to play virtually the same character in a series of "law-and-order" commercials. This way, American Express gets the identification, or rub off, as it is called, with a hit program without having to buy into that program.

Sponsors who make sizable buys are often given star lead-ins— the star of a show, usually holding the product, leads-in to the commercials by saying something like, "And now here's a word from Big Mouth the new antiperspirant tooth paste." Or they get opening and closing billboards. (A billboard is a visual and/or voice-over identification of a product or sponsor tied to the show's title and/or star billing.) For instance, an opening billboard might be, " 'On the Give,' starring Nelson Rockefeller, is brought to you by Virtue Is Not Necessarily It's Own Reward, Inc." A closing billboard alters this to say ". . . *has* been brought to you by . . ." I think these star lead-ins and billboards are meaningless in terms of audience recall or response; they are most valuable as face-saving sweeteners from the networks to the agencies.

But I can recall Mobil bringing us "Masterpiece Theatre," now that I think about it, and I have purposely sought out Mobil filling stations because of it. Billboards are most effective on public television, I think, since they are rarer, though a growing menace.

Thus, the networks decide everything—which programs will be made, where these will go into the schedules, who will be in them, and who will produce and direct and write them. The programs are generally made by the major and independent outside suppliers or by the networks themselves. The advertising agencies and sponsors acquiesce.

But are they so docile that they can only call up networks' Sales Departments and say, "Sell me a minute between 8:00 and 11:00," or "I need daytime the week before Christmas?" Not really. Yes, the smaller agencies and sponsors are not too far removed from such subservience to the networks, but the major agencies and sponsors exert considerably more clout in trying to get exactly the space they want. The networks, for their part, expend millions of dollars and manhours to court and satisfy the important agencies and sponsors.

Here, roughly, is how it works for the prime-time schedule. When the networks have chosen the programs, contracted with suppliers to make them, and have announced their fall schedules (usually around April 15) the major agencies and clients are invited to presentations of those schedules and for screenings of the pilots. From these encounters they will decide about or recommend which shows they think they should buy into.

These days, of course, most of the pilots of programs being seriously considered for a new season can be seen on the air in early spring, before the schedules are set. Here is why: In former times a television season ran for thirty-nine weeks (episodes) from mid-September until late-May. More recently, with costs ascending, it has become imperative that networks cut back the number of original episodes and increase the number of reruns, thus amortizing the costs over two plays. This shorter season leaves open time periods in the spring. Furthermore, pilot program costs have also multiplied—each network spends roughly $20 million a year to develop new programs—so it is a further economy to recoup some of these staggering expenditures by playing these sample shows on the air, with commercials. And, what better means of testing audience appeal of a new series than to play the pilot of the series for the general audience which will ultimately judge it in any case?

Even so, the pilots continue to be shown in private screening rooms to important advertisers. In the case of variety shows, where there is seldom a pilot, the star of the show or the producer or both are introduced to potential buyers via conference meetings, luncheons, dinners, or cocktail parties, at which the star or producer will talk through the show.

These are the Rites of the Television Spring, "the Selling Season," the "Mating Season," when advertising agency buyers are avidly sought by the network salesmen. In its four to eight weeks, the voices of advertisers may be heard rising in the land of Manhattan: "Wow, that's gonna be a hot show," or "What a bummer—who dreamed that one up?" "It's a winner; a breakthrough; the guy's a genius; it's perfect for my client." "It's stale; a loser; they must have something on him; I hope the producer's sleeping with the broad playing the lead so it shouldn't be a total loss; that show's a Dunkirk for my client—the *Andrea Doria,* the Edsel, the Havana Hilton, Watergate!"

Agency people pay studious heed to these programs and schedules and consider that their human involvement in the ceremony is essential. The more conscientious ones read all the available scripts and outlines for appeal (and client biases) and go watch the production or meet stars or creators in California. Some do not sleep as they sincerely ponder how to make the shows better or more creative. But all of this is really just so much making love with your clothes on. The truth is, if these people did not like the programs, believe in them, read the scripts, worry about casting, or go to California—nothing much would be different. Finally, they must buy, and they buy mostly on bloodless data, or, as one agency man told me, "Our computer calls your computer." Do I need that night or time of night or season? (Research, computer, decision.) What preceded and follows the show? What will the other networks be playing against it? What is the station line-up? Live clearance? What has been the track record of the production team? The leads? Will the star do the commercials? The lead-ins? The sales convention? Not just how many people are likely to watch, but what audience composition in terms of my product— young, old, children, women, men, educated, disposable income? How short a commitment can I make? How much will it cost? Does the network really believe in it and will they promote and advertise it? Then, finally, more practically, and a lot more humanly—what choice do I have anyway? And, maybe—maybe—I'll get a couple of tickets to the Super Bowl out of it or meet Mary Tyler Moore.

If I seem cynical or condescending, I am not spurred by any contemptuous feelings I have about agency people or sponsors whom I know, and I know lots of them. Many of these men and women are tremendously well educated about shows and entertainment. Several have been in the networks or have made shows themselves. I am defining the reality: Advertisers are only bettors at the track—not the horses, the jockeys, the owners, or trainers.

Perhaps I am being naïve or self-serving or lucky enough to have met the good guys, but, in any case, I wish there were more contact among program makers and network Program Departments on the one hand and advertising people and sponsor on the other. I seek this contact constantly since, on the whole, I think agency people and sponsors are closer to the society, more in touch with Macon and Toledo and Big Springs and Tacoma, to point of sales—with what Americans are thinking and wanting—than we are. We are too much wrapped in the wombs of our ersatz Bauhaus offices in New York and Los Angeles, shuttled back and forth between them in incubators numbered 707 and 747, talking only to each other and responding as though America is nothing more than what Nielsen, *Variety* and the *Hollywood Reporter* tell us it is.

For the year 1974, the ten largest advertising agencies in terms of television spending, or billings, as they say, were:

1. J. Walter Thompson	$246,100,000
2. Leo Burnett	202,400,000
3. Young & Rubicam	190,000,000
4. BBDO	178,100,000
5. Grey Advertising	144,000,000
6. Ted Bates & Co.	136,500,000
7. Dancer-Fitzgerald-Sample	130,700,000
8. Benton & Bowles	124,800,000
9. McCann-Erickson	113,000,000
10. Ogilvy & Mather	108,300,000

All except Leo Burnett, whose home base is Chicago, headquarter in New York City, but have offices in Los Angeles and elsewhere. Besides these, at least fifty other important advertising agencies are interested in television programming. (Check the Yellow Pages; also there is the *Standard Directory of Advertising Agencies,* published by the National Register Publishing Co., Inc., in Chicago. It is available in most public libraries and tells you the names of the important executives, gives addresses and phone numbers, and lists the clients of each agency.) All of the agencies have television departments and television executives who are looking for program ideas.

Aspiring producers and program makers should look to advertising agencies and sponsors in three major television areas: syndication, the commercials themselves, and specials.

You have seen in the chapter on syndication, with the example of "American Life Style," among other shows, how an advertising agency and or sponsor can be effective in the genesis and distribution of a syndicated series. Remember that advertising agencies and sponsors are cumulatively frustrated by years of commercial clutter and subsequent lack of program-product identification. They are actively searching, always, for programs which they can own or in which they can be more intimately involved; and with which their products and services can be better identified and remembered. Syndication is an important way to satisfy these needs.

Of course, there are the commercials themselves. Many agencies produce their own, or contract independent companies. You have heard the old saw, "The commercials are better than the programs." Too often, the old saw is well oiled and true. Do not—if you are lucky enough or good enough to get commercial production work—turn your nose up at it. There is absolutely no shame, and there is much learning and discipline in making commercials. All of the production challenges and techniques—tape and/or film—are the same and the rigidity of the frame—thirty or sixty seconds—is even more demanding.

Then there are the network specials. Advertisers play a larger role with network specials than with regular series. Advertisers like network specials for a number of reasons: (1) They can get their name in the show's title. (2) They can, if the content of the special is carefully conceived, attract exactly the audience—called the target audience—that they know will be interested in their message. (3) They can exert great control over content and creative elements and they can even own a special or share ownership: (4) They can get the desired program-product identification, since a special seldom has more than two sponsors, and ideally one: (5) They can get concentrated audience attention and publicity and, perhaps, editorial mention by television reporters and critics: (6) They can key point-of-sales campaigns and print advertising, or the introduction of a new or seasonal product or model, to a specific launch date: (7) They can get, usually, a popular time period by pre-empting a proven regular series hit: (8) They can, on a relatively limited television budget, make a bigger noise per dollar.

In their aggressive search for specials, advertisers prefer to find them on the outside rather than from a network, since they will have more control and leverage if the idea is "theirs." Also, most of these agency people are savvy program people. Frustrated by the regular-schedule network shut-out, they are eager to find ideas of their own for at least three additional reasons: (1) It looks better with the client if the agency has developed its own program for the client, rather than shopping at the networks; (2) it may promote an individual's career; (3) it certainly is more fulfilling to the human needs at work.

As a program maker, advertiser support of your program will

enhance its chance of getting on. Enhance, I said—not guarantee. The networks will have the final word. I mean it. Even if a special is fully sold, a network may reject it or, as we say, take a pass or pass. (When a show is particularly odorous, some Runyonesque program buyers say, "Pasadena." Other colorful, inside terms for supposedly dull or low-appeal shows are: *Heavy furniture, Brown socks, Medea, 5 share, Hiroshima, Sominex, Terminal yawns, Parsifal,* and a *Jerry Ford press conference.*) Networks reject specials because they do not like the ideas or feel they would damage program flow, or would constitute too many "hits on" (pre-emptions of) popular regular series, thus disrupting viewing habits. Or they have similar shows already in development or committed.

But you are, in the end, better off taking your special first to a network. Again, even if the network likes it, the idea may not get on, since all the networks are reluctant to inventory a special without knowing they have it sold first, or up front. But, of course—and this is still the prevailing condition—networks do develop and buy specials without prior advertiser commitment; moreover, if a network likes your ideas, they will become an ally in finding advertiser support—and they are better equipped for the task. Better still, from your point of view, networks are barred by law from owning your idea or sharing in its ownership. They will license it for "X" number of plays, and following these, the show will be yours for disposal as to other rights.

This is not the case with an advertiser. Depending on your relative strengths and needs, he may own you. Still, you should not be dissuaded from dealing with advertising agencies or sponsors, since 50 per cent of something, as they say, is better than a 100 per cent of *nada.*

If you approach a sponsor directly, be aware of the dangers. Nearly every major company has a vice-president of advertising and a staff. Being human, these people love nothing more than to come up with "their own" ideas for programs—zinging their advertising agency experts in the bargain. Conversely, when the company person exposes the idea to the agency, the agency will have every motive in the book—and a lot of expertise—to knock it down. If you have some special or natural access to the sponsor directly, do not *not* use it. But in using it, try to devise some way to make the sponsor's advertising agency your ally rather than your committed and formidable foe. Especially is this true if you know the agency people. They will resent it deeply that you went around them to the sponsor. With all due respect to William Congreve, it is not woman scorned but advertising person, that hath "nor Hell a fury like," when that person thinks you have given the client yet another reason to ask, "What do I need 'em for?" All considerations weighed, you are better off going to the advertising agency. Beyond the psychological and political reasons, the agency is also more professional and receptive.

When you are approaching an advertising agency, there are some basic guidelines to keep in mind. First, remember everything I will tell you in the chapter on presentations. Next, find out who the agency's clients are and try to design program ideas to fit a particular client's needs. Don't, for instance, try to sell American Airlines a special on the history of the automobile. Don't try to sell Hallmark a game show; they have a seasonal (holidays) marketing approach and a long and distinguished association with quality drama. On the other hand, you might try to convince Hallmark's agency to abandon or supplement their drama with another kind of program which could bring them a larger audience. You must be prepared to substantiate such a claim. Do try to find out what an agency's clients' competitors are doing— fear works wonders—and argue for your idea as being more exciting, more attention-getting, a better marketing vehicle. This competitor technique works especially well if the party you are pitching is not in a similar program format at all. Provide extensive—more than if you were going to a network—data as to what kinds of audience your program appeals to and relate the data specifically to a particular client's target.

Try to research what a client's likes and dislikes are. Many have regional or political or religious biases. Tailor to them. You don't pitch Shick, a politically conservative company, a Shirley MacLaine special, for instance. But Schick might be just the place to go with your "Great American Battles" series, John Wayne hosting. If you feel you have limited access to inside information—and there is more available than you might think since everybody likes to talk in *Variety, Broadcasting, Advertising Age,* and other trade publications—use what you've been doing for probably two hours a day for most of your life anyway —watching television. You will see what kind of programming clients buy and what image they project in their commercials.

Common sense, right? But be sure to observe the spirit not the letter in designing a show idea to fit the product. There are rules forbidding stations to carry a program that is really an extended commercial, unless they log the entire program as commercial time, and none of them wants to do that. I designed a special for Volkswagen once—the "First Annual Stanley Myron Handleman Miniature Golf Classic." (The idea for the show was Stanley's, not mine.) But taking it to the advertising agency was my idea: Small car, demonstrated sense of humor in their advertising, plus a play toward reverse form—"think small" complemented by a small show, a comedy spoof (mostly comedians) in a half-hour format, aimed at younger buyers, who are Volkswagen's target.

Dick Clark has designed a number of young-appeal contemporary music specials for Dr. Pepper. Smart. Dr. Pepper had sounded old and medicinal and was coming into the national soft drink market, a market in which young people were the big consumers. The Clark rock star shows (plus very clever commercials) helped remake Dr. Pepper's image, and increased sales. I am not sure whether it was Dick's idea or Art Greenfield's, at Young & Rubicam, but to pitch these half-hour shows to ABC and in the third quarter (July, August, September) was consumate program discernment: Summer months are good for soft drinks; sold specials are easier to get in the third quarter when network sales are softest; ABC was receptive because of its youth and contemporary music fix.

Lead time is the length of time that elapses between the presentation of an idea (and/or its acceptance) and the day it is aired. For network series shows, this is anywhere from ten to twenty-four months. Typically, a show might be pitched in June or July of one year and go on in September of the following year. (for daytime, six to twelve months is more typical. For "Wide World of Entertainment," three to six months).

With advertising agencies, you should add an extra sixty to ninety days to the lead time. The agency will need it both internally and with a client to get a go-ahead before it takes an idea to a network. With specials, try to pitch your idea to advertising agencies in January, February, March, or in September and October not for the coming fall/spring season but for the fall/spring season a year later. Even two full years later is not unusual. Never pitch a special that must air within three to six months.

In presenting an idea to an advertising agency, individuals can say no, but only a committee can say yes. Do not be dismayed by the committee system of approvals and rejections. Rather, be prepared so that your effectiveness in dealing with it will be increased as your frustration with it is diminished. How easily I say it, knowing that a committee is as wary as a trapped animal. I hate stalking this stony-faced monster, but I have many times and will again, and so must you sooner or later.

A committee is almost always white and male, though increasingly you will find a black part and a woman part. It wears a blue suit and has a fresh haircut. Sometimes it wears Ben Franklin glasses. The part of it with gray hair will do most of the talking. Where it is young, it will carry a manila folder and frown. It will have lots of legal-size yellow pads and freshly sharpened pencils and large weighty ashtrays, but it will not write and does not smoke. It will arrange itself around a huge conference table, buffed to a shine as if waiting for the Potsdam conference rather than for the frail television idea that you are rapidly losing faith in. And the silence is deafening.

If you are like me, there will be a moment when you want to smoke two cigarettes at once, hurl the ashtray, write something obscene on a legal pad, and go to the bathroom. But—one doesn't. Here, instead, is what you should do.

Make your presentation like a half-hour pep talk. This business is racked with insecurity, doubt, and, of course, subjective judgment, since no one really knows what will be a hit show. Your confidence and enthusiasm will stiffen doubters and excite the half-asleep. Repeatedly, I have seen good presentation pitches carry the day for programs—even those with dubious merit. Conversly and unfortunately, I have seen good ideas get lost through fumbling or unconvincing presentations. Your audience is looking for assurance. Do your best to provide it.

Generally, unless you know the committee well or are well-known, keep jokes and amenities to a minimum. Make your presentation with dispatch and in full detail. Homework is essential. Bring hand-outs—written presentations or fact sheets—to distribute to every one. When you can, provide a card presentation—large poster-board graphics (with photos if possible) set up on an easel. Advertising agencies do card presentations all the time and seem to swear by them. Show slides or film if available. Slide, films, cards look professional and provide the added effect of giving you something to look at besides the jury staring at you. These also keep the jury from looking at you constantly or seeing the soup you spilled on your lapel at lunch. All of these materials also help people see what they may miss in your oral description. Invite questions. Answer fully, but don't argue. Some junior committee members use the question period to exercise their negative power. Do not just seek out the boss; try to talk to every member of the committee. Perhaps, it is the boss who will say yes, but the juniors can harm you later with their noes. Make your presentation no longer than twenty minutes. This leaves ten minutes for questions. Chances are they have booked you for no more than this half hour. (In case lightning should strike, always book yourself for an hour.)

As you get farther along in the business, one very serviceable technique is to try to get individual members of the committee at an agency away from the group into separate one-on-one meetings, in the office, at lunch, or for drinks. In these sessions, do not knock other committee members, but rather try to get to know the individual. These humanizing encounters will give you some friendly padding in the next committee meeting. Also, listen in these single meetings more than you talk. You will learn the individual's character and his views on fellow committee members. Use nothing you learn in this way maliciously—politically, which I deplore—but only to help you understand the committee's personality so that you keep your feet out of your mouth and get approval of your idea. One-on-one meetings are also good for finding out which clients and agencies are looking for what kinds of shows. From this you will be able to devise programs especially for those needs rather than waiting for your favorite idea-child to find a smiling patron. As you get more experienced as a program maker (and better known), you will learn how to bring a buyer and an agency together on your projects, by playing their common needs in a parlay. Shorthand, "J. Walter Thompson will buy X kind of show, if you will air it. ABC will air X kind of show, if you will buy it."

A few last words. Send out mailings regularly about your own activities—no one reads advertising so carefully as advertising people. Read *Advertising Age* and *Broadcasting* regularly. These publications are thick with information about agencies and sponsors. One way to get your foot in the door is to write a fan letter to an agency man or sponsor who has written a column or been interviewed in one of these magazines, commending his remarks and asking for an appointment.

Kin Hubbard said, "It used to be that a fellow went on the police force after everything else failed, but today he goes in the advertising game." Perhaps you share that view of advertising and the Lord (& Thomas) knows there is much evidence to support such a low opinion. But, loathe and mock advertising as you will—I do not—never forget its power and presence in television.

Chapter 6
talent agencies and personal managers

Joke: "What is pneumonia?"
    "A cold handled by William Morris."

I am as ambivalent in my attitude toward agents and personal managers as I am about McDonalds' quarter pounder, though one thing is certain about both: The current market is vigorous. There have been agents, I suppose, forever. For your purposes, the business began with the establishment of the William Morris Agency and the Music Corporation of America.

The William Morris Agency was founded in 1898 by a man actually named William Morris, who represented talent in the legitimate theatre and vaudeville. The agency spread steadily, paralleling the growth of motion pictures, radio, phonograph records, and television. William Morris and other large agencies are also active in the live concert, fair, and night club fields. In addition to more traditional kinds of performers, they now frequently represent athletes, authors, politicians, and—in the case of William Morris—Julie Nixon Eisenhower, and the great thoroughbred stud, Secretariat.

During the heyday of the Music Corporation of America, the William Morris Agency was the third largest representative of talent. The Music Corporation of America was the first and second. Founded in 1924 by a physician named Jules Stein (not the composer), the company was always referred to as MCA, or warmly, as "The Octopus." If William Morris's growth was prudent, but steady over a longer period of time, MCA assaulted show business and overwhelmed it.

MCA started out as a company representing dance bands and orchestras when that counted; soon it enlarged to handle singers, actors, writers, producers, directors, composers, conductors, authors, circus and variety acts, and probably, although I do not know for sure, Rex, the Wonder Dog. (For a bitingly funny account, hear the Lenny Bruce routine about MCA handling Adolph Hitler.)

113

With the advent of television, MCA's growth exploded. What made the difference was MCA's discovery of the technique of packaging and/or owning shows as well as representing the individual talents required to make them. MCA was unique among talent agencies in possessing outright ownership of certain shows, and it pioneered in the business of setting up major clients in their own production corporations and then representing these corporations as well as the stars. They also led in the technique of packaging stars, producer, director, and writer on a single project—and all would be MCA clients. These devices were valuable to MCA in inverse order: The packaging of creative elements in a show was nice; it meant several 10 per cents instead of a few or one. Client ownership of a show through his company was better; this meant 10 per cent on the gross of the entire amount a company received for a show rather than a lot of little 10 per cents. And, of course, outright program ownership by MCA was best of all.

It was this latter juicy arrangement that lifted MCA into superpower status and brought it down. MCA established Revue, its own production company, which became the biggest in the industry; it acquired Universal-International Studios, and very nearly dictated the NBC prime-time schedule during the Robert Kintner era; it worked the same ownership-packaging technique in the recording field through MCA-Decca; and finally it caught the eye of Uncle Sam.

In 1962, the United States Department of Justice took a long and jaundiced look at MCA. What they saw was a show business mammoth that was both buying and selling talent. As it turned out, the government had two Acts of its own that MCA did not represent: Sherman and Clayton, and it invoked both of them to bring an antitrust action. It told MCA it could buy talent or sell talent. It could not do both.

Since MCA's income from television program ownership and packaging was five times more lucrative that its fees from representing individual talents, the choice was easy. MCA stopped being a talent agent and became a full-time program supplier. Today, MCA is a thriving and diversified conglomerate, but still very much in the network television business through its owned subsidiary, Universal. In the spring season of 1975, Universal was providing 8½ hours of regular series programing out of a combined three-network total of forty-seven such hours. In addition, Universal supplies a sizable number of made-for-TV movies. This is impressive considering that there are only sixty-three total prime-time hours on all three networks. Their regular series were: On ABC, "Six Million Dollar Man," "Marcus Welby, M.D.," "Kolchak, The Night Stalker," and "Baretta." On NBC, "Adam-12," "Lucas Tanner," "Emergency," and the "Rockford Files." On CBS, "Kojak."

It has been noted that the networks are sensitive about maintaining a dignified mien so as to minimize the taint of show biz and gain the gray admiration of bankers, Wall Street, and their somber corporate peers. This is also true for the major talent agencies—in spades. They will stop at nothing in their efforts to look respectable. MCA was particularly obsessed. The offices were wood paneled (real) with eighteenth- and nineteenth-century English hunting prints (also real) and antique furniture (I am not sure). It was rather like meeting in the office of Queen Victoria's solicitor.

All MCA agents wore suits that were not merely dark—they were black. And their ties were black (four-in-hand) and all of the shirts white. Somehow for me the clothes never achieved the desired effect. No matter how good the cloth or careful the tailoring or likable the occupant, the clothes always reminded me of chauffer uniforms at a Mafia funeral. Most of the agents these days are still quietly turned out, except for a few of the Hollywood and/or rock-and-roll agents. These latter types are to clothing what Caesar's Palace is to architecture.

When an agent enters with teased hair, orange-tinted air force glasses, a body shirt, and wet pants studded with metal nails, all of it teetering on five-inch heels, it is hard to take seriously the content of his remarks.

With the withdrawal of MCA from the talent representation business, William Morris became the largest agency and remains so. Foreseeing MCA's trouble in its Icarus flight to the sun of total program ownership, Morris has always stopped short of becoming a producing or ownership entity. It does, however, represent producing companies and packagers, and it assembles talent packages, as well as representing individual talents.

Consider the effects of this representation. If William Morris represents a TV series star, whose salary if $30,000 an episode, its commission is $3,000. If it represents all the talent whom it has assembled into a package—stars, producer, director, writer—whose combined incomes may be $90,000, its commission is $9,000. If it represents the packaging company which may get $200,000 to make the hour, its commission is $20,000 per show. You readily see the incentive for being the agent to a company rather than to the individual talents.

Two items which relate: (1) In the event that an agency represents the owning company and takes a commission on the gross, the agency does not then take commissions from individual talents whom it may represent within the package. For instance, when I was producing "Candid Camera," both the show and I were represented by the Ashley-Famous Agency. Since the agency took a commission of the show's gross, it did not take a commission on my salary. (2) The William Morris Agency has been getting more than 10 per cent commissions for a long time. They take a ninth.

In our example of the hour show bought for $200,000, you can see clearly (keep it at 10 per cent) that the company, before it starts, has only $180,000 to produce its $200,000 show.

This gross packaging less commission arrangement is the sorest lesion between program buyers and sellers on one side and talent agencies on the other. In the example, the agency collects $20,000 per episode in the first run; after that, the 10 per cent arrangement goes on forever on whatever monies are derived from all uses of the episode.

The owner and/or producer of the series is almost certainly making less—say $15,000—or may even be going into debt on the first run, in which case he hopes to make his money back and a profit on syndication and foreign sales. This, by the way, is becoming harder and harder to do as the syndication and foreign markets get cluttered with product and the hours get fewer. In many of these situations the agency is making more on a show than the people who own or make it.

Program sellers and makers contend that an agency has little to do with the show's conception and bears no risks of production; therefore, it gets a hugely disproportionate share for its efforts, which may have consumed as little time and sales initiative as a couple of phone calls, an office meeting, or a lunch. In fact, if he has several clients, the agent may not have devoted even the entire phone call, meeting, or lunch to the client in question.

Program buyers contend that the money which the agency takes out of the gross price they are paying for a show never gets on the screen; they are shortchanged on the product they are spending for.

The talent agencies defend the gross fee system by saying their unique and powerful services are costly and on-going. They say they spend much of their time positioning clients for a sale; further, they must absorb costs for the time and effort wasted on failures or rejections of clients' projects which far outnumber the successes. Agencies say they do all the dirty work and have to be the bad guys with regard to selling, negotiating, and clinching deals; with handling objective and emotional grievances. They are always available to, and frequently do, intervene during the run of a show to smooth out problems that arise with the stars and other creative people in the package, as well as with the networks and advertisers.

With so many shows being offered—and several rather much alike—it is because of the agency, the agencies say, that a particular show will be bought. The agency's bigness gives the clients added weight, especially its less powerful clients.

Further agency arguments run that they offer legal, tax, and accounting advice in addition to show business expertise. Occasionally (very occasionally), they have on their own loaned or advanced money on projects to clients if they cannot find outside resources. With the larger agencies you get offices and service on both coasts as well as in key cities throughout the country and abroad.

And, for whatever he makes in commissions, the most impassioned point of all in the agent's arguments: I *am* creative. We *do* make creative contributions to projects, despite what the creators say to the contrary. This sense of creative inferiority rides a talent agent's back like the hump of Richard the Third.

None of these points put forth by agents is without merit. Still, none supports the gross price commission and it remains, I believe, an excessive tax on all program budgets.

Some moves have already been made to mitigate the gross price commission practice. Powerful clients and/or buyers have sometimes forced reduction of agency commissions to 5 per cent; in other cases the commissions are 10 per cent on only the above-the-line portions of program costs rather than the total budget.

Many suppliers do without the services of an outside agency and hire (or handle themselves) program salesmen internally on salary. More and more, suppliers are turning to lawyers who specialize in television and show business to take on some of the traditional agency functions. These lawyers are paid on a per deal basis or through annual retainers which are less than any 10 per cent of sales—and can be terminated and left unentangled with other projects.

The agencies themselves have often reduced or waived their commissions, especially in marginal situations where budgets were extremely tight and the program might not otherwise get made or newer talents be given a chance.

I look forward to a system in which an agency gets a one-time commission on a sale or is paid on a declining graduated scale over X amount of time in the life of a series or show. Furthermore, I think it is coming.

The second largest talent agency these days is International Creative Management, a subsidiary of a company called Marvin Josephson Associates. International Creative Management was born in January 1975, via the union of the previous number two and number three agencies, International Famous Artists (IFA) and Creative Management Associates (CMA).

IFA has had more names in the last fifteen years than Howard

Hunt. It was called Ashley-Steiner, Ashley-Famous, Ted Ashley Associates, and some others I have forgotton. Ted Ashley, a nephew of Nat Lefkowitz, the president of William Morris, started his career at that agency in the mail room. It caused hurt family feelings when Ashley left William Morris to go on his own, not just because as a nephew to Lefkowitz he was real family, but because of the family philosophy at William Morris which applies to all of its agents. While the sons and daughters of William Morris leave frequently these days, it is not uncommon for agents there to begin in the mail room and stay at the agency for their entire working careers.

Ted Ashley was a *Wunderkind* agent who specialized in putting television and movie packages together and finally packaged himself into the presidency of Warner Brothers. (He retired in 1974.) He is a prime example of an agent becoming a creator.

CMA was born in the ashes of MCA. Ex-MCA agents, Freddie Fields and David Begelman founded the company and got off to a good start by promoting the revival of Judy Garland's career, which after months of painstaking preparation happened in a single night— her famous Carnegie Hall Concert of April 23, 1961. CMA quickly absorbed GAC, General Artists Corporation, the only other sizable agency around and became very strong in movie packages and rock and roll. Fields remains in the merged ICM and Begelman has gone on to become president of Columbia Pictures.

Of all agencies, for creativity and style, I prefer ICM. In my experience, their top agents on both coasts smoke fewer and smaller cigars, are more innovative than their competitiors and frequently are more talented than their clients. Their approach is Ivy League cum *New York* magazine. One gets the immediate impression that they actually know and care about what their clients do and that their world extends beyond the boundaries of *Variety,* Las Vegas, and the Friar's Club. They sell on rational arguments rather than friendship or "Do me a favor" or engaging guilt.

Why do people have agents? Why should you? There is a cliché in the business that runs, "By the time William Morris wants to sign you, you don't need them anymore." There is a dust of truth on that. A big agency will be least interested in you—and who can blame them?—when you are beginning your career and not making much money. It certainly does not mean, despite the implication, that you cannot make use of a big agency even after you are making it, when they will want to handle you. Moreover, agencies do a rather comprehensive and commendable job of searching out young talents and signing and working with them in the early stages of their careers.

I suppose a performer's need for an agent is more obvious, but a program maker needs one too. Program makers are seldom handled, however, by small agents or personal managers, but rather mostly by William Morris and ICM. If you can sign with one of these larger agencies—or with one of the known and respected smaller agencies, independent agents, or personal managers—do it. The most compelling reason for having an agent probably is emotional immaturity. Many people—all of us at times—simply cannot or will not face the full range of realities that constitute our professional lives, let alone our personal ones. It is comforting to have a surrogate doing these things for you. There are also any number of practical reasons for having an agent.

What does an agent do for you? First, the good things.

In pitching you and your ideas, an agent makes calls and contacts for you with buyers both at networks and the advertising agencies, as well as with station groups and syndicators. He can do the same for you at the major supplers: Universal, Warner's, Fox, Paramount, Col-Gems, and MGM, and with the smaller suppliers such as Quinn Martin, M-T-M, Filmways, Four Star, Talent Associates, Goodson-Todman, and so on. He comes along to steer you through the shoals of these meetings. When he is associated with a larger talent agency, especially, he has the most priceless commodity of all: information. William Morris has thirty agents covering both coasts, calling on everybody who is important and representing lots of important people. This constitutes an intelligence-gathering force which is quite beyond the resources of any single individual. At William Morris this information is shared among the various agents at "The Television Meeting" which takes place two mornings a week—Tuesday and Thursday—in New York and Los Angeles. These agents have a much better overview of the television business than individual networks even, since they call on all three networks and since networks have no similar, systematic exchange of information, even internally. I am forever astonished at the speed with which agents learn what is happening is some particular television situation.

What else? An agent can say all those glowing things about you which you know are true, but, since you are also possessed of a glowing modesty, you hardly can say about yourself. He can sell you.

Also, an agent with lots of clients has lots of meetings with the right people, thus he has continuing access to them. Even if you get an initial meeting on your own with a lot of buyers, it is difficult to follow up without making a nuisance of yourself. In fact, even if you make a sale, who is going to be making the next sale while you are out completing the first show? An agent who is always in contact with the buyers can work like dripping water to wear them down. His continuing presence also works to keep you from simply being forgotten, which can happen, since buyers are bombarded with submissions of ideas and talents. So, instead of pestering the field, you only have to pester one person—your agent.

Because of other more powerful clients on his list whom a buyer wants, an agent can use this leverage to get you into a package or a sale.

Of course, once a show is picked up or ordered, your agent negotiates the deal. He haggles over all the terms of the agreement or contract, from money to billing, to length of license, to creative controls, to approvals, to number of runs, your dressing room, expenses, hotel accommodations on the road, transportation, wardrobe, hairdresser, make-up artist, and—in the case of particularly arrogant rock groups, what kind of wine or beer or "toys" must be put at their disposal. And on and on and on and on.

All of this is such a loathsome and boring business it is marvelous to have someone do it for you; it is of particular relish if the going gets really tough. What then happens is that you have the luxury of maintaining good relationships with buyers, having them think you are one hell of a nice person, while your agent gets tagged as the heavy.

Another of the protective duties of an agent includes saying no for a client to everybody and everything the client wants to avoid; again, it must be said in a way that preserves the good face of the client.

Still more good news: An agent, when he gets you a job, is getting you 90 per cent of something.

Moreover, many of the agents I know are seasoned show business professionals, with much knowledge and taste and their advice about career moves and the handling of situations and people are invaluable.

Still another positive quality in a good agent is his support and encouragement as a friend. If he is good, he will tell you the truth, or at least as much as you can take and when you can take it. He will be realistic in appraising the industry's honest views about you. He will not run to buyers with your ideas when he believes they are bad or wrong. And, when life in this business really is stinking he will give you knowledgeable emotional support to help you get back up just when you are sure you can't.

Then, there are the bad things.

They take 10 per cent of what you earn—sometimes when you have done all the work.

They sell you out to a buyer. For instance, you are one of many clients on the agent's list. He will go by you fast if he gets a no from the prospective buyer and will quickly move down his list to other

clients in the same category, using superlatives—your superlatives—
to describe each of them, to sell the next or the next or the next. You
get washed out on the laundry list of clients. Remember, the agent's
job is to sell—someone or something. If it is you, fine; it is just as fine
if it is the next client.

Another way: If he is not sure about your idea himself or doubtful
of the buyer's reaction to it, he will separate himself from the idea.
(Never browbeat your agent into going to a buyer with an idea that
he has told you he does not like.)

Still another: When push comes to shove in a situation where
your agent is representing your interests against a network, he will
usually cave in to the network's position. After all, you are only one
client among many; a network is one buyer among three. You are
temporal. The network is permanent and the talent agent will have to
go back there tomorrow, next week, next month, next year, next
decade, long after your star has faded. It is only natural for him to
favor the network's good will rather than yours. Obviously, this is not
to the advantage of your negotiating position. If your show is sagging
and in danger of being cancelled, do not believe for a moment that
your agent is in there fighting to the last to save it; faced with the
inevitable, he is more likely to be in there pitching replacement shows
from other clients. (If he is good, he will tell you the truth about the
impending death of your own show and ask you to come up with a
replacement for it.) Still, there is every likelihood that in disaster, it
is to hell with that business of women and children first—the lifeboats
will be filled with agents.

Since the majority of agents have no talent, you will often get
terrible career advice from your agent, simply because he is ignorant
or insensitive about show business. Worse, sometimes you will be
pushed into projects that are disasterous (or pushed over good ones)
because of the conscious and venal needs of your agent to turn a fast
buck for himself.

Do you recall talking about all that information your agent has
access to? It can become a bludgeon when he withholds it from you
or uses it against your best interests.

Again, since agents have no particular talent of their own, they
mostly become agents through attraction to the glamour of show
business. Because of this, if you are famous, your agent will seek to
get whatever glow may spill from your light, and he will almost
certainly use the influence of your name or position to enhance his
own stature, whether it is to sign other clients, make more money, or
simply to get a better table at Sardi's or drop a little tantalizing gossip
on his mother's canasta table.

Some other agent negatives: He will lie to you. He will tell you the truth. He will make emotional demands on you and will probably ask you to do a show for his kid's school. More seriously, since he is a representative of what you are, he may give a totally false picture of you through his own obnoxious or overzealous selling techniques or personality. You have to ask yourself honestly—Would I buy me from this person?

One thing more: If your agent has lots of clients, you may feel ignored or that he is too busy to give the kind of service that you want. For this reason especially—and for all the other negative aspects about an agent—you may want a personal manager.

Personal managers perform the same general functions as agents, but service is much more concentrated. They have fewer clients—ideally only one, or only one in each category of talent. This relationship can become very intense, with the personal manager frequently becoming the talent's alter ego. Too, the personal manager can be very vulnerable to the talent if he has only one or two clients on whom he is depending for income. Too often, I have seen talent reduce personal managers to carrying the wardrobe bag.

A personal manager's piece of you can range as high as 50 per cent or more or go as low as 5 per cent. Mostly, a personal manager gets 15 per cent. (You must be thinking: 10 per cent to the agent, 15 per cent to the personal manager—that is a quarter of everything I make! Relax. If you are making it and did not give it to them, you would have to give it in taxes to the government. Besides, if they are good, they will get you more than enough for yourself and themselves.)

Now I have told you that people have both agent and personal manager. It is true—and not necessarily idle luxury. An agent, especially as a member of a large agency, will not always be looking out for you; his first loyalty is to the company; nor will he have the time to devote to you even if he has the desire. A personal manager gives you custom service—even to protecting you from your agent. Still a personal manager alone cannot provide all those valuable services that are available through a large agency. So, people have both.

There are some more things you should know. An agent will try to sign you to a blanket contract agreement and for a long term—three years at least. You do not have to sign with an agent for everything. If one is better for television, another better for movies or the theatre, you can have separate agreements for all of these. If you are a producer, writer, director, or packager, again you may exclude some or all but one of these various categories from your agreement. You can sign with an agent to handle some of your projects, not all of them. You can set the term of the agreement at one year or two years.

Do not depend on an agent to do it all for you. You cannot sit at home in isolation waiting only for the agent's call. You have to supplement his activity with your own.

Do not let your agent or other people's agents interfere in your work, or make the final decisions. They do not run the ultimate risks and therefore have no rights, unless you have had to agree up front. For instance, I once threw a performer's agent out of a control truck when he began making producer-director noises. My parting advice was, "Get your own show." On the other hand, I once gave Cat Stevens's manager, Barry Krost, whom Stevens had entrusted with the responsibility, the right to make final judgement on the sound and look of how we were recording Stevens, since this was the only way to get Stevens for the show—and because I trusted Krost's taste and fairness (as well as our own). I was not disappointed. But I certainly would not grant such a right willy-nilly to agents and managers, even if it meant not getting a particular talent or not doing the show at all. Most simply could not be trusted with such power.

Do not be surprised if agents create irrational scenes. Their role is often uncertain and this creates a lot on anxiety. They will and do seek to justify their presence.

Do not be afraid to change agents. I knew one successful producer who as a matter of course changed agents every two years. "Throw the rascals out," he said, "Keep 'em on their toes. I vote the same way."

So. Many times, just when I have given up on agents and am moved to ask God for their removal along with mosquitos, one of them will, by being creatively dedicated to our electronic derangement, turn me full-around so that I end up asking blessings on all of them.

All right, I told you I was ambivalent about agents. Where does this leave us? In an attempt at a final word about agents I will say, I admire many; will never forgive some; and believe most can be judged skeptically because the category of their work is psychologically the hardest and worst part of our business and because, mostly lacking definite creative gifts themselves, they are tempted to deal in the make-work and the emotional smoke screens of our business rather than in substance.

As W. C. Fields has said about death on his tombstone, "On the whole, I'd rather be in Philadelphia," so do I feel about agents: On the whole, get one.

Chapter 7
the business of television

A thorough understanding of television requires knowledge of unions, budgets, contracts, performance rights, insurance, and the government's role. What follows is only a beginning, but let us begin.

UNIONS

In big-time television, nearly everyone from the star to the parking lot attendant belongs to a union. Each network has a full-time department responsible for labor relations and negotiations and for keeping track of its hundreds of union contracts. Even these specialists are hard put to know all the provisions of all the contracts. The unions themselves are in constant internecine combat over jurisdiction. All of this seems absolutely paralyzing at first, but, amazingly, in daily practice, it seems to work.

Membership in more than one union is common for thousands of television professionals; in my own career I belonged to four different unions at the same time. Let's start with those.

AFTRA—the American Federation of Television and Radio Artists—and SAG—the Screen Actors Guild—are the two unions representing performers. AFTRA has jurisdiction to represent performers in all live or electronically recorded television and radio. This applies to news commentators, reporters, and sports announcers as well as to entertainers—principal performers, singers, dancers, specialties, and animal acts. After one gratis appearance, everyone must join the union. AFTRA also represents performers in commercials.

SAG, which began as a theatrical motion picture performers' union, retains jurisdiction in that category, but also represents performers in all television shows and commercials that are made on film. For years, these two unions—with much pressure especially from

AFTRA members—have been trying to merge, a logical step which must eventually be taken.

Minimum salaries established by these two unions are high, but the formulae are so complicated and change so frequently that I will not list them. To get exact information for any specific situations, write or phone the union offices in New York or Los Angeles. This applies to all unions I will be describing. Also, many of the larger local libraries keep copies of the SAG and AFTRA agreements; certainly the Library of Congress in Washington, D.C., has the information, and the Labor Department.

AFTRA and SAG establish minimum wages—called scale—with minimum rehearsal days and hours for a day and for a week. Wages and hours are tied to length of show and use—local, regional, network. There is one scale for principal performers, another for those speaking fewer than five lines—under five—and various other scales for extras, specialty acts, voice-over, dancers, singers' groups and choruses.

The contracts define guaranteed days of employment, meal and rest periods, credit, wardrobe, hair and make-up requirements, retakes, understudies, stand-ins and dance-ins, stunts, vacations, holidays, overtime, remotes, auditions, travel requirements (always first class), dressing rooms and other working conditions —in all for AFTRA, 44 pages of 105 paragraphs of terms and conditions. SAG's network contract is 60 paragraphs in a 48-page contract.

AFTRA and SAG have also won for their members a pension and welfare plan (7½ per cent of each paycheck) and a health and insurance plan, both of which producers must pay for totally, as well as residual payments when a program is rerun. This payment is 75 per cent of the original compensation for the first and second replays; 50 per cent for the third, fourth, and fifth replays; 10 per cent for the sixth; 5 per cent for the seventh and all additional replays. Both contracts also call for payments for international use.

The initiation fee for AFTRA is $300 and for SAG, $300 plus $40 for the first year's dues. You must have a covered job before you can join. The AFTRA annual dues for the first year are $47.50 and in subsequent years, like SAG, they are related to covered income. It is alleged that 80 per cent of the membership of these two unions make less than $2,000 a year in the field.

DGA—the Directors Guild of America—represents directors, associate and assistant directors, stage managers, and production assistants. DGA has jurisdiction in television for live, tape, and film; also radio. DGA has contract rights governing wages, working conditions, and most of the specifics in the AFTRA and SAG contracts. DGA has a health plan and pension and welfare plan totally supported by employers. DGA guarantees directors the first cut of their picture or program in editing and defines credit. It may be instructive to quote the paragraphs covering such a simple item as credit to give you a glimpse of the complexity and detail in all of these contracts.

—You shall give credit to the Director for each program he directs. You shall not delete such credit on replays or delayed broadcasts. You shall require by contract with licensees, buyers, and all other persons who obtain broadcast or exhibition rights that they shall not delete such credit on any play, replay, delayed broadcast or theatrical exhibition or otherwise, and you shall use your best efforts to secure compliance therewith.

—The Director shall be given credit on television programs and documentaries on a separate title card which shall be the last title card before the first scene of the program or the first title card following the last scene of the program.

—However, in the case of split credits, where credit is given to any person before the first scene of the program, the Director shall be given the last solo credit card before the first scene of the program. For the purpose of this clause, the credits of the established stars playing a continuing role in the series, or of well-established stars in the motion picture industry, or a bona fide producing company credit shall be considered credits of a person. No commercial or other material shall intervene between the Director's credit card and the program.

—No commercial or advertising matter, audio or visual, shall appear on or above the Director's card either as background or otherwise.

—The Director's name on the screen shall be no less than 40% of the episode or series title, whichever is larger. If any credit is larger than the foregoing, the Director's credit shall be equal in size to the largest credit.

—The Director's credit shall be in such contrast to the background and/or such color as to be clearly visible, and shall be not less than two seconds in the clear.

—Whenever credit is given in paid advertising to any persons other than the stars appearing in the program, the Director of the program shall receive credit in such paid advertising of equal size and prominence as such other person(s).

—The credit shall read "Directed by _____" without the addition of any qualifying or descriptive language whatsoever.

—Whenever audio credit is given to any other person, the Director shall receive audio credit in addition to video credit.

And that is an easy part!

DGA has various contracts covering free-lance members and staff members at the networks and local stations. There are separate rules governing work on documentaries and commercials. The initiation fee is very high—$3,000—and it is hard to become a member. Annual dues are related to income, but the minimum is $100 a year.

WGA—the Writers Guild of America—represents writers in television for film and tape or live, and in radio. It has two independent chapters—WGA, West, and WGA, East. As one might expect of writers, the WGA contract is the longest—over a hundred pages. It covers many of the same items as the AFTRA, SAG, and DGA contracts. It, too, defines the writer's creative rights and credit. It forbids members to write on speculation. WGA also has a pension and welfare plan paid for by producers, and rerun residual payments. These latter are: first reuse, 100 per cent of the minimum basic compensation; second reuse, 75 per cent; third and fourth, 50 per cent; fifth, 25 per cent; sixth, 10 per cent; all others, 5 per cent. WGA provides its members with a registration service for recording and protecting scripts, stories, outlines, treatments, titles, and ideas. The initiation fee is $300. Again, dues are related to income, but the minimum is $50 annually.

AFM—the American Federation of Musicians—represents all musicians working in live or tape or film television, and radio. AFM is a national union with local chapters. AFM sets wages and working conditions, gets 5 per cent of gross for its pension and welfare fund, and also makes producers pay into a medical plan. It establishes rules governing performances, rehearsals, vacations, overtime, holidays, minimum session calls, rest and meal periods, special wardrobe or make-up requirements, arrangements, orchestrations, and copying and librarian services. Leaders get double scale and players who double—play more than one instrument—get additional compensation.

These are the artists' unions. Just to give you a quick idea of the scale of compensation, here are some random per-day figures:

AFTRA: *half-hour show*

Principal performer:	$191.48
Under 5	90.20
Extras	50.64
one-hour show	
Principal performer	$242.65
Under 5	110.78

Extras		64.36
P&W (Pension and Welfare)		7½%
DGA: half-hour dramatic show, once a week		$342.88
one-hour variety show, once a week		$1,055.00
P&W		5%
WGA: half-hour show		$1,475.95
one-hour show		$2,248.21
P&W		7%
AFM: half-hour show		
variety	$38.19 for program + 2½ hours rehearsal @ $15.88	
Dramatic	$40.42 for program + 2½ hours rehearsal @ $15.88	
P&W	5% of gross, including overtime	

Keep in mind that these are scale prices only and that name performers and talents get considerably above scale for their efforts.

Then, there are the below-the-line unions. These represent cameramen, technical directors, sound people, electricians, stagehands, make-up artists, wardrobe, hairdressers, publicists, tape and film editors, scenic designers, art directors, decorators, carpenters, painters, and truckers.

Again it is impossible to give all the salaries of all these categories or the formulas that determine them, but as an indication, stagehands receive:

Head stagehand: $237.32 per week + overtime @ $8.90 per hour.
Stagehand: $227.44 per week + overtime @ $8.52 per hour.
Pension and Welfare: 7% of gross weekly compensation.

Electricians earn over $400 a week and their P&W is 7½ per cent.

The principal unions representing the crafts are IATSE—called "Yatsey" or "the IA," which is the International Association of Theatrical and Stage Employees—and its chief competitor, NABET—the National Association of Broadcast Employees and Technicians. Each network's craft situation is different. At ABC, for instance, IATSE represents stagehands, while NABET represents electrical technicians.

Within IATSE, which is the older union and which has powerful jurisdiction in theatre and motion pictures, there are scores of locals that represent separate job functions. Each of these requires a separate contract, and each specifies wages and working conditions, pension and welfare, and health plans, as well as many of the other items we have discussed. NABET, to a lesser extent, has this same locals setup, for various categories of jobs.

IATSE and NABET are powerful unions and those with which, frankly, I have had the most difficulty. The majority of their members are enthusiastic, well-trained professionals, but there are individual members and some leadership who have a negative attitude about themselves, their work, and management. Management, for its part, is frequently snobbish and makes an enormous mistake in avoiding dialogue with labor. Nothing could be healthier for television than continuing encounter sessions between the two parties.

In New York especially, the crafts are high-priced to the point of diminishing return and often highhanded. There would seem to be a self-contempt for their work which dissembles pride of craft and tempts leadership into ever-increasing and unreasonable demands. Example: I tried to do "In Concert" from Broadway's Palace Theatre and, twenty-four hours before the taping, IATSE demanded residual payments for stagehands. This under-the-gun, out-of-the-contract demand sent the show to California—to stay. That is what has happened to a lot of New York production. Another example: A provision of our ABC New York contract says that a man must be allowed forty-five minutes to set up a tape machine and fifteen minutes to take it down—just for screenings. The machine actually requires no more than five minutes to set up properly and a minute to knock down. To screen an hour show, one must book two hours! This harms everyone. One more example: I had to screen a show once on Saturday and rather than book a screening room I went directly to the tape machine to view. The machine was one of two in a small room. After the tape operator had started my show, he flopped down in front of the other machine and switched his monitor to "on air" and began watching the World Series—on another network. When I asked him to turn it down, please, since I was having trouble hearing my show, he went into a rage—and turned it up, and complained to his supervisor! Reluctantly, the supervisor agreed the man was not being paid to watch another network's program.

The Teamsters represent drivers. They get $30 an hour in New York, $15 in Los Angeles. On the average, the same show in New York will cost 25 to 30 per cent more than it does in California. The New York unions' response to this? They are trying to get California to raise its prices.

BUDGETS

It is impossible to provide much hard information about show budgets, as pricing changes frequently. Roughly, a prime-time hour dramatic show costs $230,000 to $250,000; a half-hour situation comedy, $90,000 to $110,000; a variety hour, $150,000 to $250,000; a big special from $200,000 to $700,000 and weekly made-for-television movies, $475,000 to $800,000. ("QB VII" cost $1.2 million.) Tape production is generally cheaper than film production. Game shows for instance, cost $35,000 to $45,000 for five half-hour programs and a soap opera may cost $90,000 for five half-hour episodes. Hour-long network documentaries range from $50,000 to $200,000.

It is a matter of economic fact that most prime-time programs and movies—especially those with heavy action—lose money on their first run. That is, if the network has given a company $250,000 per one-hour episode, it may in fact have cost the producing company $300,000 to make the show. For a long time companies did not mind this deficit financing of network programs, since with a hit series they were destined to make millions in domestic and foreign syndication sales. An hour show in domestic syndication can gross $150,000 per episode. But series are dying faster these days which means the companies have fewer episodes to sell—they generally feel they need at least a hundred episodes to succeed in syndication—and the syndication market is drying up. Since the prime-time access rule has taken away hours, the cumulative inventory of series has made finding a place in the schedule that much more difficult. All of this will probably encourage videotape production which remains less costly.

The most important consideration in making a budget is to make sure that every item is included. Producers frequently forget things—pension and welfare obligations, for instance—which can come to thousands of dollars. As one apprentices upward in the business, pricing and budgeting become more familiar and less frightening. Specialists who do the hard figuring are available. There are specialists, in fact, who will budget a show for you on a free-lance, fee basis.

Here is pretty nearly the fullest possible budget check list which I use to keep all possible items in mind. (I figure the overhead item at 20 per cent and a contingency at 15 per cent.)

CREW	NUMBER OF DAYS @	OT	P&W	ESTIMATE	ACTUAL
Director					
A.D.					
Prod. Manager					
Cameraman					
Ass't. Cameraman					
Sound					
Grips					
Electrician					
Gaffers					
Props					
Make-up					
Hairdresser					
Wardrobe					
Script					
Home Economist					
Prod. Ass't.					
Teamsters					

TALENT	SESSION	OT	P&W	WARDROBE		
Casting Fee						
Principals						
Under 5						
Xtras						
Hand Models						
V.O.						
Animals						
Music						

SETS AND PROPS

	ESTIMATE	ACTUAL
Designer		
Scenic Artist		
Stylist		
Outside Prop Man		
Painters		
Carpenters		
Construction		
Supplies		
Equipment		
Accessories		
Props		
Furniture		
Artwork		
Cue Cards & Prompting		
Trucking		
Miscellaneous		

WARDROBE

	ESTIMATE	ACTUAL
Costume Designer		
Manufacturing		
Rental		
Accessories		
Shipping/Trucking		

Schedule	Prep	Survey	Travel	Shoot	Post
STUDIO DAYS	DAYS @			ESTIMATE	ACTUAL
Construction					
Shoot					
Strike					
Supplied Equip.					
Phones					
Electricity					
Refreshments					
Miscellaneous					
LOCATION DAYS					
Survey					
Fees/Permits					
Transportation					
Gratuities					
Lodging					
Per Diem					
Travel					
Shipping					
Miscellaneous					
EQUIPMENT					
Camera					
Mounts					
Lenses & Filters					
Motors & Power					
Miscellaneous					
Sound					
Recorder					
Mikes & Booms					
Power					
Miscellaneous					
Lighting					
Units					
Power					
Grip					
Miscellaneous					
Trucking					
RAW STOCK					
Film					
1/4" Tape					
LAB FEES					
Developing					
Wk. Print or Dailies					
Coding					
Inter. Positive					
Inter. Negative					
Slop Print					
Answer Print					
Miscellaneous					

SOUND	TIME	STOCK	ESTIMATE	ACTUAL
Recording				
Narration				
Music				
EFX (effects)				
Transfers				
16mm Mag.				
Optical				
35mm Mag.				
Optical				
Mix				
Transfers				
Stock EFX				
Transfers				
Music				
Stock/Rights				
Transfers				
Original/Rights				
Composition/Arrangement				
Musicians				
Cartage Fee				
EDITING				
Editor				
Assistant				
Equipment				
Supplies				
Negative Matching				
OPTICALS				
Effects				
Artwork & Titles				
STOCK FOOTAGE				
Rights				
Master				
MISCELLANEOUS				
Pension & Welfare				
PAYROLL TAXES				
CONTINGENCY				
OVERHEAD				
Staff				
Phones				
Space				
Travel				
Messengers				
Shipping				
Entertainment				
Insurance				
Miscellaneous				
TOTAL				
COMMISSION				
PROFIT				
TOTAL BID TO CLIENT				
WEATHER DAY				

COMMENTS:

INSURANCE

So many risks are involved in television production that plenty of sane people, considering them, immediately choose other professions, which fortunately permits us insane people to have the field to ourselves.

Even we, however, try to protect ourselves. We must by law provide workmen's compensation and liability insurance—and pay social security. Beyond these, the principal insurance coverage includes errors and omission insurance—or E&O, as it is called—negative insurance and cast insurance.

Errors and omission insurance for producers of network shows must cover pilot programs and each program episode. It must provide a minimum of $500,000 for a single party's claim arising out of a single occurrence and $1 million for all claims arising out of a single occurrence.

E&O insurance protects the producer or packager from people who claim the program idea is theirs, or claim the program has defamed, libeled, slandered, or held them up to ridicule; who claim the program has invaded their privacy; and various other frightening possibilities. My E&O once stood between me and a countess, a member of a famous family who threatened suit because she thought I had sullied the family's good name in producing, directing, and writing a documentary about them. She gave up, finally.

Negative insurance is vital. All networks require it of all packagers and producers, but even if they did not, producers would be fools not to have it. Negative insurance protects the producer against losses arising from damage to, defect in, or destruction of any negative or program. For tape, this would cover your original recorded material. Coverage should begin on the first day of shooting and continue until a composite print or edited master is completed and stored in a safe and separate place from the original negative or tape.

Negative insurance saved at least two producers I know. One had taped a program in the Midwest and had entrusted a production assistant to hand-carry the tapes back to New York. The production assistant did, but, at the Midwest airport, walked the tapes through the electronic hijack detection devices—which mutilated the tapes' content. The producer had to retape the show, of course, but the insurance company paid for the remake.

In another situation, the producer had finished a week's shoot in California and returned with his film to his office in New York. There, a messenger picked up the film to take it to the lab. Getting out of the cab, the messenger set the film carton on the sidewalk and turned away to pay the driver. When he turned back, the film was gone—stolen in thirty seconds. The producer had to go back to California to reshoot the entire show, but was totally reimbursed by the insurance company. This story has a bizarre second ending. Several months after the original incident—there had been four rolls of unexposed film in the package—the producer got a call from a second producer saying, are you so-and-so and did you shoot such-and-such in California? Yes, the producer said, how did you know? The second producer said, because your show is under my show—double exposed.

Apparently, the thief sold the stolen film to a film house which specializes in selling recanned film, or rolls left over from a shoot. (Recanned film is film that has been loaded but not shot and then put back in the can. I never use it. It is too large a risk, since it may have been exposed to light and dirt in the handling. Many producers, however, do buy it, since the cost is cheaper.) With the four new rolls and what he thought was recanned film, the second producer went forth, shot his show, and only in development realized another show had already been shot on the film. Toughest still, this producer had no negative insurance. Cheap is costly.

Cast insurance covers talent. In our business, which is frequently dependent on names, death, injury, or illness to any of these people is disasterous to a production. Even with an unknown, the consequence to a production is severe, if a lead is incapacitated during the shoot. Imagine the chaos when Elizabeth Taylor is indisposed. Stanley Kramer has told me that his cast insurance payments on *"Guess Who's Coming to Dinner"* were astronomical since it was known that Spencer Tracy was terminally ill and might not live to complete the picture.

There are other production insurances. Weather protection is one, but the expense is ghastly and most producers avoid it. Most networks require more liability insurance than states require. Minimum bodily injury limits of $500,000 are required for any single individual's claim arising out of a single occurrence. Minimum property damage limits are set at $100,000. Most producers likewise insure against equipment loss or damage. Too, they usually have life, health, and accident insurance on all participants in the production. Of course, all these items must be included in a show budget.

CONTRACTS

Producers and packagers make contracts in two directions—with the networks or other buyers; with their employees—performers, writers, directors, and so on. All contracts with employees or subcontractors must conform with the buyer. Networks have Contract Departments whose members report through their head to the head of Business Affairs.

While many provisions have become standard, it is, of course, unwise to enter any contract without legal counsel. There are many firms in New York and Los Angeles which specialize in theatrical and television law and contracts. A network contract can run anywhere from three to fifty pages depending on the complexity of the deal. Let us examine the provisions of a typical one. The contract is called an agreement and is made between the network and the packager or producer's company. While the contract may call for steps in development—outline, script, pilot—and will spell out the prices and dates for these various steps, it will anticipate success for the project by establishing terms and conditions for an overall deal. Assume the program in question is an hour-long dramatic series to be shot on film.

The agreement would set forth that the packager will develop the sixty-minute series in color and on film and to be titled such-and-such, which title and subsequent titles become elements of the series.

Next, the pilot would be discussed. The contract would declare that the network has agreed to order from the packager a sixty-minute, color television pilot to be shot on 35mm film. The network would have the exclusive right to make two network broadcasts of the pilot program over a period of three years commencing on the date the network gets delivery of the pilot. A network might require the option to run the show a third time during this same licensing period for which right it would pay verifiable out-of-pocket costs—union residual payments.

For the rights to the pilot, the network would pay the packager one-third of the agreed gross price twenty days prior to commencement of principal photography, one-third within twenty days after completion of principal photography, and the final one-third within twenty days after delivery of the completed pilot.

There would be pay or play provision. This means that the network must make all applicable payments whether it airs the program or not.

Next, there would be set forth a timetable of delivery dates for scripts, rough cut, viewing print, and final answer, or air print.

The broadcast area would be defined. Usually, the network requires exclusive license to broadcast in the United States, its territories, and possessions (excluding Spanish TV in Puerto Rico), Bermuda, Tijuana, Mexico, and the Bahamas. Some restriction is placed on Canadian sales the packager might make, since many U.S. and Canadian television markets overlap.

Then would come a paragraph defining series start dates and

orders. Networks require at least three different possible start dates for a series: fall, or September–October of the coming year; midseason, or January–February of the following year; and, fall, September –October of the same following year. This gives the network flexibility in placing the series in the schedule. Notification dates to provide the packager with reasonable start-up time are clearly spelled out for each possible start date. Ninety days is minimum.

The number of episodes to be ordered is set forth. Let us say, the initial order is for thirteen programs. There would be an option allowing the network to order a certain number of additional programs by certain pre-established dates.

Similar terms would be defined for a second year's order—usually more episodes than the first year's order. Say it is twenty-two for the second year. The packager assumes responsibility for keeping all relevant talent—performers, writers, and so on—available to the package.

The overall term of the contract would be for anywhere from three to six seasons, with the exact number of episodes to be ordered for each season set forth. Networks, of course, like to make the term of an agreement as long as possible, with out options at regular intervals. Packagers, on the other hand, like to keep the term short, so that if they have a hit, they can negotiate up sooner.

Next would come a payment schedule—perhaps in one-third installments as we have seen or in lump payments made on delivery of each program. Prices will be spelled out for each season of the term. There is always a 5 to 10 per cent increase per season.

Now the network's approval paragraph. Networks retain prior discretionary approval over all creative elements in the package including cast, directors, line producers, writers, story editors, story outlines, and scripts. The packager further must promise to consult with respect to dailies, or rushes, rough cuts, and trial runs. Again, timetables are laid out for these. Often, a packager must agree to screen test potential cast members at his expense. Usually, scripts must be delivered two weeks before shooting and rough cuts must be available for screening within ten to fifteen days after principal photography. The network can require the packager to replace any creative element prior to delivery of the show.

Delivery of the final program must be made in accordance with a separate technical specifications schedule and must be delivered at least fourteen days before the scheduled original broadcast.

The network insists on property exclusivity, including spinoff series from the original series.

The packager guarantees the network performers' exclusivity

during each broadcast season as well, and restricts performers from appearing in competing commercials. Most talent will be permitted three guest appearances during the season.

Networks may try to insert a paragraph binding cast members to do commercials for the series' sponsors at minimum union compensation. Most strong agents or lawyers knock this out—or up the ante.

A further provision calls for the packager to give the network first negotiation/first refusal rights. On a specific timetable the network gets the right to negotiate first for a continuation of the series. If this negotiation fails, the packager may try to sell the series to a third party, but the network retains the right to meet this new offer equally and retain the series.

Union scale increases or government-required increased payments will be paid for by the packager but will be reimbursed by the network upon proof of such additional payments, during the term of the contract.

The packager must provide the network with music cue sheets which must include title, type and duration of use, names of composers, lyricists, publishers, copyright proprietor, performing rights licensor, and syncronization rights licensor.

The packager agrees to use his best efforts to provide that no program will include "objectionable material" and that all material must be approved by the network's broadcast Standards Department.

The network is given the right to air the program on any day of the week at any time, on behalf of any commercial sponsor.

The network may modify, reduce, edit or alter, the program in any way.

The packager is responsible for including copyright notices in the program and for maintaining copyright protection in the program.

There are additional rights granted to the network to use any and all portions of the program for advertising, promotion, sales sampling, and audience market testing.

The packager must warrant that he has the right to grant the rights he does in the agreement and that he has secured all the necessary union contracts, licenses, and talent contracts. He further warrants that he has violated no laws and will pay all taxes and other financial bills due.

Usually, there is a full page in the contract defining specific and general indemnities which the packager provides the network and its affiliates, holding them harmless relative to all claims, damages, liabilities, suits, costs, and expenses.

The packager further agrees that he and the network are independent contractors and nothing binds them in association, partnership, joint venture, etc. All persons hired under the contract are clearly employees of the packager.

A "name and likeness" paragraph grants the network the right to use and grant to others the right to use the names, likenesses, and voices of all creative personnel in the package. This is mostly for advertising and promotion.

There is a page requiring the packager to provide the insurance coverage we have discussed.

There are paragraphs defining how and where notices are to be given and how and where disputes are to be settled. An assignments paragraph grants the network the right to assign the contract to any third parties, but restricts the packager's rights to do likewise.

A further payola paragraph binds the packager and his best efforts on behalf of employees and subcontractors to comply with the provisions of the Communications Act of 1934 and other Federal Communications Commission regulations, with specific attention to the disclosure Sections 317 and 508. These, in essence, say one should not get money, gifts, or other considerations for doing favors—without disclosing the facts.

A supplemental section of the contract spells out technical specifications of delivery of the show material and physical elements.

When a producer makes a contract with his talent employees, he must be sure to get rights for subsequent use in all media. He must also include a moral turpitude paragraph. This would void the contract if the particular talent were involved in a scandal that might effect the value of the property.

Many of the items in the network contract are not subject to negotiation. Several others are—especially the overall terms, payments, and rights to performers' services. In these areas a good lawyer, an agent, or you yourself can improve your deal.

Networks can no longer share in ownership of your property for subsequent uses or for ancillary benefits such as merchandising. However, certain powerful stars, writers, and directors may insist on part of the action.

MUSIC PERFORMANCE RIGHTS

Copyrighted works, under the copyright law of 1909, are protected for a period of twenty-eight years from the initial publication or copyright date. This protection is renewable for a second twenty-eight-year period. After this total of fifty-six years, a work is considered to be in the public domain and no further payment is required for its use. There is a long-standing move to extend copyright to the life of the creator plus fifty years, which strikes me as a more equitable system.

Musical works, of course, can be copyrighted and their use must be paid for.

There are two major music-licensing organizations, ASCAP—the American Society of Composers, Authors, and Publishers—and BMI —Broadcast Music Incorporated—which is a direct outgrowth of broadcasting's fight with ASCAP in 1939.

ASCAP was founded in 1914 (by a group of composers headed by Victor Herbert) as an organization to collect fees for the public performance for profit of copyrighted musical works belonging to the members. ASCAP holds no individual copyrights and does not publish music. Rather it is a clearing house for collecting performance fees for its more than sixteen thousand members. It provides blanket licenses to all users of copyrighted music and this, of course, includes television—and radio. ASCAP licenses networks and individual stations and collects millions of dollars a year from these sources. It is privileged information as to the exact pricing structure, but the structure is based on the use of music by and the size of the organization being licensed. Obviously, a small station pays much less than a network. These licensing fees are negotiated and cover a set period of time. A licensee need not pay for each individual use of a piece of music under this arrangement, but he must clear and report each piece of music performed. Based on these reports, ASCAP collects funds and, after subtracting the cost of its operation, disburses the funds to its members according to the total number of plays of a composer's works in a year, or by quarter. A single performance of a classical work gets as many points in the system as many performances of a popular song, in order to encourage serious work. A featured performance of a work earns more points than use of the piece as background music.

As little as four bars of music may be copyrighted and playing it can constitute a performance. This explains why composers are so eager to write program theme songs and incidental music. The constant repetition builds up performance points impressively. Last year, ASCAP members had over $80 million distributed to them.

BMI, which was founded in 1940 by broadcasters as a result of a dispute with ASCAP over what the broadcasters felt were excessive monopolistic powers and unreasonable license fees, is structured very much like ASCAP. It has thirty-five thousand members. BMI, unlike ASCAP, also publishes music.

Both organizations have cross-licensing agreements with foreign licensing organizations to receive monies from performances in their various territories.

Every good production office has ASCAP and BMI indexes for

compiling accurate logs and cue sheets of all music performed, in order to avoid copyright violations. New arrangements of public domain music may be copyrighted, so these, too, must be reported.

THE GOVERNMENT

Though it is hard to see it, the air waves are owned, it is said, by the people. That is amorphous. More realistically, they are controlled by the federal government and regulated by an agency of the government called the Federal Communications Commission. The underlying authority for the Commission is the Congress-voted Communications Act of 1934.

As a practical matter, the privately owned corporations which are assigned licenses to operate on certain specified channels and wave lengths by the Commission have a hammer lock on their dial positions. Rarely do they blow it and lose their licenses. Still, there is a lot of paper work to go through each three years to win renewal and the FCC exerts great residual power with its license revocation sword hanging over the broadcasters' heads.

The FCC is made up of seven commissioners appointed—no more than four from one political party—by the president of the United States and confirmed by the Senate. They serve overlapping seven-year terms. The commissioners establish policy and preside over a civil service staff of nearly two thousand, and an annual budget in excess of $20 million.

The FCC assigns bands of frequency, allocates licenses, advises on international regulation of air waves, designates call letters, monitors programming and signals, demands that stations keep accurate logs of broadcast material, has quasi-judicial powers, and regulates all telephone, cable, and telegraph service—the whole in a philosophy of what is called "the public convenience, interest, or necessity." (You make your own mind up as to what that is.)

Of course, the work of the FCC is much more complex and detailed than you will learn about here, but, in fact, it affects a producer's day-to-day life very little; and frankly, it has done virtually nothing to improve the aesthetic quality of American broadcasting. More's the pity.

As we saw in the Nixon era, a president can bring enormous pressures on the television industry, but over the long haul, it is Congress which has the power through legislation to make substantial changes in television. So far, it has not done much with the power. Occasionally, it scares hell out of the broadcasting establishment by trotting the big guns down for a Senate or House hearing. When things are slow, it is always worth a few headlines to scald the television industry, since everybody has an opinion on that. There is nothing like deploring television's "sex and violence" to distract the constituents from the real hell taking place in the world.

Oh, well, I should not really complain. For the most part, government regulation in the rest of even the free world is worse. In the communist countries, it is suffocating, and boring to boot.

THE NAB

Broadcasters in 1922 established the National Association of Broadcasters, more to fight ASCAP at the time than to watchdog their own activities.

These days, the NAB provides a number of worthy services to the industry, not the least of which is the Television Information Office. The NAB also channels information to members on employee regulations and costs, formulates engineering standards, lobbies on behalf of the industry before Congress and government agencies, initiates broadcasting research, and, of course, through the NAB Code, establishes standards for programs, commercial formats, and other industry practices.

The NAB Code calls attention to broadcasters' responsibilities in the use of television as a tool for extending education and culture, sets forth principles (often ignored) to aspire to in relating to children, the community, and broadly accepted social mores. For example, "Suicide as an acceptable solution for human problems is prohibited." Or, "Illicit sex relations are not treated as commendable."

In trying to satisfy the needs of so many audiences within the mass television audience and at the same time not too severely pinch the profit-making motives of its members, the NAB Code is a successful document, with far more integrity than most servants trying to please so many masters.

THE NATIONAL ACADEMY OF TELEVISION ARTS AND SCIENCES

The Academy gives out the Emmy Awards. While my fellow members and governors—I am a governor of the New York Chapter—will not like my saying it, the Emmy Awards are why the Academy was founded and why it continues to be tolerated by the industry establishment. I hope my fellow members do get angry. Maybe together we can change things. I would like to see the organization become an Academy-in-fact and a potent industry force made up of professionals, rather than a social club that has too many peripheral members eating too many meals together and giving out too many awards. There is a new guard at work in this direction. Join if you will. The initiation fee is $45 and it costs $30 a year in dues.

Chapter **8**
presentations

A good idea for a television show is only the beginning. It is a long, complex, and often torturous journey from the pure idea to the realization on screen. First, it must be presented in the right form to the right buyer in a right manner. What is more, there is no one right form, right buyer, or right manner. The formula varies with each situation and I have seen seasoned professionals squirm like errant schoolboys when they are presenting ideas for shows. Small wonder. The odds for success are high enough to make Jimmy the Greek seek social security.

In my job at ABC, for instance, I receive 30 written submissions a week and more than 100 phone calls from people with ideas for shows, which translates to some 6,760 submissions a year. I program only (only!) 240 nights a year. A long shot in anybody's book. How do I sift through these ideas to select what I need?

First of all, I speak most often and listen most carefully (while I do try to return every phone call and respond to every written inquiry) to those packagers and producers whom I either know personally or who are very well known in the profession. I cannot stress this factor of track record too strenuously. It is why I urge beginners to work first for established producers and companies before venturing forth on their own. Track record is a first priority in every buyer's thinking and deciding as he weighs a show idea. The buyer knows that even with an experienced professional team, the risks involved in producing a good, even acceptable show are extremely high; with a beginner, the risks are boundless. Often, I have rejected an idea that I have liked merely because I did not feel sanguine about the people proposing it.

If you are a known supplier, say, you merely pick up the phone, call the prospective buyer, and arrange a meeting in accord with your personal style and your relationship with the buyer. You might arrange a luncheon at LaFayette or Scandia or breakfast at the Plaza or Bel Air or meet for drinks or simply go to the buyer's office. You might even make the first pitch on the telephone. "I've got the rights to the Chinese Acrobats. Are you interested?" Or, "Liza's doing a concert at Versailles. How 'bout it if I can get it?"

There was one time I recall, when David Susskind set up a luncheon through his agent, Gary Nardino of ICM (International Creative Management). His main target was Michael Eisner, the vice-president of prime-time program development for ABC. Michael brought me along as vice-president, program development, East Coast, which at the time I was.

The formalized ritual of such a luncheon includes a superficial discussion of family, truth or rumor about personalities in the business, the state of current shows and the other networks (something is always being cancelled or somebody fired), sports (though not in this group), and the most recent or most forthcoming trip that one or more of the participants has just returned from or is about to make, with details about hotels and restaurants. There is remarkably little talk about sex and quite a bit in New York about politics and the theatre. In Hollywood, it is television and movies, period. Never is the business at hand discussed immediately. There is hardly any drinking. When there is these days, it is white wine, now very chic. This day, when he finally got to it, Susskind had two projects in mind.

"If I can get Katharine Hepburn, I'd like to do the *Glass Menagerie.*"

"If you get Hepburn, you got it," Eisner said.

Nardino, typical and correct as the agent, took notes, so that later he could follow through.

The other project was more complicated. Susskind had acquired the rights to a splendid journalistic history called "The Mafia at War," which had been running in six episodes in *New York* magazine. He outlined the series orally as he saw it being adapted to television, after he had talked at length about the content of the written pieces. He knew the material well. He had copies of the magazines with him in case Eisner had not read them. (He had.) In an accompanying written presentation, Susskind had included ideas for casting, writers, and directors. Several choices for each. He further proposed that the series have a big-name host who would appear in each episode and narrate around the dramatized scenes. (This was a good idea since characters would be different in each hour drama and television people are wary of anthology series. They much prefer a continuing character.)

The series was to be presented in six one-hour shows—a mini series. This was the season of the mini series. "Masterpiece Theatre," the impressive BBC series, had made the form voguish with its initial

American hit, the "Wives of Henry VIII." NBC had bought Joseph Wambaugh's *Blue Knight,* CBS had purchased Mark Twain's *The Gilded Age,* and we had Joseph Lash's *Eleanor and Franklin.*

Eisner and I both responded to the idea enthusiastically. Curiously, that morning I had sent Michael a memo stating that we ought to check into the series of articles. It was a natural. It could be prestigious, popular, and highly promotable—all prerequisites for a mini series. *The Godfather* movie was breaking box office records. The Mafia was a star. To deal with the subject factually seemed a way to achieve maximum audience appeal and industry stature without undue sensation.

Eisner agreed on the spot to a step deal. This means that any agreement, while written out in contract to anticipate all steps, goes through a series of cutoff points. The network has the option to drop the project at the end of any one of these steps. In this case, the first step was to write two scripts, fully, and four extended outlines. If these were satisfactory, we would go to six scripts. Liking these, ABC would go to series—we would shoot the six hours. Susskind went over his list of suggested writers and pushed hard for Robert Alan Aurthur. We approved Aurthur, if he were available, and Susskind could work out terms. An overall budget figure was proposed, discussed, and tabled for negotiation by Business Affairs. A rough timetable for delivery was set forth. The lunch was concluded, Susskind said goodby and left. Nardino walked us back to the office. Good agents always like to stay behind after the client has left. They get a better indication of the real interest on the part of the buyer as opposed to politeness. Also, they usually start pitching on behalf of other clients —especially if the first client's idea gets a no.

This deal, "The Mafia at War," has not been produced for a number of reasons. Certainly, it was not Robert Alan Aurthur's fault. He wrote two beautiful scripts. In any case, the incident is a fair example of how ideas are presented.

In the case of the Hepburn-*Menagerie* project, the presentation could not have been simpler. One oral sentence. It could have been handled on the telephone. There was a known property and a known producer, offering a much-sought-after star. If Hepburn agreed to play Amanda (she had never made a show or even a movie especially for television), it was yes or no, details to be worked out. And—odds on yes, given the palatable ingredients.

Being known and successful, Susskind had several advantages on both projects, projects that a newcomer would have had difficulty in putting together. He had weight and acceptance when he called Hepburn and Tennessee Williams, indeed when Nardino called to get the lunch date. To secure the rights to "The Mafia at War," he had his well-established credentials as a producer, plus cash to buy the property. Further, through his own television show, David has some sheen as a performer-personality himself. This is not a small asset. I have seen Merv Griffin, Dick Clark, Alan King, and others use their visibility as public figures to great advantage when, in the role of businessmen, they are trying to sell another project. After all, buyers are human and quite vulnerable to saying to wives or friends that evening, "Guess who was in the office today?" or "Guess who I had lunch with today?"

Failing to have an original concept or program, a new producer is well-advised to acquire an established property. Adaptations are as popular as Ping-pong in China. In our business, a tense game, the success of a property in another medium naturally offers at least some tissuey security and, in the event of failure, a reasonable excuse—"It was a best-seller, you know." Of course, it will not be easy for the newcomer to get a property—especially if it is new or very successful —because he will lack reputation and probably cash. Still, it is possible.

In my own early days when I was still a talent coordinator on the "Jack Paar Show," I was wildly enthusiastic about Arthur Schlesinger, Jr.'s *The Age of Roosevelt* and wanted desperately to convert it into a television series. One of the volumes was on the best-seller list, so I thought my chances were zero. I did not even know how to begin. Through a friend, I got to Mort Becker, an honorable show business attorney of the honorable firm, Becker and London. He said he would see me through the early stages without a legal fee. He asked me, as a first step, if I thought Paar would be interested in having Schlesinger as a guest on the "Tonight Show." I said I was sure he would. Then, Becker said, "Why don't you book Schlesinger? This will give you the chance to meet him in a professional setting, and it will help establish your credentials. Later, you can approach him about the series."

I booked Schlesinger as a guest. We got on nicely, and sometime after that I wrote him a letter (I had his home address) asking if I might come to Cambridge to discuss a television version of his work. He agreed. My wife and I drove to Cambridge in a whimsical car borrowed from George Kirgo, a television comedy writer now living in Hollywood. I had made George a transient TV personality by booking him several times on the Paar show. He was funny. Plugging a second book based on his experiences with the first—*How to Write Ten Different Best Sellers Now in Your Spare Time and Become the First Author on Your Block Unless There's an Author Already Living on Your Block in Which Case You'll Be the Second Author on Your Block and That's Okay Too and Other Stories*. He was asked by Jack what killed his first book and George replied, "Word of mouth." Why were there so few copies available? "My publisher used monks." Anyway, we met with Schlesinger over lunch in a Cambridge coffee shop—his choice. I wasn't that cheap!

I knew the books very well, and spoke of them with love and understanding. I had them fully outlined as to how they should be produced in thirteen one-hours on television. And, as Mort Becker had further suggested, I proposed that in lieu of option money, Schlesinger would get a percentage of the program ownership and profits. I made this figure much larger than any established producer would have. We parted with an oral agreement. I was ecstatic.

Back in New York, the following week, I read in *Variety* the ABC announcement of a thirteen-part series on FDR—without Schlesinger and certainly without me. I was crestfallen; my series was meaningless now. Still, the point is valid: It is possible and it does not cost very much. Later, I acquired certain rights to John Steinbeck's work in a similar fashion.

Let us assume that you have a project, either an original concept or an acquired property. How should you proceed? First, set forth the project in writing. If you are new, it will be necessary for you to go into much more written detail than if you are established. One presentation of a dramatic concept I received from Universal was a single, rather mangy page, badly Xeroxed. Other veteran suppliers query me on the phone or submit ideas in a brief letter or memo. For the newcomer, that is not sufficient.

A written presentation will vary depending on the nature of the project. If it is an original concept for an hour-long dramatic series, it should contain considerable detail with certain items as musts. I will give you some examples for an hour dramatic series, a variety program, a game show, and a documentary series.

First, let us suppose you are presenting a series I once used for illustration at the New School in New York. (Please, do not do what one breathtakingly impudent student of mine did: He submitted my idea four months after the class as his own idea—to ABC! And to me!)

The series is called the "Kinsey Report." The lead character is Joe Kinsey, a forty-year-old television investigative reporter who does a weekly show called, you guessed it, the "Kinsey Report." Joe, originally from the Midwest, fought in Korea and covered the war in Vietnam. In Vietnam he married a French plantation owner's daughter, who later was killed along with their only child in a Viet Cong attack. Restless, cool, courteously cynical and quixotic, Kinsey cannot make the adjustment to a settled life in New York. The network tries unsuccessfully to make him its nightly news anchorman. "Anchors're for ship in port. I got to move." He is assigned a film crew and is permitted to travel the country—the world—in order to dig out his own stories.

All right. No better or worse than many shows now on the air or soon to come. This is not a series I feel deeply about. It is slide ruled to achieve many television necessities and to impart these to the students.

The title is willful. It is already familiar and carries sexual implications. (It might not be clearable.) At the beginning this will draw a curiosity audience. Later, it will be accepted or forgotten, depending on whether the show is a hit or a miss.

Joe Kinsey is consciously drawn to exploit what I know is desirable in an action series lead. He is strong, attractive, adventurous, and a loner—but no fag. He has a past, sad and romantic. This is the stuff of television heroes. Kinsey is designed to have strong male audience appeal: He is tough, an action type, free to roam anywhere and get involved with anyone, guilt-free, since the wife is dead. (Have you ever wondered why most series leads are widows or widowers? Married, the audience cannot fantasize. Divorced, the audience might disapprove.) And, he is successful and establishment; he is working. Women will like him, also guilt-free, and feel, in addition to their sexual attraction, a certain mothering response. Somebody has to look out for this wandering widower. They also like the employed and the successful. Security.

For both sexes, he is an authority or father figure, as shown through his relationships with the other running characters and with the guest characters he meets each week. There is additional strong male and female audience appeal in the fact that he is in a glamorous business, on the side of right, and gets involved in weekly life and death situations. The young will like the action and the fact that he is a film maker. The old will like the action and the preservation of values they grew up to believe in. Of course, Kinsey must be likeable. In an action series, he need not be as creamy-likeable as Allen Ludden, but he cannot go beyond Peter Falk's eccentricity as "Columbo" or David Janssen's aloofness as "Harry O." Even Telly Savalas's "Kojak" has a heart of gold.

Before going to the actual form and content of the written presentation, I would like you to digest the above facts, and then I urge you, in a similar way, to think carefully about the kinds of ideas you are devising for television. Never forget that commercial television is a business, an advertising vehicle that must reach out to its maximum mass audience. A reminder of this thought toughly and daily will save yourself and a lot of buyers a lot of time.

For instance, if you are writing a downbeat series lead, forget it. It won't go in television. One student of mine submitted a program idea that had a black ex-con as the series lead. In the story line, he had just come out of prison and now, every week, was going to help another ex-con make it in society. In some episodes, he failed, and the object of his philanthropy would land back in prison! That is anathema! Perry Mason must win every week. So must Dr. Welby. Comedians and social critics may scoff; we ourselves know life is not like that. So what? People, masses of people, do not watch television to learn what life is like, but rather to escape it. Defeat and dreariness are what happen to you during the day. At night, in front of the box, most people want to share in victories, associate with winners, be transported from reality. Reality is waiting in the bill box, in your spouse, in your boss's frown, in your kid's lousy report card, at a dark and lonely bus stop, in the broken car, refrigerator, furnace, or, heaven forbid, television set.

My student's too-real hero is poisonous for television, particularly in a series. (In one-shot specials you can deal more honestly with life, though even here a positive resolution is desirable.) Moreover, there are other problems in this series idea. Does a mass audience really want only to see ex-cons every week? I think not. (If my opinions seem harsh, remember they are not my private views, but those forged in me as a television professional.) Do they want such a man to be black? White audiences will not—ranging from red-neck who-gives-a-damn to liberal guilt. Blacks themselves will not much care to be reminded that so many of their brothers are going through this trip in real life. And what of the general atmosphere of the series? Desperate struggle, mental anguish, crushing poverty, and potential violence which is all too close to daily reality. I believe audiences prefer clearly defined hero/villain characters in exotic or glamorous settings (or at least middle-class) and cartoon-type violence. As one other student said, pithily, about the proposed series, "You can get all that real crap on the news."

My student's idea was not a bad one. It came out of his experience and his most honest feelings. He had developed it in substantial and persuasive detail. It was simply not right for television. I urged him to write it as a novel, screenplay, or play.

What about comedy? Here, I think the television audience is hungry for reality. "Maude," "Rhoda," "All in the Family," "Sanford and Son," "Mary Tyler Moore," "M.A.S.H.," "Bob Newhart," "Chico and the Man," "Barney Miller"—all deal right on with the gut, mature, and contemporary issues—and succeed. We have been through the bruising sixties, when every issue was dragged kicking and screaming into the light, when every value, supposedly fixed in granite, was challenged and frequently seen to be made of chalk. We elevated our mediocrities and killed off our wise men. For the first time, we "lost" a war. We were forced, as in *Clockwork Orange,* to have our eyeballs taped open and to see the enormous problems which we had pretended did not exist and to see that most of them resisted solution.

In the numbing and more resigned seventies, audiences know, and know that everybody else knows, what all the difficult, even insoluble, problems are. What does one do in such cases? Laugh.

What to make of all of this? If you are devising a drama, make it escapist; if you are creating a comedy, make it real . . . cartoon real. For both, keep a close watch on our society. It is subject to rapid change. I predict that silliness is coming back within a year or two.

Let us go back to Joe Kinsey. Joe will need supporting, regular, or running characters. (Also called continuing characters.) Quite naturally, he has the film crew, his boss editor back at the network in New York, and a film editor. You will not have to invent idiots who live next door. I made the crew a cross-section of types. His cameraman: a young, sexy, clean hip-type. A med school drop-out, upper middle class, searching for himself. The assistant cameraman: black, happy to be getting up out of the ghetto into the middle class. The sound person: a luscious, feminine women's libber. The gaffer: a crusty, older, lovable type who has been everywhere—he was in Nam with Kinsey. He is very physical and street-wise. Fists first. The editor in New York: bright, buoyant, and Brooks Brothers-suited, torn between his respect and affection for Kinsey and his role as a pillar of the establishment. And so on. Make up your own.

The written presentation must contain such obvious information as the show title and the show length. It must also include lead characters and a description of each as to personality and physical characteristics. You must give the back story, that is, all the events in the central characters' lives which have led up to the point where the story is to begin. Next, you must—especially if you are a newcomer—present an extended treatment of the first hour's story, paying particular attention to the introduction and establishment of the continuing characters. Then you should have paragraphs describing the stories for the next six episodes; and, finally, one-line or one-sentence story lines for six more episodes.

These should all be on separate pages—more on this later. On a following page you should have suggested casting, subject to availability and acceptance. (*Their* availability; acceptance belongs to the network.) Always say, "suggested." This allows the buyer to become your creative partner and leaves room for his hates. As much as possible, do homework. Try to find out whom the individual buyer and his network are hot for—and whom they hate or failed with last season, and therefore have not yet forgiven. Even if you think someone is right for the part, do not put him on the list if you know he is in another series or play or film—or too important for the role. Sure, John Wayne would be perfect for the gaffer in the "Kinsey Report," but he does not do television and certainly he does not do supporting leads. You have got to know such things. Otherwise, you will get tagged as an amateur and the buyer, already wary of you as a newcomer, will put you down yet another notch. I once had an assistant whom I tried to use for casting suggestions. He would inevitably list all of the major movie actors and actresses and all the leads in current television series, knowing full well that these people were unavailable. Or did he know? I began to doubt it, and this undermined my confidence in him in all areas.

Next, set up pages in a similar manner for directors and writers. Suggest other creative people if they are appropriate to the idea. A musical show should include a list of musical directors and choreographers. If it is a hardware show, (e.g., "Mission: Impossible") that depends strongly on physical gimmicks, list special effects experts when you know about them.

If you have a novel idea for a show opening—such as the instructions on the self-destructing tape recorder each week on "Mission: Impossible"—be sure to describe this on a page, near the beginning of your presentation.

If you have any professional credits, include a brief biography of yourself. Indicate, if you are, your willingness to put your idea into a partnership with a more established producer or packager.

Do not give a budget figure—and never give a detailed budget breakdown.

Written presentations begin and usually end with a heavy helping of hyperbole. We call it by a grittier name. This opening and closing statement intends to tell the buyer why the idea is the hottest thing since Polaroid and why it is socially significant and needed. Avoid this trap. Most buyers either flip past it or bog down in it and never get on to the idea.

There is reckless and epidemic talk that program buyers are illiterate. Divorce yourself from this fancy. Network programmers, aside from college literature department members, are as well-read and educated as any group of men and women I know, and a good deal more worldly-wise. Sadly, in fact, most of them routinely deal in material that is far beneath the levels of their own tastes and pleasures.

Nearly all are college-trained. Many hold advanced degrees. They read new books and the classics, attend theatre, ballet, concerts, lectures, movies—foreign as well as U.S.—digest a bouillabaisse of newspapers and periodicals, meet a wide cross-section of their countrymen, travel extensively in America and abroad, and are extremely sophisticated about food, wine, business—self-survival. Theirs is not a ship of fools. Approach with respect.

They are, however, inundated with reading matter. That is, in part, how they get the reputation for illiteracy; that and the self-salving rationales of rejected suppliers that buyers are Philistines, cowards, cretins, and children of questionable parentage. Because of the mountains of material and the producers' panting ancipations, it is true that buyers are always slower to respond than suppliers like and, occasionally, we do forget or confuse characters' names, story points, or novel bits and devices. Remember also, please, that much of what programmers read is trash and, therefore, should for sanity as well as for sanitation be flushed from the mind immediately.

Your task in approaching a programmer or in presenting ideas to him is not to curse him—though you might—but to assist him in giving the fullest and fastest consideration possible to your submission. You can expedite this in a number of ways.

One thing to keep in mind is that no matter how extraordinary your idea may seem to be, the programmer has seen it. There are no new ideas. There is only, contrary to the Lord's advice, new wine in old bottles. That's all right. No one is expecting or wanting anything else. Television deals in simple formulae; buyers like to keep it that way, since that is how the audiences like it.

Imagine, if you will, that all ideas are small chips of tiles and that there are a limited number of these tiles. We are all playing with the same tiles. The programmer has seen them all. Your job, his job, is simply to rearrange the tiles in a fresh mosaic. Television is taking known elements and fitting them together into a pattern that seems fresh. If it is not Bing Crosby or Perry Como, then it is the Smothers Brothers or Glen Campbell, John Denver, or Cher. There will always be a new likeable, low-key, middle-of-the-road variety star.

One friend of mine, Bernie Brillstein, an intelligent and jolly talent manager and producer, had tried for months to sell a prestige series he believed in. Zero. He was getting absolutely nowhere. Also, the stars on his roster were beginning to bug him with unreasonable demands. In frustration, he grabbed up a copy of *Variety* to see what the hell was selling. In the top ten shows he saw "Beverly Hillbillies," "Green Acres," "Glen Campbell," and "Laugh-In." Consciously, maliciously almost, he sat down and grafted all of these programs onto his one giant nerve end of frustration. When he had it, he called CBS (the rural network in those days), got an appointment, and in two minutes sold the show. It was "Hee-Haw." New cider in old jugs, if you will, with the added advantage of being a concept show—no stars on which you were dependent.

A year later, Bob Wood, the president, saw CBS losing the youth and urban audiences and he threw out all of those clodhopper shows and announced to the affiliates' meeting a "brand-new," "young" schedule, although he brought in Bob Eberle and Helen O'Connell, two forties band singers, to entertain the affiliates. As Samuel Goldwyn is alleged to have said, "I'm sick of these old clichés. Get me some new ones."

We have seen that "All in the Family" is a let-it-all-hang-out "Honeymooners" or "Life with Riley." "M.A.S.H." is a cool and cynical "Bilko." "Marcus Welby" is fifty different doctor shows. The "Streets of San Francisco" is "San Francisco Beat." The "Rookies" is "Mod Squad" in a time that moved quickly from youth rebellion to law and order. "Sanford and Son" is hip "Amos 'n' Andy." "The Waltons" is "One Man's Family" and *The Grapes of Wrath.* The "Six Million Dollar Man" is Superman made with a Lockheed cost overrun. And Howard Cosell is sent in for Ed Sullivan.

The point of all of this is that a seller should examine those ingredients which have been recurrently successful and reshape them, without shame, into new programs, or with today's personalities. This is step number one in helping the programmer and thus yourself.

Step two: Go to the buyer who needs your idea. Do not take a documentary to the entertainment buyer or a daytime soap to nighttime news. Study a network's structure and personnel, and also determine what that network's strengths and weaknesses are. Where are the soft spots? The vacuums? For at least two seasons, ABC had a chronic 8:00 P.M. lead-in problem on Tuesday and Wednesday nights. This was extremely serious to the network since its "Tuesday" and "Wednesday Night Movies" were important properties right behind the lead-in times. For the most part, these movies could generate their own strength, but if they were marginal, the low lead-ins would get them behind and they could never catch up. ABC was searching hard for half-hour situation comedies. Smart producers zeroed in on those time periods.

Step three: The written presentation. For a dramatic series, I have already listed the items which should be included. What about form? First, remember that the programmer has too much to read and too little time. Keep it simple. One good rule—lots of white space. Do not cram everything onto one page. Put two or three paragraphs at most—double- or even triple-spaced—onto a single page. This way he can be reading your idea while he talks on the phone, without getting drowned in a sea of print.

Get to the point fast. A title page—with your name and where you can be reached—or rejected. Then bang—-the idea in its simplest definition. Then, who should be in it. Who will be the production team. And who you are. For openers, that is enough. If he likes the idea at that point, he will make you flesh it out later. But—for this he will probably pay you. If it is a drama, he will pay you to develop a detailed treatment or bible or even a script, maybe all of these. If it is a game show, he will ask first for a live run-through. Then if he likes it, he will pay for a pilot taping. Networks have sizable budgets for development. Do not spend any more of your own money than you have to. Work on theirs.

Now come three presentations which are models: a variety special, a game show, and a documentary. Do not judge them on their content, but rather on their form; and keep in mind that these are initial presentations—the first exposures of the ideas.

Each of these presentations came bound in either a plexiglass or pressed cardboard folder (available in any stationery store for about twenty-five cents apiece) or in a specially designed folder with the company's logo on it. I recommend such a folder to you. Do not send the presentation stapled or simply paperclipped together. The clips get stuck onto other presentations in the pile, stapled pages can be torn loose, and unbound presentations generally have a way of getting torn and reshuffled, with key pages lost. Again, make sure—and you would be astounded at the number who don't, even veteran professionals—to put your name and/or company name and address and phone number on the title page. Submit at least two copies. All buyers must register ideas and submissions. With two copies, the buyer can read one while the other is being registered.

The presentations follows. First, for a variety special:

THE FIRST ANNUAL B.L.U.N.T.* AWARDS

A 90 Minute

Satirical Comedy Special

Created By:
                Carolyn Raskin
                Eric Lieber
                IFA

                March, 1974

*"Better Luck Next Time"

Never in history has there been a society that is so
award conscious. All year round, the media,
newspapers, magazines, radio and television bombard
us with announcements of awards in almost every
conceivable area of human endeavor.

The Oscar Award
The Emmy Award
The Grammy Award
The Tony Award
The Heisman Trophy
The Cy Young Award
The Most Valuable Player
The Davis Cup
The Stanley Cup
The Car of the Year
The Motor Trend Award
Miss America
Miss Universe
Miss World
The Model of the Year
The Best Dressed List
The Nobel Prizes

The list of awards to the "best this" or "best that"
goes on and on.

But in this day when more things seem to be going wrong
than right, the worst is at least as noteworthy as the
best. It is high time that we paid tribute to these long
over-looked accomplishments.

To this end, and so that we might learn from our mistakes, we present . . .

THE FIRST ANNUAL "B.L.U.N.T."* AWARDS
A Ninety Minute Satirical Comedy Special

*"Better LUck Next Time"

The First Annual B.L.U.N.T. Awards will be hosted by David Steinberg . . . and will present awards for undistinguished accomplishments in such categories as . . .

1. Television "The Keefe Brasselle Award"
             Presenter: Tony Randall
2. Sports   "The Charles O. Finley Award"
             Presenters: Howard Cosell
             Billy Jean King
3. Science   "The Masters & Johnson Award"
             Presenter: Barbara Feldon
4. Literature "The Erich Segal Award"
             Presenter: Erica Long
5. TV Commericals "The Carmelita Pope Award"
             Presenters: Joe Namath
             Ruth Buzzi
6. New Faces "The Senator William Proxmire
             Award"
             Presenter: Phyllis Diller
7. Fashion   "The Alice Cooper Award"
             Presenters: Robert L. Green
             Edith Head
8. Business   "The Robert Vesco Award"
             Presenter: Mort Sahl
9. Fads   "The Golden Hula Hoop Award"
             Presenter: Alice Cooper
10. Music   "The Lawrence Welk Award"
             Presenter: Fabian
11. Romance   "The Henry Kissinger Award"
             Presenter: Suzanne Pleshette
12. Motion Pictures "The Myra Breckinridge Award"
             Presenter: Rex Reed

In addition to these categories, there will be some
special awards, such as . . .

1. <u>The Who Cares Award</u> To the golfers in
   Melbourne, Australia who while looking for a
   stray ball, found a giant toadstool weighing 22
   lbs.
2. <u>The Presidential Award</u> To Phillip Milhaus,
   first cousin to the President, who declined an
   invitation to the Inaugration because he was
   too poor to make the trip from his home in
   California to Washington.
3. <u>The Comeback of the Year Award</u> To San
   Francisco topless dancer, Carol Doda, who, by
   increasing her already silicone inflated bust
   from 36″ to 44″ increased her annual salary from
   $36,000 to $44,000.
4. <u>The Quote of the Year Award</u> To Margarita
   Moran, Miss Universe 1973, who said after her
   election "I think President Nixon is the
   greatest person in the world."
5. <u>The 'Til Death Do Us Part Award</u> To Tony Perkins
   and his bride, Berry Berenson, for having
   Tony's pet collie, Murray, serve as best man at
   their wedding.

And, of course, this program will explore some
indepth questions like . . .
                "Who <u>Is</u> Carmelita Pope?"
The winners in each category will be selected by a
panel of America's trend-setters, who will vote from a
list of pre-selected nominees. (Write-in votes will
be honored.)
The panel will be comprised of persons such as . . .

Fashion:	Earl Blackwell
	Robert L. Green
Sports:	Jim Murray
	Dick Young
	Howard Cosell
	Jim Bouton
	Billie Jean King
The Arts:	Rex Reed
	Charles Champlin
	Judith Crist
	Vincent Canby
	Gene Shalit
	Cleveland Amory
	Sue Cameron
	Artie Shaw
	Carl Reiner

```
                                 Mike Nichols
                                 Joyce Haber
                                 Gore Vidal
                                 Rona Barret
News & Public Affairs:           Art Buchwald
                                 Jimmy Breslin
                                 Shana Alexander
                                 Herb Block
                                 Oliphant
                                 Bill Mauldin
                                 Martha Mitchell
                                 Russell Baker
                                 Jack Anderson
                                 William Buckley
                                 David Schoenbrun
                                 Bess Myerson
Society:                         Suzy Knickerbocker
                                 Charlotte Curtis
                                 Amy Vanderbilt
                                 Hugh Hefner
                                 David Reuben
                                 Barbara Howard
```

POSSIBLE PARTICIPANTS OR PRESENTERS

Selma Diamond
Dick Clark
Ron Carey
Minnie Pearl
Jimmy Dean
Roger Miller
Bobby Goldsboro
Sam Levenson
Rich Little
Frank Gorshin
Totie Fields
Bernadette Peters
Soupy Sales
Stiller & Meara
Henny Youngman
Nancy Wilson
Fanny Flagg
Milton Berle
Norm Crosby
George Hamilton
Liberace
Barbara Feldon
Vincent Price

FORMAT

I. The program will open with an introductory
monologue covering the following points:
1. The reasons why the B.L.U.N.T. Awards are
important.
2. The standards of judgement used in determining
the winners.
3. Some examples of possible winners in previous
years.
4. A brief explanation of the voting procedures.
II. Preceding many of the awards, a special
"B.L.U.N.T. Hall of Fame" Award will be made in
the corresponding category. These segments will
take the form of a blackout, musical tribute or
historical re-enactment.

For example: Preceding the award for Romance . . .
we will present a sketch involving
Martha Mitchell and her first
husband.

Preceding the award for TV
Commercials . . . we will present a
medley of television's most
irritating commercial jingles.

Preceding the award for Fashion . . .
a sketch on unisex.

Preceding the award for Science . . .
a sketch on Kouhoutek, the Comet
nobody saw.

Preceding the award for Television
. . . a sketch based on what a 1994
episode of "Gunsmoke" might look
like.
III. The presentations themselves will be short
monologues based on the nominees in a given
category, ending with the announcement of the
winners.

In some cases the recipients will be on hand to
receive their award.

In any case, a specially designed award will
be at hand. It will either be given on the show or
mailed to the recipient.

161

RUNDOWN - (90-Minutes)

	Segment Time	Running Time
1. Opening of show Glamour shots, Billboards, Guest stars, Titles		1:30
2. Commercial #1	1:00	2:30
3. Intro Host Host MONOLOGUE	7:00	9:30
4. Commercial #2	1:00	10:30
5. a. Host intro Category #1	1:00	11:30
b. Hall of Fame for Television "Gunsmoke" SKETCH	2:00	13:30
6. Intro Presenters	2:00	15:30
7. Award #1—Television Award	:30	16:00
8. Commercial #3	1:00	17:00
9. Host Intro 1st Nominated Song	1:00	18:00
10. SONG #1 "_____" Joanne Worley	2:00	20:00
11. Commercial #4	1:00	21:00
12. a. Intro Category #2	:30	21:30
b. Hall of Fame for Sports— COMEDY	2:00	23:30
13. Intro Presenters	2:00	25:30
14. Award #2—Sports Award	:30	26:00
15. Commercial #5 & #6	2:00	28:00
16. Station Break	1:00	29:00
17. Host Intro Song #2	1:00	30:00
18. SONG #2 "_____" Roger Miller	2:00	32:00
19. Commercial #7	1:00	33:00
20. a. Intro Category #3—Science	:30	33:30
b. Hall of Fame—Science SKETCH on Kouhoutak, the Comet nobody ever saw	2:00	35:30
21. Presenters	2:00	37:30
22. Award #3—Science	:30	38:00
23. Commercial #3	1:00	39:00
24. Host—MONOLOGUE on Special Awards—"Who Cares"— "Comeback"—"Quote"—"Til Death Do Us Part"— "Presidential", etc.	6:00	45:00
25. Commercial #9	1:00	46:00
26. Intro Category #4	:30	46:30
27. Intro Presenters	1:00	47:30
28. Award #4—Literature	:30	48:00
29. Commercial #10	1:00	49:00
30. a. Intro Category #5— Commercials	1:00	50:00

```
          b. Hall of Fame—Commercials
             MEDLEY of memorable, but
             irritating jingles—Ruth
             Buzzi                                 2:30        52:30
31.Commercial #11                                  1:00        53:30
32.Presenters                                      1:00        54:30
33.Award #5—TV Commercial                           :30        55:00
34.Commercial #12 & #13                            2:00        57:00
35.Station Break                                   1:00        58:00
36.Intro Song #3                                    :30        58:30
37.SONG #3 "_____" Tony Randall                    2:00        60:30
38.Presenters                                      1:00        61:30
39.Award #6—New Faces                               :30        62:00
40.a. Host Intro Category #7                        :30        62:30
    b. Hall of Fame—Fashion
       A short SKETCH on Unisex                    1:30        64:00
41.Presenters and Award #7                         1:00        65:00
42.Commercial #14 & #15                            2:00        67:00
43.Intro Song #4                                    :30        67:30
44.SONG #4 "_____" The Letterman                   2:00        69:30
45.Intro Presenters                                 :30        70:00
46.Award #8—Business                               1:00        71:00
47.Intro Presenters                                 :30        71:30
48.Award #9—Fads                                   1:30        73:00
49.Intro Song #5                                    :30        73:30
50.SONG #5 "_____" Fabian                          2:00        75:30
51.Presenter—Fabian—Award #10
   —Music                                          1:00        76:30
52.Commercial #16 & #17                            2:00        78:30
53.a. Host Intro Category #11                      1:30        80:00
    b. Hall of Fame—Romance
       SKETCH on Martha Mitchell
       and her
       first husband                               2:00        82:00
54.Presenters                                       :30        82:30
55.Award #11—Romance                               1:00        83:30
56.Host—Final Category
   Hall of Fame—Movies "Great
   Moments in History"—
   COMEDY                                          2:00        85:30
57.Presenters                                      1:00        86:30
58.Award #12—Movies                                 :30        87:00
59.WRAP UP—Host                                    2:00        89:00
60.Credits                                         1:00        90:00
```

PROPOSED WRITING STAFF –SEVERAL OF THE FOLLOWING

Hal Kanter
Gene Perret
Jay Burton
Tom Whedon
Jack Burns
George Bloom

In this case, Carolyn Raskin and Eric Lieber are known to me, so it was not necessary for them to include biographies of themselves. This presentation came in an agency binder. I would only have two reservations about this presentation: Pages one and two should be stretched more evenly and with more white space; more white space throughout. I would have left the buyer more flexibility in choosing the host. Otherwise, I think it spells out in quick but adequate detail exactly what the concept is, how some of the ideas would be handled and whom they would hope to have as guests and production team.

Next, one I have made up as an example for a game show.

"ARMCHAIR QUARTERBACK"

A Once-a-Week

Half-Hour Quiz Game

Submitted By: Bob Shanks
              Company Name
              Address
              Phone Number
              Date of Submission

"Armchair Quarterback"

"Armchair Quarterback" is a quiz game focused on calls
a quarterback makes in various football situations.
Only pro football is covered.

There is a host.

There is a celebrity panel—3 permanent members and 1
alternating guest from the sports world. Each
panelist plays for a home viewer selected at random
through mail-in.

THE FORMAT

1. Host is introduced

2. Host introduces panel

3. Host introduces guest quarterback

4. Guest quarterback's career is reviewed in brief interview, with statistics, anecdotes and film highlights of his career. He has brought filmed plays from his own career to test the panel as "armchair quarterbacks."

GAME—PLAY #1

1. We view the play on film that preceded the play in question and get filled in by V.O. from host on what the situation was.

2. We run the play-in-question up to the center snap. Freeze the frame.

3. Panel is offered choice of 5 plays to choose from— shown by diagram slides. Each panelist writes down his choice and also indicates if he thinks the call was successful.

4. The play "unfreezes" and we see what happened. We see the play in question again—in slow-motion. The panelists choosing correctly get:
   6 points for calling the right play
   1 point if the play was successful
   3 additional points if the play scored
   Scoring is cumulative and the panelist with the most points at the end is the winner. The home viewer whom the panelist is playing for gets the point total in cash, 2 tickets to an NFL game and transportation to the city where the game is being played.

5. The game process is repeated 5 more plays with the guest quarterback.

6. A new quarterback is introduced and the process is repeated.

The show could run from the first week after Labor
Day until the end of January; approximately 20
weeks of shows. Or—year round for those ravenous
football fans who get TV anemia from January to
August.

There are 20 teams in the NFL, each with a quarterback
and a good back-up quarterback; for instance, Earl
Morrell, Colts; George Blanda, Raiders. Not to
mention some outstanding quarterbacks now retired:
Y.A. Tittle, example.

This is a plentiful supply to pick 40 from for our
annual series of shows.

HOST SUGGESTIONS:

    Joe Namath
    Don Meredith
    Jerry Kramer
    Kyle Rote
    Howard Cosell
    Alex Karras

And, I know all the best game players.

This game could be adapted to pit colleges against
each other:

Texas vs. Notre Dame

(coach & quarterback)   (coach & quarterback)

The next presentation, a documentary, is by my wife.

THE AMERICAN WORD

Six 1-hour television programs

(an initial offering)

to

illumine

The Giants

of

American Literature

June 11, 1972   Presented by:

COMCO PRODUCTIONS, INC.
850 Seventh Avenue
New York, New York 10019
(212) 765-4898

Ms. Ann Zane Shanks

<u>THE AMERICAN WORD</u>
stars
MARK TWAIN
F. SCOTT FITZGERALD
ERNEST HEMINGWAY
EUGENE O'NEILL
WILLIAM FAULKNER
JOHN STEINBECK

with the distinguished American actor,
E. G. MARSHALL,
as host and narrator

The soul of a nation is revealed through its authors and is frequently transformed by their visions.

As America has inspired the inventions of its writers, so have its writers invented America. Life imitates art. We perceive realities, take on attitudes and initiate action because of our writers' visions and definitions of the way we are.

America is different because Mark Twain saw and celebrated the uncooked boldness of the emerging nation and, by the power of his talent, pricked the pomposity of an America tacking toward aristocracy in the Gilded Age, thus keeping it true to its democratic and common folk character.

Steinbeck did nearly as much as the New Deal to persuade us from the human cruelties of the Depression.

Hemingway was the Prophet of American Internationalism and the protean model for American masculinity, which otherwise was losing its faith in itself as it lost the frontier and individuality to its new-found factories and machines.

This television series, THE AMERICAN WORD, then, is, simply, the revelation of America through its major literary figures: How we live and how we think, as substantiated and projected by these six men.

Focusing on each writer, intensely and personally, THE AMERICAN WORD will indirectly shed light on the entire flow and flavor of the American culture and time in which each man worked, thought, felt; and which each helped to shape.

One program, One writer

Each hour will be a sight and sound biography of one
writer.

A mixture of television techniques will be used. (The
recent Italian production, <u>Leonardo</u>, is helpful for
envisioning the format.)

Some events will be dramatized, with a "name" actor
playing the central character. George C. Scott as
Hemingway, for instance; Jason Robards as Eugene
O'Neill or Lee Marvin as Steinbeck.

Visual emphasis will dominate. Films, "stills,"
prints, and paintings will be used where appropriate.

If we are "reading" from Faulkner his description of a
Mississippi summer day, the camera will see such a
place and day. We will learn of Faulkner's alcoholism,
his struggle with Hollywood and the New South from
people who knew him. Twain's River, Hemingway's
Paris, Fitzgerald's Jazz will be seen and heard.
Certain living people who knew the authors will be
interviewed.

None of these men was a bronze Saint, nor will any be portrayed that way. Their triumphs and failures were human and their humanity is what will be on display.

Their humanness is our source of strength and identification. Our oneness. Their genius has been not to confound us but rather to make us say, "Yes. That is right. That is true. That is the way I feel. The way things are—or ought to be."

THE PACKAGER

THE AMERICAN WORD will be produced by Comco
Productions, Inc., New York, which has won 2 Emmys, 3
CINE Golden Eagles, and Gold Medals at The San
Francisco, American and The New York Film and TV
Festivals for its work on various productions—THE
GREAT AMERICAN DREAM MACHINE; AMERICAN LIFE STYLE;
DENMARK, A LOVING EMBRACE; CENTRAL PARK; TIVOLI; and
FALL RIVER LEGEND.

Ann Zane Shanks will serve as on-the-line producer.

DIRECTOR SUGGESTIONS

It is proposed that established directors of stature
be sought and employed for this project:

PETER BOGDANOVICH
SIDNEY LUMET
JOHN HUSTON
ARTHUR PENN
ANTHONY HARVEY
STANLEY KRAMER
HAROLD PRINCE
ELIA KAZAN

WRITERS

It is recommended that scripts be written by such able
craftsmen as:

GORE VIDAL
JAMES COSTIGAN
ROBERT ALAN AURTHUR
LANFORD WILSON
JAMES DICKEY
ARTHUR LAURENTS

Technical and research assistance will be sought from
leading biographers of each writer to be a subject for
THE AMERICAN WORD.

Production will be in color and shot on 35MM film.

Costs for THE AMERICAN WORD are reasonable and consistent with current industry pricing for such a project.

The packager would be open to a partnership production arrangement.

THE AMERICAN WORD, designed first for American
commercial network showing, will have enduring value
for a sponsoring company in public television, use in
schools and colleges, foreign markets and libraries
and community organizations.

The programs would make an ideal book or series of
books, adapted in the way of Alistair Cooke's AMERICA
or Kenneth Clark's CIVILISATION.

Again, setting aside the merits of the show idea, I believe Ann has devised an excellent presentation:

1. Title page—the title, indication of the project, date of submission, information as to who has submitted the idea.

2. A lot of white space—for easy reading and for a buyer to make notes in.

3. Substance—quick explanation of the basic idea and the techniques to be used. Further, and wisely, she has related her approach to a known project —"Leonardo"—which a buyer may have seen or could arrange to see, and which was a big prestige success. This latter point is important since she knows that only advertisers or buyers who want prestige products will be interested in this project in any case.

4. Packager—briefly she says who she and her company are and what they have done.

5. Creative elements—she has suggested going a blue-ribbon route with cast, directors, and writers; though note that she has only proposed or recommended, thus leaving herself and a potential buyer flexibility in these areas. Doing this, however, achieves positive effects: She communicates her seriousness and respect for the project. Further, since she herself is not a "big name" producer such as David Wolper, she gets rub value—stature-by-association—in the categories of performers, directors, and writers.

6. Price—she has acknowledged it but has left the fixed figure for later negotiation when a buyer shows genuine interest. Price will vary in any case, depending considerably on the talent who might finally be signed up and on where the show is finally placed—network, syndication, public television. The way she mentions price does communicate her awareness of this factor and that she knows what the market place is paying generally for such projects.

7. Other uses—she has shown a potential buyer benefits he may derive beyond the initial television airing—and may not have thought about. Such factors should be important to a Xerox, IBM, Exxon, or Mobil, for instance, and demonstrate her ability to think with a corporate view or overview.

She has been firm in the presentation about only two important ingredients: the writer-subjects of the programs and her choice of host —E. G. Marshall.

All right, in the matter of writer-subjects, one buyer might want Carl Sandburg, another Thomas Wolfe and so on, to replace those she has listed; and she would be willing to flex if this will make the sale, but, even so, she knows she has stayed very much in the American mainstream and has communicated that by her selections. First, her choices are all safely dead and generally noncontroversial. All are in the marbleized category. There is middle-brow familiarity with them which makes them attractive for television. For a project start-up, they are particularly good choices. Later, if the series is successful, she could make bolder or more esoteric choices. Moreover, even with these six, television has done very little thus far to examine their lives and works.

As to Marshall—it is wrong to be this specific about a host, since the buyer might not like him or Marshall might not be available for the project; therefore, the host page should only recommend, and it should give more than one name. She, in this case, has to be specific, since she and E.G. evolved the project together. Do not get me wrong: E. G. Marshall is a splendid host; she and a buyer could not have a better one.

One more thing about this presentation. You could say that there is some hyperbole in it, contrary to my advice to keep such material to a minimum. So? (A) She has kept it to a minimum. (B) Prestige buyers want more why and what than buyers looking for grind products. (C) She has to anticipate buyers questioning her writer-subject selections and buyers unfamiliar with angles on each of the writer-subjects listed as to what makes them interesting historical and dramatic choices.

Once the initial written presentation is complete, what does one do with it? It will be helpful to describe the circumstances of approach taken on the Carolyn Raskin-Eric Lieber presentation.

In the case of the "B.L.U.N.T. Awards," the procedure was simple. I make frequent trips to Southern California, for the prime purpose of meeting with members of "the creative community." Plainly, this phrase lumps together packagers, producers, directors, performers, writers, and their representatives. Many of these people —nowadays most of them—live in and around Hollywood, the catch-all name for that pastel, Panglossian area that sprawls across the Southern California coast. Despite the fact that much of the area looks like a circus that went broke on the road, it is the show business center of the world and, if you work in television, sooner or later, you will work there; what's more, you will probably like it. If you yearn for Paradise and are not too demanding, Southern California will suffice, even if there is a crack in the foundation and your eyes smart.

On one of my trips I had a meeting with Carolyn Raskin, who conceived the "B.L.U.N.T. Awards" show. I had never met Carolyn but knew about her from many people in the business and respected her reputation and credits—she produced "Laugh-In," among other shows. Our meeting took place in one of the guest offices of ABC in Beverly Hills, which I had been assigned to use while I was in California. The date had been arranged by phone by Sandy Wernik, Carolyn's agent who worked in the West Coast offices of IFA (now ICM). He sent the written presentation to me in advance (a good idea) and accompanied Carolyn to the meeting.

Since we had never met, Carolyn kept the amenities to a minimum—we did discuss mutual acquaintances and did affirm that it was good at last to meet each other because we had heard "so many nice things" about each other for a long time. Quickly, she got to the business at hand and began describing the show verbally. She elaborated on each award and how each segment in the show would be treated as to technique, with special emphasis on comedy.

Raskin and I then went over her list of presenters and performers and I told her those I did not like. (Read "would not be right for the show" for "like." "Like" mostly has nothing to do with your professional judgment. You do not have to like someone to hire that person. There is an old show-business saw that cuts, "I'll never work with that son-of-a-bitch again—until I need him.")

We discussed her writer suggestions in a similar way. I wanted to know her choice of director, and we agreed on the desirability of two or three. Wernik, properly from his point of view, pushed for those who were IFA clients.

I said I did not like the title—the "B.L.U.N.T. Awards." It did not focus on the content of the show, took too long to explain, and did not sing. She said she was not wedded to it.

I took time, since Raskin is a respected professional, to explain what I think works and what does not work in terms of late-night viewer preferences, not only for this project, but to stimulate her thinking toward other ideas for "Wide World of Entertainment."

I wanted the "B.L.U.N.T. Awards" for late night, and I had confidence in Carolyn Raskin. For a number of reasons, however, having nothing to do with the merits of the project—I had made too many other commitments and I was running perilously close to over-budget—I had to say no to the project, for now. Keep that in mind. Frequently buyers say no for a lot of reasons that have no direct connection to a project.

With Carolyn Raskin, the buyer-seller meeting had been routine and easy to set up. I spoke to Sandy Wernik frequently, since he had a number of solid professionals as clients. Raskin herself is an established producer, so I was very amenable to hearing about any ideas she might have.

From their side—Raskin's and Wernik's—they had made a proper approach. I am not sure which came first, her idea or her examination of the needs of "Wide World of Entertainment," but, in any case, she had devised a good marriage of program need and program idea. I must assume that she or her agent had studied "Wide World of Entertainment," saw that we did specials, and had found out that we especially were looking hard for good comedy or entertainment concepts that had some reality basis to them. She saw also that we took chances and that we might be receptive to the spoof form, since we had already done one successfully—a spoof of the beauty pageant form in our "Unofficial Miss Las Vegas Showgirl Beauty Pageant" show. Too, we would be receptive to her producing such a show, given her "Laugh-In" credit.

Before I go on to give you an idea of how to find a buyer for your idea, let me recount a few unorthodox approaches—and the varying success they met with. For instance, I remember how Dick Cavett got his first television job, on the "Jack Paar Tonight Show." His approach broke all the rules—particularly when you consider Paar's shy and reclusive private personality.

Cavett, a copy boy for *Time* magazine, began writing Paar letters every day—on *Time* stationery, it should be noted. Then he started to hang around the studio. Paar was one of the most powerful and controversial men in television in those days. After a few times, Cavett found it increasingly easy to get close to the Inner Sanctum, since by now his face was familiar to everyone and if they did not know what he did, they assumed he did something on the show or at the network. Finally, he was able to confront the Great Man Himself. It happened at NBC, in the sixth-floor corridor which Paar had to use to get between his office and Studio 6B where the show was taped. The corridor was a hangout for anyone connected with the show. I was there and saw it happen. Dick Cavett suddenly moved to block Jack's path. That was unheard of! Cavett did it, though, and said, "I think you're the best and I'm talented—and I want to work for you. I'm Dick Cavett—who writes you all those letters—from *Time* magazine? Here are some jokes I've written." Words to that effect.

Paar was moving again by the time Cavett finished speaking, but he did take with him Dick's material and, later, in his office, Paar read it. A week later Dick was hired as a talent coordinator and junior writer. If that is your style and you can, like Cavett, back it up with talent, try it. But if those jokes had not been good, I can assure you that Dick Cavett's career would have begun elsewhere.

Enjoy the story, but do not take from it that you should approach buyers this way. The buyers will think you are an idiot 99.9 per cent of the time you try such bizarre contacts. But here are a few other unorthodox approaches before we get to the more acceptable ways of doing business.

In the Westinghouse days, the "Merv Griffin Show" was taped at the Little Theatre, a converted Broadway house on West Forty-fourth Street in New York City. Our production offices were upstairs and we got to them via an alleyway which gave access from the street to the stage for performers, technicians, and scenery. One day I was told that a huge crate with my name on it had been delivered by Railway Express; it was sitting in the alleyway.

I did not go down right away, but when I did, I passed the crate several times on my way in and out of the building. I figured it contained some kind of practical joke or promotion item, neither of which has ever much amused me; having read about the Trojan War and knowing my business as I do, I had a pretty good hunch that the contents of the box might better stay unrevealed in the interest of my mental health. For others, however, the crate became a great curiosity; all day people knocked on it, listened for sounds, speculating as to what it might contain. Finally, after the taping that night, pestered by nearly everyone, I opened the crate on the side marked *Open Here.*

There are guys just right for some kissin',
And I mean to kiss me a few.
Oh, those guys don't know what they're missin'.
I've got a lot of lovin' to do!*

A perky girl singer, dressed in an evening gown, stood inside singing her little lungs out. With her sat a young man in tuxedo accompanying her on a Spinet piano and singing along. Okay. Novel and harmless. But you do not have to work that hard. And, no, they did not get booked on the show.

Another time, during my stint at the "Tonight" show, I returned from lunch and my secretary started going over the phone messages with me, calling particular attention to one.

"A Mr. Van called and said I should give you this message precisely," she said. "The case has been settled out of court. Mr. Shanks should send me the check for three thousand and if I get it by 5:00 P.M. Tuesday, everything'll be fine. Tuesday at 5:00—you got that? No later. I'm leavin' town and I don't want any screw-ups. If Shanks has any questions, have him call me at (he gave me a phone number)."

I did, indeed, have questions. I called the number immediately. What case? What $3,000? What Mr. Van?

Mr. Van turned out to be a young, unknown comedian named Vinnie Van who was looking for an audition and thought he would be unable to get me on the phone. His apologies were Niagaran and I must say I was so relieved I gave him the audition. When I met Van I liked him, but I thought that nothing else he did was as funny as his phone joke.

Here now are what I consider to be appropriate ways to approach buyers. Just keep in mind that what I tell you has worked for me or reflects what I have heard other buyers say about how they prefer to be approached. Again, we are not dealing with a pure science; all of this happens in a context of complicated human needs and perceptions, actions and reactions, not the least important of which is your personal style.

If you are truly unknown, stick your ideas in a drawer, get the best job in television you possibly can, and work your way up to a level where buyers will respect your experience. When you are ready for the approach, do your homework. The first and most important question is, What buyer needs my idea the most?

It is easy to find out who the particular person is whom you properly should see within the target organization. All you do is phone the company and ask the operator, "Who is in charge of so-and-so?" Too many people exhaust themselves trying to find some clever access to the buyers. When you have the correct person's name, phone him. It is one in a million that you will get through on the first phone call. When you do not get through on the first call, do not despair and do not get annoyed. This is fatal. Continue to call at least twice a day; always be pleasant and try to make friends with the secretary. By this latter bit of advice I do not mean that you should come on or try to make out. Save your libido for leisure hours. Such a tactic, aside from being boorish, will most likely turn her off anyway. What she does not get is warmth, courtesy, and sympathy. If you use a civilized approach consistently, she will become your ally in getting through to the boss. Imagine the scene from the secretary's point of view: A constant bombardment of phone calls and she is the harrassed front line of defense. If you engage her sympathy by in turn being sympathetic to her, she will nag the boss to speak to you: "Oh, talk to him. He's so patient and nice." (Women's Libbers: Please excuse the genders used here, but it is simpler and still mostly the way things are.)

If you cannot get through the secretary, try calling during lunch hour or after 6:00 P.M. Most secretaries go out to lunch and leave by 6:00; the boss frequently is there alone. He might pick up his own phone. If you do get the boss, be polite and brief. Do not start by saying, "You're harder to get than the president of the United States." A line we have all heard too often. (When did you last attempt to call the president of the United States?) State your name—chances are the boss will know it by now, since you have called so often. If you're lucky, the boss may even think he knows you. Try to get an appointment (at this stage do not try for a lunch date or drinks). If he will not see you, suggest that you are willing to describe the idea briefly on the phone or come in to see one of his associates or assistants. Failing all of this, say that you will mail in your program idea.

Always be willing to see an associate, if you must. Having started with the boss, you can say, "Boss so-and-so asked me to call you"; given the bad communication, sloppy organization, and crush of activity in most companies, you have an automatic foot in the door. Moreover, associate-types are more willing to take meetings because they are for the most part ambitious and hungry for ideas to take to the boss. Never sneer at associates; eventually they may be the boss. One major executive I know goes out of his way to establish relationships with these younger executives as a hedge against the future.

If you get your appointment, be there on time. If you are kept waiting without explanation for more than half an hour, ask, politely, for another appointment, and leave.

When you do get in, be succinct and get out as quickly as possible. You should try to make some human contact, but keep it safe. Comment on the view, the wall art, a necktie. Do not hand over the written presentation until you have finished making your oral pitch; otherwise, the buyer will be half-listening, half-reading, and not doing either very well.

If the buyer says no at this point, do not continue to sell or press, unless the buyer gives a signal that he really wants to be sold and needs additional reasons as to why he should say yes. When the answer is no, either then in the meeting or later on the phone or by mail, accept it graciously, thank the buyer for the chance to submit your idea this time and say you hope it will be possible to see the buyer again with subsequent ideas. Try to get the buyer to talk about the kinds of projects he is looking for. It is easier to sell him his own idea.

Somewhere along the way, do not hesitate—subtly now—to flatter the buyer and/or his company. Pick something you genuinely admire. We all believe something we are doing is worthwhile and we love to hear about it from others.

Some do nots: Do not drop by an office without an appointment, unless you know the buyer very well or have checked the secretary and found out that the buyer is in a mood for company. Even then, the truth is that he will resent your stalking him or interrupting him when he is not mentally prepared for you. Do not accost buyers outside of their offices—at restaurants, on commuter trains, in theatres, on golf courses, in dark bars. That is anathema.

Do not keep selling after the buyer has said yes, since this can just as quickly unsell your idea. (Apparently, Darryl Zanuck, despite his success, was notorious in this regard, hence the title of his book, *Don't Say Yes Until I'm Finished.*)

Do not promise more than you can deliver, and do answer all the buyers' questions as honestly and as fully as you can. I am especially hard on these points. I seldom buy twice from a supplier who inflates his claims, or lies. Yes, there are suppliers who employ bribes of every sort to get a yes; frequently they are successful. Don't try most of us, however. We have our own hairshirts tailor-made and detest the bribe approach.

In summary, I suppose what I am urging on you here is common sense and common courtesy.

Chapter **9**
production–before, during and after

Once a program maker has sold a show, all of his gall is divided into three parts: preproduction, production, and postproduction. Preproduction has to do with all of the planning prior to production. Production is the recording on tape or film of actual show content. Postproduction is the process of assembling and editing the recorded content into the final and polished program.

Jumping into your first shooting day without preparation or planning is packing your parachute after you have jumped out of the plane. Even in those "real" documentaries that beginning people are so fond of making, planning is essential. We have long passed the day when unintelligible sound, shaky and blurred camera work, bad lighting, and undigested dialogue and ideas can hold our attention or warrant consideration as statement.

Each program is different and dictates its own interpretation of the rules for preproduction. Always, first, there is the idea. The idea may be a concept—"Let's do a show about how the Pentagon sells itself"—or a personality—"Let's do a show starring Cher."

In a continuing program such as "Good Morning, America," "Today," game shows, "Tonight," or the "Merv Griffin Show," the problems and planning in production become routine. Here is a typical day for the "Merv Griffin Show" producer and staff:

OFFICE

10:00 A.M.	staff booking meeting
11:00 A.M.	routine show; meet with writers
12:00 P.M.	production staff meeting
Lunch	meetings with agents, talent, PR people
2:00 P.M.–	phone calls, mail, auditions, appointments,
5:00 P.M.	show rehearsals, administration
5:00 P.M.	preshow meeting with Griffin, staff, writers

193

5:30 P.M.	preshow meeting with production crew
6:00 P.M.	meeting: producer and Griffin
6:30 P.M.– 8:00 P.M.	VTR show
8:30 P.M.	postshow meeting with censor

STUDIO

12:00 P.M.	ESU (electrical set up) and crew call
12:00 P.M.– 2:00 P.M.	lighting
2:00 P.M.– 5:00 P.M.	orchestra and talent rehearsals
5:30 P.M.	preshow meeting with producer
6:00 P.M.	camera registration—chips
6:30 P.M.	VTR show

Perhaps no other activity of the "Merv Griffin Show" staff day was so important as the 10:00 A.M. booking meeting, since this program's fundamental business was the presentation of talkers and performers. The meeting, held in the producer's office, would include the producer, associate producer, three talent coordinators, two associate talent coordinators, a press contact, and the production assistant. The central focus of the meeting was the information contained in the "Talent Status Report." The report was published daily, Monday through Friday, and was divided into four categories: "Confirmed," "Available," "Unavailable," "Future."

Under "Confirmed" were listed those names of guests who had been booked definitely for the program, the date of the booking, the guest's contact and, in parenthesis, the initials of the show's booker. For instance:

CONFIRMED:

Jack Lemmon; Mon. 3/12; William Morris (TG)
Jackie Gleason; Wed. 4/3; ICM (PS)
Tom Seaver; Fri. 4/5; Mets PR office (RM)

Under "Available," set up in similar form, would be listed all the people being pitched to come on the show or those who could and were recommended by the staff. Here, too, would be included certain feature ideas, such as a new products demonstration or a fashion show.

"Unavailable" seems clear enough. Actually, here were listed those we had gone after and could not get or whose date of availability had changed from an earlier date.

In "Future" were listed people and ideas from the talent coordinators or bookers that they wanted to see on the show and which were being discussed for the first time. Such as, "Pilot who led Japanese air attack on Pearl Harbor has found religion and lives in Seattle. Good idea for Dec. 7 anniversary. Should I go after?" (JM)

Everyone in the group had a booking book. On loose-leaf pages, one for each week, mimeographed lines were drawn to separate days, Monday through Friday, and the names of the confirmed guests would be penciled in accordingly. The book had pages for about twelve to fifteen weeks ahead. In my booking book, I not only wrote the names of the confirmed guests, but the names of possibles, in order to see what a particular mix of guests might look like on paper. To me a perfectly booked show was a big-name movie star to lead off, a good comedian, both stand-up and at the panel, a pretty girl, a singer who could also talk, and a newsmaker—athlete, politician, or sports figure. If I thought the movie star was dull, I would bring him out after the comedian or another regular who could interrupt amusingly.

As availabilities or mixes changed, I would scratch out the names and write in new ones. By the time a show was actually set and ready to tape, my booking book sheet for that day would look like a bad Jackson Pollack painting. Fortunately, my secretary would daily retype an orderly booking sheet which she kept herself so everyone would have a legible record of the guests booked for the show. Other producers work differently. Woody Frazer and Roger Ailes, then at the "Mike Douglas Show" and Rudy Tellez and Perry Cross, then producing "Tonight," employed a large cork board, lined off Monday thru Friday, for five weeks, and showing the guests for each program on index cards pinned to the board.

The booking meetings were vicious sessions of talent evaluation. "Old," "Boring," " 'Bout as funny as Auschwitz," "Sings like a cat caught in a screen door." Often the bookings were negotiated settlements. "Danny Thomas'll only come on if you book this tenor he's discovered." (Ever since Eddie Cantor patroned Eddie Fisher, big-name comedians have been infected with the disease.) "Can he sing?" "He's terrible, but Thomas thinks he's great." "Okay, one song— near the end of the show—and make clear in the intro he's Thomas's find, not ours."

As well as determining future bookings, the meeting was used to go over information on the guests for that day's program. Each talent coordinator was responsible for a preinterview and would submit a written introduction and page of talk leads for Merv to use in questioning. He counted on these leads to pay off in a story that was interesting or funny. He never knew the ends of the stories before he heard them on the air; we wanted to keep his reaction fresh.

When the meeting was over, the bookers went away for meetings with now and future guests, auditions, or to redo their notes on guests for that night. The production assistant stayed on to get my routine for the show. Routine, or rundown, it is called. It means establishing the running order and time given to each guest or segment. She would then get it typed and distributed.

At 11:00 A.M. I met with the show's writers. We went over the notes on the guests so they could write one-liners, discussed feature ideas and items in the morning news that could be incorporated into Merv's opening remarks. We always settled on the opening. This would include opening lines for Merv and then some feature—a monologue or audience game. Whatever.

At noon I went to the studio to meet with the production staff —the director, the assistant director, the technical director, the scenic designer, the lighting director, and the production assistant, who gave out the show routine. We would run down the requirements for that evening's show, including comedy pieces, props, songs, sets, special bits, and wardrobe for all the people on the show. We would do the same for the next four upcoming shows. Then, the production staff would go to work and I would go to lunch.

Lunch was nearly always for business. The large talent agents; performers, politicians, writers; press interviews; and so on. I spent most of my time after lunch on the phone. I preferred to stay away from the rehearsals—I watched them on closed circuit—allowing the production staff and the particular booker to handle matters. I would come in if there was trouble. I found my presence then was always more effective than if I had been hanging around.

Usually, Merv arrived around 4:00 P.M., earlier if he were singing or working in a sketch. Other business matters and a production company kept him busy during the earlier parts of the day. I would see him around 4:45 P.M. This was normally his first look at what was planned for that night's show. At 5:00 P.M., all the bookers and writers would join us in Merv's office to talk down the show. Frequently, changes were made or someone would add information to a booker's notes. "Hey, Lemmon has a great story about when he was in the navy in Virginia and beached an aircraft carrier. You should add that."

At 5:30 P.M. I would meet again with the production staff to go over changes—theirs and mine.

I spent from 6:00 P.M. to tape time at 6:30 P.M. with Merv—just bulling mostly and trying to keep him loose and up for the show.

So much for preproduction on a show like this. Since much was planned but very little was rehearsed or scripted, production was a living animal. We taped the show straight through, ninety minutes without stopping. I sat in the front row, in a direct visual line with Merv. Next to me were an on-air monitor, so I could see how the show would look on the air, and a telephone to the control booth. Merv and I had devised a series of signals as intricate as those between a batter and third-base coach. We tried to pace or orchestrate the show as it happened. We conferred during every commercial break. If a guest was dying, we would try for whatever up we could get quickly and then go immediately to commercial. We used the commercial breaks as an electronic hook. Also, we frequently rearranged the order of guests or other items as we went.

Merv's talents as a singer and pianist were further tools. Once, when a really big-name comedian was our opening guest and drifted into a numbing and endless paean to an unknown old actor friend of his who had died, I signaled Merv to the piano. He caught it and said to the comedian, "Hey, remember, all those great songs from that Broadway show you were in? How 'bout one or two."

Oh, Merv, I don't feel up to it."

"Well, let me then—in your honor. I'm sure the audience'd love to hear them—wouldn't you, audience?"

I, of course, started to applaud—one person can easily do that, you know; the audience joined in, Merv sang and played and then went to commercial.

Since the program was taped straight through, there was almost no postproduction, except to edit out what the censor would not pass. These were most often audio bleeps.

The real tension in a show like this comes from the human factor. With an average of twenty-five guests a week, and show types at that, you get some crazy actuarial tables of temperament, alcoholism, divorce, and missed planes. Sometimes you get lucky. Mostly, you have to have planned backups. When guests did not show, plan number one was to call a member of a pool of regulars to run over and fill the spot. If they were unavailable, we would call celebrity watering spots to see who was there. I once pulled Bea Lillie out of Sardi's—picking up the tab, of course—and thrust her onto the Griffin stage. Another time Merv himself got sick an hour before show time and I tried everywhere to find Gary Moore to replace him. I just missed him at his agent's who said he was on his way home. I called the highway toll booths and asked that they intercept him. They did and he drove back to the city and hosted the program. Another time, I had used all my trump cards. We were two guests short and I was still on the phone trying to book somebody when the opening theme was playing. One of the bookers rushed up to me and said, "You'll never believe this, but Ginger Rogers is in make-up."

"Terrific. She'll go on second," I said.

"But she's supposed to be here tomorrow."

"I won't tell her if you won't." Another booker ran up and said, "Dick Shawn's wandered in and's standing in the back of the theatre. He was rehearsing across the street and . . ."

"Good. Send him to make-up." It was one of the best shows we ever had.

As to a more preplanned kind of program, during the time I was producing, directing, and writing for the "Great American Dream Machine," I wanted to do an essay on "a day in the life of a rock band." This idea preceded having any particular rock group in mind. As I began to investigate groups, I learned that the lead singer of Blood, Sweat and Tears, which at the time was at the height of its popularity, was a man named David Clayton-Thomas and that he had served time in prison on a serious felony conviction. I further discovered that the group planned to end one of its concert tours with a free performance at a prison in California. I decided that this prison connection was the extra angle I had been searching for.

I contacted the group's management and had at least three meetings to discuss my idea. They had been suspicious of television, but knew the "Dream Machine" and liked it, as well as what I wanted to do. In these meetings I also found out as much as I could about the individual members of the band and about the interaction as a group. I measured this against having read all I could find about Blood, Sweat and Tears. (Since television time and money are always severely limited, I have learned to use every opportunity to sharpen the focus for actual filming.)

The managers of Blood, Sweat and Tears did not make the final decision. The nine members of the band did that. They had equal votes as to what the group would do—though some votes turned out to be more equal than others. It would be necessary, I was told, for me and the cameraman to audition for the group before they would vote on whether to be filmed for the program. Especially in documentaries, such is frequently the case, you spend a lot of time and energy building up trust in the people you want to shoot before you are allowed to come near them with a camera. I don't mind. Whoever it is, if they have granted you this trust, will be much more open and revealing during the shoot, so of course you get better content.

I had selected Ted Churchill as cameraman for this shoot (this, too, is part of planning) because he was an experienced rock music film maker—Woodstock, etc.—loved the rock world, spoke its language, and was close in age and attitudes to the members of Blood, Sweat and Tears.

If the group wanted to see us before the filming, we also wanted to see them. Again, an opportunity to be together, prior to shooting, in a similar situation, could hone our approach later—and save money. When I had looked at the group's itinerary, I suggested we join them on their trip to Saratoga Springs, New York, where they were to give a concert at the Performing Arts Center. Since "Dream Machine" operated in New York City and the group would be leaving from New York for Saratoga by chartered plane and returning the same day, this day in the life of the group would keep my survey costs to a minimum.

We learned a lot on the Saratoga trip about how to shoot the band in concert and about individual personalities. We knew what to go after in the documentary filming. For its part, the group learned to trust us and decided to let us film.

Fine. Now all I had to do was figure out how, on a painfully limited budget, we could get to California to shoot the prison concert and the day in the life of the band. While I believed the group was good enough and interesting enough to warrant a full-hour treatment, the policy of the "Dream Machine" required a magazine approach; that is, several features in a single program; so, to go to California to shoot only one fifteen-minute film essay was an unjustified expense. How could I shoot the Blood, Sweat and Tears piece and make it price out?

For a start, I gave up the idea of taking the usual film crew from New York and decided to use California personnel instead. Only Churchill and the associate producer would go with me. This was a big savings in transportation, hotel, and per diem costs.

I made up a new budget and saw that it was still too much. But, I began to think, if one story into the cost of the trip was too expensive, two or three or four film stories into the cost—while adding to the gross figure—would make the cost of each individual film piece tolerable. I began to think of other pieces that could be shot on the same trip in the days just before or after the fixed date of the Blood, Sweat and Tears prison concert.

I had been talking to David Steinberg about doing something for the program, but neither of us had come up with an idea in New York that he liked and, besides, he had to leave for work in California. His being out there was now a plus, so I went back to a file of notes for ideas that I always keep and found one called "Kalifornia Kar Kulture." The notion was to show, satirically, the pre-eminence of automobiles in our society by asserting that it was possible in Southern

California to get through an entire day's activities without ever getting out of your car. This idea, idle before, seemed right for Steinberg— and for the budget. I spoke to David. He liked it and he was free for two days later in the week after the Blood, Sweat and Tears concert. David agreed that if my research proved out, we would do it.

At the New York Library I went through a Los Angeles Yellow Pages and scanned the ads in a Sunday *Los Angeles Times.* I found mobile homes, drive-in banks, movies, photo stores, shoe stores, liquor stores, car washes, a wedding chapel, a Jack-in-the-Box fast food outlet (rather new then and only in the West), a church, and a wild animal preserve. The drive-in mortuaries where you could pay your respects to the deceased from your car, flourishing a few years earlier, had unfortunately gone out of business. The only one of these left in the country, I found was in Atlanta—rather far off my budget. Still, there was plenty to shoot (the drive-in church turned out to be a pure Fellini and a lion jumped onto the roof of the car at the drive-in zoo). Now I had two ideas. Better, but not enough.

I had long wanted to interview Dr. Arthur Janov, *The Primal Scream* man, and to visit his Primal Institute in Los Angeles. I contacted Janov, whom I had met, and asked if he would be available at the time I had in mind and if he would agree to our filming. He was available and agreed.

Also, I had been talking to comedian Albert Brooks about adapting to film his *Esquire* magazine piece, "The Famous School for Comedians," which was a funny take-off on correspondence schools. By the time I called Albert, the dates of shooting were coming up fast and he was reluctant to get the piece ready so quickly.

I argued that since he virtually had the script written, we could easily cast it and get the proper location and props in time and that if we did not do it now, we might never get around to it, since he had a long tour coming up and my shooting season would be ending. As a final persuader, I said that if he would do it now and did not like the results, I would agree to reshoot it later when he was in New York. (With at least three pieces set to lay against the budget, I could afford to take a chance. Besides, I had every confidence that the Brooks piece would be right the first time.) Albert said okay. We set the date and began to prepare the piece.

Satisfied now that I had enough to shoot to justify the cost of the California trip, it was icing on icing when Linda Finson, my associate producer, handed me a letter from the curator of the Atom Bomb Museum in Albuquerque, New Mexico, wanting us to film there. This was a perfect "Dream Machine" idea. Since Albuquerque was between Los Angeles and New York, going there would not add significantly to the shooting costs; this idea would also serve as a hedge against the Brook's piece perhaps not making it. I wrote back to tell the director we would be there. I am glad we went. The place was surreal. I will never forget the vision of this fragile woman mothering over those doomsday monsters and keeping them sparkling by spritzing them with Fantastik. "It works best," she said, adding, "You've heard of the clean bombs, haven't you? Well?")

Now that I had the ideas, the major casting, the basic production team, and the shooting dates set, I did a lot of producing on the telephone, without the expense of actually going to California. By phone I hired a recommended California production manager to work the entire shoot and to start the advance work of negotiating for and surveying all the locations prior to our arrival. He also hired California crews and arranged for equipment based on the requirements of the shoots. I provided him with a rough calender—a shooting schedule—that could flex somewhat depending on what he needed and where. Only the talent days were rigid.

Day 1—Fly New York to Los Angeles, arriving early enough to have a production meeting with the California crew during working hours and to allow Churchill to go over the equipment. If anything was wrong (several things were), the equipment houses would still be open and changes could be made (and were) that day.

Day 2—Blood, Sweat and Tears. In the morning we would pick them up as they arrived at the Century Plaza Hotel where they were to perform for the CBS Records annual convention. Then, onto the bus—filming as we went—for the journey to Chino Prison and the concert. We would keep filming open-ended till the day was over back in Los Angeles. At Chino we worked with three cameras. The crews for cameras number 2 and number 3 and the concert sound recordists had gone to Chino early in the day to shoot pickups and get set for the concert, while Churchill's crew and I stayed with the band.

Day 3—In the morning, more Blood, Sweat and Tears. This time, long interviews with individual band members. In the afternoon, the long interviews with Dr. Janov and his wife, Vivian, who run the Primal Institute. Only one film crew is required for this day —and all the days except for the concert. I had scheduled the last three Blood, Sweat and Tears morning interviews outdoors, so the lighting man can break early to go to work at Janov's. When we arrive there the lights will be ready. The film was to be shipped back daily to New York for lab processing and syncing by the editor.

The Janov piece was bothering me—even more so as I made up the schedule—since I wanted to show not merely Janov talking about primals but to show actual sessions of primal therapy as well. I knew this latter was impossible to film in my constricted shooting time, and there was no money to buy the long time to film which I knew the sessions demanded.

I called Janov and shared my problem. He told me about a two-hour film of primals that had already been made. I found out from him who had made it, contacted the person, arranged to screen it while still in New York and I made a deal to buy fifteen minutes of it. With this action footage, I intercut the talking heads material of the interviews with Janov and his wife. The intercutting technique lent vigor and drama to the straight interview portions and to the primal sessions, clarity about what was happening.

Day 4—The Albert Brooks piece—five major sets and fourteen camera setups, but all in and around one building at UCLA. I put on an extra lighting crew to light the four interiors during the afternoon of the previous Day 3.

Day 5—David Steinberg. Six locations. Widely separated. Tough, but possible, since all but one of the locations are exteriors. Start day with interior, give lighting crew early call, then dismiss them.

Day 6—David Steinberg. Two locations. One of them forty miles from Los Angeles. Both exteriors. Leave late afternoon for Albuquerque. Arrive there in time to survey Atom Bomb Museum for shooting the next day. Send lighting crew ahead to Albuquerque early this day to rough in, be ready for the following day.

Day 7—Atom Bomb Museum. Late flight back to New York. It was an ambitious schedule and I added a contingency day.

Amazingly, the entire shoot went according to plan and we were able to stick to the seven-day schedule. We shot the five ideas successfully and all five pieces aired—forty-eight minutes worth. The entire shoot, including talent-at-scale and postproduction editing (I had a good idea beforehand of how I wanted pieces to look so I shot with editing in mind—this is called editing in the camera) cost $15,000 (16mm, color). Five ideas into $15,000 is $3,000 per piece. I had budgeted the original Blood, Sweat and Tears piece alone at $7,500. The per-minute cost of air material came to $312.50. You cannot run stock footage as cheaply as that.

The only curse of good planning, if things go wrong, and they nearly always do, is inflexibility. You have got to adjust to the real not the paper situation. Once I had to flex so much that I thought I would break, but I got lucky—which is the only reason I can stand to tell this story.

In the course of doing an hour-long documentary special on Joan Baez, I knew it was a must to shoot at LaTuna Federal Penitentiary near El Paso, Texas, on the day her then-husband David Harris was to be released after having done sixteen months in prison for resisting the draft. I got my budget approval and arranged to arrive in El Paso with my New York film crew on the afternoon of the day before Harris was to be released.

We got there early enough to survey the prison entrance and film all the necessary insert shots. We drove the proposed route from the prison to the airport, where Joan, David, and their infant son, Jason would fly to San Francisco. We walked the airport from curbside to check-in gate, measuring lighting needs and the physical characteristics. Again, we filmed insert shots. I left nothing to chance. When David came out it would be an emotional and one-time occasion.

The crew and I went back to the motel—the same motel in which Joan was staying. I called her to say hello, shared her happiness about the next day, and confirmed with her that David would be released at 7:00 A.M.—exactly. We agreed that it certainly would not be before 7:00, knowing authorities, and that it might well be later for the same reason.

Everything had been seen to. Smug and snug in my thorough preproduction planning, the crew and I went to Juarez, Mexico, just across the border, had a proper and relaxed dinner and got back to the motel early—to bed.

The next morning we saw Joan in the motel coffee shop just before 5:45 A.M. It was a twenty minute drive from the motel to the prison. She was just leaving as we entered.

"I know it's early," she said, "but—I want to be there."

That made me nervous. A premonition churned in my stomach. However. What could possible go wrong? She left. We ate breakfast and started for the prison at 6:15 A.M.

As we arrived and were parking in the visitor's parking lot near the prison entrance, I saw an agitated knot of people moving from the entrance to the parking lot.

"Hey," I yelled, "It's them! He's out! He's out!"

"It's only twenty till," the assistant cameraman said.

We spilled from the station wagon like Thieu's army leaving DaNang. Equipment scudded along the paving, we tripped over each other. Sound never did connect with picture. By the time the cameraman got himself together, David, Joan, and the baby were in their car and underway. All we got were blurred shots of them through the car windows as they roared off. Who could blame them for wanting to be out of there fast? And this was certainly not a situation where you could ask for retakes.

Joan Baez is a swift and certain driver. We raced back to our car.

As I jerked the wagon out of the lot, I was afraid we would miss them at the airport. I was already furious with myself for having missed the single moment that was the cause for the whole trip. As I U-turned, I barely avoided hitting another film crew that was loading their van. Not conscious of it at the time, I did see the call letters of the local NBC station on the side of the truck. I ignored their curses and chased after Joan.

We caught up to her car on the expressway and my cameraman got traveling road shots. At the airport, everything went beautifully. We got touching and emotional moments of David, Joan, and the baby. The sync sound was good and true, as David spoke and reacted to his new freedom.

When their plane had left for San Francisco, I was grateful that we had gotten some footage, but I was in shock from having missed the moment at the prison. I have seldom felt so helpless—or foolish. What would I tell my bosses in New York? I could just hear them: "You went two thousand miles to El Paso with a full crew for one shot and didn't get it?"

As we started to drive away from the airport departures area to take the station wagon back to the car rental area, my cameraman said, "Those dudes from the local TV must think we're the Keystone cameramen."

"Hunh?" I said.

"That other crew. Over there. They got the whole thing, man—and did you see that old Auricon he was usin'? Musta been Matthew Brady's."

I looked up, finally, and saw the van from the local television station. It's crew was loading up. They, too, had been filming at the airport.

"Big razzle dazzle Whamo Harley crew from the Big Apple and we blew it," my cameraman said. "Those yokels had the prison shot on a tripod, man—on a tripod."

I woke up. They had it. *They had it!*

To save money by avoiding another night in El Paso, I had scheduled us out on a plane that was leaving in an hour. There was no chance to go to the local television station and I certainly did not want to approach the crew directly—especially since I had almost run over them. Besides, I knew they would not have the authority to grant me what I wanted.

"Stop the car," I said.

"Hunh?"

"You take it back. I gotta make a call." I ran from the car, called and got the news director of the local station. I told him who I was, but not how we had goofed. I said his guys had had another angle of the whole scene—*especially the prison*—and I would like to buy his footage so I could intercut two angles. And held my breath.

"Sure, hell—we just throw it out after the 10:00 O'Clock News tonight."

"Fine. Fine. How much do you think you'd want for it? This is public TV, remember."

"Aw, hell, I don't know—$25? It'll cost me $5 to mail it to you."

I said that seemed reasonable—and my knees buckled.

When I saw the film in New York, it was perfect. There it was —that beautiful, once-in-a-lifetime moment at the prison entrance. I cut it into our own El Paso footage and when I showed the sequence to my bosses, they were estatic. (Till they might read this, I have never had the courage to tell them.)

"You were right, Shanks. Sure glad you went down there. That moment when he comes out—beautiful—priceless."

Not quite. My shoot—editing included—had cost three thousand, two hundred—and twenty-five dollars.

Sometimes, flexibility can be planned. A simple example. If you have exteriors and interiors to film or tape, always make certain that you have arranged to have interior setups available on those days when you are planning to shoot exteriors. In case it rains, snows—or a pneumatic drill suddenly arrives on the scene—you can move inside quickly and stay on budget. When I have a mix of interiors and exteriors, I always plan to shoot my exteriors first. If there is bad weather, you can keep falling back on interiors until it clears. If you shoot interiors first—especially on clear days—you may be stuck with all exteriors and bad weather at the end.

About the pneumatic drill and other such man-made menaces, I have a private paranoia that in every construction or utilities office there is a bulletin board which provides announcements of production crews in the area, so all the noisiest work gangs can rush to the site of your shoot. Even so, when I have set a date for shooting exteriors, I risk calling the local highway and building departments and the water and electric companies to find out if they have plans to be in the area at the same time. This has occasionally spared me the agony of sound or picture pollution.

I also survey every location—exterior and interior—for lighting needs, electric sources and power, cable runs, caterer, local peculiarities. While most of us have adapted in our everyday life to a kind of deafness about noise in our environment, noise is nearly inescapable everywhere these days. I have got to know ahead of time if my location is within the landing patterns of an airport, for instance, or near an expressway with a hill where trucks shift gears for the climb; or whether the fellow next door has a power mower or a model airplane. Once, I thought for certain I was shooting in an absolutely soundproof pastoral location, only to learn later and ruefully that the local kids used the harmless looking road nearby as a drag strip after school. (I shot there in the morning, as it turned out.) Knowing up front gives you the opportunity to find alternate locations if you can or if you cannot, to plan at least the best possible use of a bad site.

I always call the police, too. It is "bush" to avoid getting permits, if necessary, and to enlist municipal help. Mayors' offices and cops have spared me much expense and aggravation; indeed, they have enhanced productions by their enthusiastic cooperation and knowledge of local conditions.

Planning includes booking studios or locations and setting dates; setting talent and crew calls; making schedules for construction, setup, and lighting; arranging transportation, lodgings, and meals for locations and studios; setting lab schedules for film and edit sessions for film and tape; meeting delivery dates to make air dates.

For situation comedies and regular variety series, the schedule is roughly like this:

Monday   first read through and rehearsal hall blocking
Tuesday   rehearsal hall: blocking and rehearsal
Wednesday   rehearsal hall: rehearsal
Thursday   studio: on camera blocking and rehearsal
Friday   studio: rehearsal and VTR

For dramatic series:

Monday   first read through and blocking
Tuesday   filming or VTR in studio (location, if required)
Wednesday   filming or VTR in studio
Thursday   filming or VTR, studio
Friday   filming or VTR, studio

In the situation comedies and dramatic shows there are frequently two producers who alternate weeks, and many directors. An executive producer and script supervisor maintain characters and style overall and keep ahead on scripts. Alternating editors put the shows together. For some game shows, these days, they usually tape all five half-hour episodes in one day.

Each program should have a production book or production schedule. In the following very professional examples, I have eliminated addresses, phone numbers, and salaries, in certain cases, for obvious reasons. The first set of schedules and sheets were for an hour dramatic series to be shot on location. The first sheet is the Staff and Crew List. I have shown one page of it. Actually, there were four pages, but I think you will get the idea. Next is the Confidential Cast List. Then a Contact List. If you will notice, the only name to appear on all three is the accountant. This will give you a further idea of the importance of money in production. Then comes the Shooting Schedule—part of it—the daily Cast Call Sheet and the Crew Call Sheet. "Nightside" is the series name; "A Very Special Place" is the name of this particular episode of the series.

EXECUTIVE OFFICE		PRODUCTION OFFICE
HBL PRODUCTIONS		

TITLE	NAME	ADDRESS & PHONE
EXECUTIVE PRODUCER	Herbert B. Leonard	
PRODUCER	Paul Leaf	
DIRECTOR	Richard Donner	
WRITER	Pete Hamill	
PRODUCTION MGR.		
1ST ASSISTANT DIRECTOR	William C. Gerrity	
2ND ASSISTANT DIRECTOR	François Moullin	
SCRIPT SUPERVISOR	Renata Stoia	
PRODUCTION COORDINATOR	Diane Katz	
ASS'T. TO PRODUCER	Carolyn Compton	
SECRETARY TO PRODUCER	Rebecca Osofsky	
PRODUCTION ASSISTANT	Jay Felton	
DGA TRAINEE*	Bruce Pustin	
ACCOUNTANT	Dror Shnayer	
DIRECTOR OF PHOTOGRAPHY	Bernie Hirshenson	
CAMERA OPERATOR		
1ST ASS'T. CAMERAMAN	Maurice Brown	
2ND ASS'T. CAMERAMAN	Ron Nealy	
SOUND MIXER	John Bolz	
BOOM	Art Bloom	
RECORDIST	Jim Perdue	
ART DIRECTOR	Bob Gundlach	
SCENIC ARTIST	Sante Fiore	

*Directors' Guild of America apprentice.

"NIGHTSIDE"
"A Very Special Place"
CONFIDENTIAL CAST LIST

CHARACTER	ARTIST	HOME ADDRESS	PHONE NO.*
CARMINE	JOHN CASSAVETES		
SMITTY	ALEXIS SMITH		
ARAM	MIKE KELLIN		
VENTURA	JUNE HAVOC		
GABLE	RICHARD JORDAN		
JABBO	JOE SANTOS		
ACKY	F. MURRAY ABRAHAM		
MORT	PETER MALONEY		
GEORGE	EARL HINDMAN		
SGT.	NORMAN BUSH		
FOREMAN	HY ANZELL		
ACCOUNTANT	ALEK PRIMROSE		
SEAMAN	LOUIS CRISCUOLA		
BARTENDER (DAY)	ED BARTH		
CON ED MAN	BEN SLACK		
HEALTH INSPECTOR	SHANTON GRANGER		
WOMAN IN CAR	MARGE ELIOT		
BARTENDER (NIGHT)	JOHN SCANLON		
SAMMY THE COOK	CONSTANTINE KATSANOS		
GRUDIN	JOSEPH WISEMAN		
MATCHES	VINCENT DUKE MILANA		

*Under phone numbers would be listed the personal number and the agent's number
or an answering service.

"NIGHTSIDE"
"A Very Special Place"
CONTACTS

POSITION	NAME & ADDRESS	PHONE NO.
ACCOUNTANT		
ATTORNEY		
BANK		
CAR RENTAL		
EQUIPMENT		
FILM		
HOTEL		
LABS (film)		
LABS (sound)		
MAYOR'S REPRESENTATIVE		
POLICE		
STATIONERS		
TRUCK RENTAL		
DOCTOR		

UNIONS:
IATSE
WGA
DGA
SCREEN ACTORS GUILD
Local 52 (Stagehands, Props, Electricians, Carpenters, Sound)
Local 161 (Script Supervisors, Production Coordinators)
Local 817 (Teamsters)
Local 306 (Projectionists)
Local 829 (Scenic Artists, Costumes)
Local 644 (Cameramen)
Local 764 (Wardrobe)
Local 771 (Editors)
Local 798 (Make-up, Hair)

SHOOTING SCHEDULE

HBL PRODUCTIONS
"NIGHTSIDE" "A Very Special Place"   2/1/73

DATE/ DAYS	LOCATION/ SET	SCENE	DESCRIPTION	CAST	PROPS/ EFFECTS	PAGES
Thurs. 2/1/73	Ext. Vulcan Heating	34	Aram tells Jabbo that Acky is the rat man	Aram Jabbo Acky	sign on garage paper pads pencils 3 old cabs 1 equipment truck Chrysler	3 2/8
1st DAY	Day					
	Int. Vulcan Heating	40	Aram is held prisoner	Aram Acky Mort Jabbo George	adding machines guns checks	1 1/8
	Night					
	Int. Vulcan Heating	53-55	Aram winning at poker	Aram Acky Mort George Matches	coffee containers playing cards money kerosene cans Matches' car Jabbo's car	1 6/8

END OF FIRST DAY

211

SHOOTING SCHEDULE

HBL PRODUCTIONS
"NIGHTSIDE"   "A Very Special Place"   2/1/73

DATE/ DAYS	LOCATION/ SET	SCENE	DESCRIPTION	CAST	PROPS/ EFFECTS	PAGES
Fri. 2/2/73	Int. Vulcan Heating	60	Aram escapes	Aram Mort George Acky	money guns balsa wood? stunt?	5/8
2nd DAY	Day					
	Ext. front of Vulcan Heating	61, 62, 63	Aram chased by gangsters	Aram Acky George Mort Woman	guns car for woman stunt drivers?	5/8
	Day					
	Int. moving car	64	Aram in car with woman	Aram Woman	purse	7/8
	Day					
	Int. Police Headquarters	25, 29	They discover the rat man	Aram Seaman Accountant Con Ed Man Atmos—Clerk Detective Policemen Lady Victim	mug shots, Acky's mug shot files etc.	1 4/8
	Day					

END OF SECOND DAY

212

SHOOTING SCHEDULE*

HBL PRODUCTIONS   2/1/73
"NIGHTSIDE" "A Very Special Place"

DATE/ DAYS	LOCATION/ SET	SCENE	DESCRIPTION	CAST	PROPS/ EFFECTS	PAGES
Monday 2/5/73	Ext. Gable's Office	27	Carmine arrives at Gable's	Carmine	cab	2/8
3rd DAY	Day					
	Ext. Construction Site Day	38, 56-59, 59a, b	Jabbo tells Gable they should burn the building. Carmine talks to Gable	Jabbo Gable Carmine Grubin Atmos—Workmen Foreman	sign, "Gable Construction Company" earth moving equip. Grubin's limo	3 7/8
	Int. Gable's office Day	28	Carmine and Gable have argument over Smitty	Gable Carmine Atmos—Office people	blueprints drafting table 3 phones construction models	2 3/8

END OF THIRD DAY

*These are published for each shooting day and are revised as changes occur.

213

HBL PRODUCTIONS, INC.   2/8/73
"NIGHTSIDE" "A Very Special Place"

SCHEDULE: Cast Call Sheet

DAY/DATE	SET/LOC.	D/N*	SC. #	CHARACTERS	PGS.
FRI. 2/9	INT. DENTAL OFFICE	D	28,A,B,C	CARMINE RALPH RALPH'S WIFE	1 5/8
	EXT. GABLE'S OFFICE	D	26	CARMINE SMITTY (taxi)	3/8
	INT. GABLE'S OFFICE	D	27-28	CARMINE SMITTY GABLE	3 1/8
	EXT. FINLEY WALK	N	19	CARMINE SMITTY	2 2/8
MONDAY, FEBRUARY 12TH		HOLIDAY			
TUES. 2/13	EXT. SMITTY'S	D	67,68,69	ARAM LADY IN CAR MATCHES POLICE-FIRE	1
	INT. SMITTY'S	D	70,72	ARAM MATCHES	5/8
	INT. SMITTY'S	D	21,23	SMITTY ACKY BARTENDER SEAMAN CON ED MAN ACCOUNTANT HEALTH INSPECTOR	5 3/8
WED. 2/14	INT. CAVETT STAGE	N	45,47	CAVETT VENTURA	1 7/8
	INT. CAVETT CORRIDOR) & DRESSING ROOM AREA)	N	42	CARMINE VENTURA SHANE RALPH PROD. ASST.	1 2/8

CONT'D. . . .

*Day or night.

HBL PRODUCTIONS, INC. 2/8/73
"NIGHTSIDE" "A Very Special Place"
SCHEDULE CONT'D
2.

DAY/DATE	SET/LOC.	D/N	SC. #	CHARACTERS	PGS.
WED. 2/14 CONT'D	INT. DRESSING ROOM	N	43,44	CARMINE SHANE VENTURA RALPH PROD. ASST.	1
	INT. BACKSTAGE	N	46,50,53	CARMINE VENTURA PROD. STAFF	3/8
SECOND UNIT WED. 2/14	EXT. VULCAN HEATING	D	61,62,63	ARAM ACKY LADY IN CAR	4/8
	INT. MOVING CAR	D	64	LADY IN CAR ARAM	7/8
THURS. 2/15	INT. SMITTY'S BAR	N	8 thru 8G 9A & 10	CARMINE SMITTY ARAM VENTURA SHANE BARTENDER RALPH ARTHUR MAN	6 3/8
FRI. 2/16	INT. KITCHEN	N	9	CARMINE SMITTY COOK	1 1/8
	INT. SMITTY'S		15, 15A	ARAM SHANE SMITTY CARMINE VENTURA RALPH	1 4/8
	EXT. CAVETT THEATER	N	41	CARMINE VENTURA SHANE RALPH	3/8

CREW CALL SHEET

CAST	CHARACTER	MAKEUP	SET CALL	PICKUP
CASSAVETES	CARMINE		6:00	
HAVOC	VENTURA	5:30	7:00	5:00
ALLEN	SETH		7:00	REPORT TO LOC.
MIKE LA PADULA	PHOTOG.		6:00	" " " " " "
JOHN STEWART	REPORTER		6:00	" " " " " "

STANDINS	ATMOSPHERE	SPECIAL PROPS
CASSAVETES 6:00 AT LOC.	3 REPORTERS 6:00 PM LIMO DRIVER 6:00 PM PORTER 6:30 PM COMPANION 6:30 PM	HELICOPTER

CREW CALL

5:30 PM AT LOCATION

DIRECTOR & STAFF

SPL EQUIP/MISC.

1st ASS'T. DIR. _____ CONSTRUCTION _____
2nd ASS'T. DIR. _____ PROPS—DRESS _____
PROD. ASS'T.—SET _____ PROPS—SET _____
SCRIPT SUPER._____ SOUND—MIX _____
CAMERAMAN _____ SOUND—REC _____
CAM. OPER._____ SOUND—BOOM _____
ASS'T. CAM. _____ WARDROBE _____
STILLMAN _____ MAKEUP _____
GRIPS—SET_____ HAIRDRESSER_____
SWING _____ SCENIC ART _____
ELECT.—SET _____ TEAMSTERS _____
ELECT.—RIG _____ CARPENTERS _____
LOCAL CRAFTS _____

ADVANCE SCHEDULE

(to be determined)

TRANSPORTATION

TRUCK AT LOC. 5:30 PM
CAMPER 5:30 PM
STATION WAGON PICKUP HAVOC 5:30 PM
LIMO AT LOC. 6:00 PM
10 YEAR OLD CAR AT LOC. 6:00 PM

Next are some examples from Jacqueline Babbin for her "Crime-time" productions shot for "Wide World of Entertainment." Jackie was doing five ninety-minute mystery dramas in five weeks. Here is how she set up the schedule. (Jackie went on to produce "Beacon Hill" for CBS.)

```
                              CRIMETIME
                              SCHEDULE
I. THE MURDERERS
Director   Gloria Monty    REHEARSE    9/22, 9/23, 9/24, 9/25, 9/26, 9/27*
P.A.   Nancy Horwich       STUDIO      9/28, 9/29, 9/30, 10/1
Writer   Art Wallace       EDIT        10/2, 10/3
                           MIX         10/4

II. THE SATAN MURDERS       REHEARSE    9/29, 9/30, 10/1, 10/2, 10/3, 10/4
Director   Lela Swift       STUDIO      10/5, 10/6, 10/7, 10/8
P.A.   Christy Welker       EDIT        10/9, 10/10
Writer   Irving Gaynor      MIX         10/11
  Neiman

III. THE SPY WHO RETURNED FROM THE DEAD
Director   Henry Kaplan     REHEARSAL   10/6, 10/7, 10/8, 10/9, 10/10
P.A.   Nancy Horwich        STUDIO      10/12, 10/13, 10/14, 10/15
Writer   William Katz       EDIT        10/16, 10/17
                            MIX         10/18

IV. LEGACY OF BLOOD
Director   Gloria Monty     REHEARSE    10/13, 10/14, 10/15, 10/16, 10/17
P.A.   Christy Welker       STUDIO      10/19, 10/20, 10/21, 10/22
Writer   George Bellak      EDIT        10/23, 10/24
                            MIX         10/25

V. SHOCK-A-BYE, BABY
Director   Lela Swift       REHEARSAL   10/20, 10/21, 10/22, 10/23, 10/24
P.A.   Nancy Horwich        STUDIO      10/26, 10/27, 10/28, 10/29
Writer   Henry Slesar       EDIT        10/30, 10/31
                            MIX         11/1
```
*Underlined dates indicate Jewish holidays and Columbus Day.

Next come one-page examples of a rehearsal schedule and a studio schedule. Each of these actually covered five pages.

(REVISED 9/12/73)

CRIMETIME
PRODUCER: JACQUELINE BABBIN   DIRECTOR: GLORIA MONTY
ASSOC. PRODUCER: DOROTHY J. GLOBUS   P.A.:   NANCY HORWICH
                                                TITLE: "THE MURDERERS"
                                                ADDRESS:
                                                PHONE:

TENTATIVE REHEARSAL SCHEDULE*

Saturday, Sept. 22	10:00-12:00	READING & MEETING	Entire Cast, NOT Officer Blier, Radio Announcer, Willie, 13-Year-Old Girl
	12:00-1:00	LUNCH	
	1:00-1:30	BLOCK Act I, pp. 1-4	Pat, Ben
	1:30-2:00	BLOCK Act II, (1) pp. 9-14	Pat, Susan, Dan, Nora
	2:00-2:15	BLOCK Act II, (3) pp. 17-19	Pat, Susan, Nora
	2:15-2:30	BLOCK Act III, (2) pp. 27-30	Pat, Nora
	2:30-3:00	BLOCK Act III, (3) pp. 30-33	Pat, Nora
	3:00-3:15	BLOCK Act V, (3) pp. 52-54	Nora, Dan
	3:15-3:30	BLOCK Act V, (4) pp. 54-56	Pat, Nora
	3:30-4:15	BLOCK Act VI, (1 & 2) pp. 60-71	Nora, Pat, Susan
	4:15-4:30	BLOCK Act VII, (1) pp. 72-74	Pat, Dan, NOT Bartender
	4:30-4:45	BLOCK Act VII, (2-4) pp. 75-76 pp. 78-79	Pat, Ben
	4:45-5:00	BLOCK Act VII, (3) pp. 76-77	Nora, Dan

*This is a partial of the whole, but I think the form is clear.

CRIMETIME   (Rev. 9/18/73)
SHOW #1: "THE MURDERERS"

TENTATIVE STUDIO SCHEDULE*
SUNDAY, SEPTEMBER 30, 1973

9:00-9:30	BLOCK & RUN ACT VII, Sc. 3, p. 77	Dan, Nora
	Entry Hall (Nite of 4th Day)	
9:30-9:45	TAPE	Same as above
9:45-10:15	BLOCK & RUN ACT VII, Sc. 6, pp. 80-82	Pat, Nora
	Living Room (Nite of 4th Day)	
10:15-10:45	TAPE	Same as above
10:45-11:00	BLOCK & RUN ACT VIII, Sc. 1, pp. 83-84	Pat, Nora
	Kitchen (Nite of 4th Day)	
11:00-11:15	TAPE	Same as above
11:15-11:45	BLOCK & RUN ACT VIII, Sc. 3, pp. 87-88 & Sc. 5, pp. 89-91	Pat, Nora, Willie
	Living Rm. (Nite of 4th day) Entry Hall	
11:45-12:00	TAPE	Same as above
12:00-1:00	L U N C H	
1:30-2:00	BLOCK & RUN ACT IX, Sc. 2, pp. 98-101	Pat, Nora, Willie
	Living Room (Nite of 4th Day)	
2:00-2:30	TAPE	Same as above
2:30-3:00	BLOCK & RUN ACT IX, Sc. 5, pp. 104-108	Nora, Pat, Dan
	Entry Hall (Nite of 4th Day)	
3:00-3:30	TAPE	Same as above

(MORE)

*Partial of the whole.

Next are samples of planning for a project of gargantuan logistics —"California Jam." Jørn Winther who produced the event that became four television shows is a meticulous planner. Here you will find the entire day reduced to a one-page routine, the detailed breakout and stage plan for one of the groups, Earth, Wind & Fire; and notice particularly his detailed check list.

<u>CALIFORNIA JAM/IN CONCERT</u>

ACT	STAGE	SET LENGTH	TIME OF DAY
INTERVIEWS: LEE KOLBREK, ONTARIO, CALIFORNIA, POLICE CHIEF JACK ROSE			
TV HOST OPENING REMARKS			
INTRO'S. DON B.			
DON B. INTRO'S RARE EARTH			
ATLANTIC RECORDS BALLOON ASCENDS			
1. RARE EARTH	GREEN*	:45	10:00-10:45
TURNAROUND		:30	10:45-11:15
ATLANTIC RECORDS HELICOPTER FLIES OVER DROPPING SUN VISORS			
INTERVIEWS: SHELLY FINKEL			
BILL KOPLEK			
2. EARTH, WIND & FIRE	RED	:45	11:15-12:00
TURNAROUND		:30	12:00-12:30
INTERVIEWS: NARSAI DAVID, JERRY RUBENSTEIN			
SKY DIVERS: REMARKS DURING SKY DIVING EVENT			
3. EAGLES	GREEN	:45	12:30-1:15
TURNAROUND		:30	1:15-1:45
PLANE FLY-OVER			
INTERVIEWS: PEOPLE AT RANDOM IN AUDIENCE			
4. SEALS AND CROFTS	RED	:60	1:45-2:45
TURNAROUND		:30	2:45-3:15
HOT-AIR BALLOONIST INTERVIEW			
ANTIDRUG SPOT (BLACK OAK ARKANSAS)			
5. BLACK OAK ARKANSAS	GREEN	:45	3:15-4:00
TURNAROUND		:30	4:00-4:30
INTERVIEWS: SKYDIVER			
KLOS DJ: SHOULD HAVE BEEN UP IN BALLOON SO HE CAN TALK ABOUT			
6. BLACK SABBATH	RED	:60	4:30-5:30
TURNAROUND		:30	5:30-6:00
INTERVIEWS: LENNY STOGEL, MEMBER OF DEEP PURPLE			
7. DEEP PURPLE	GREEN	:90	6:00-7:30
TURNAROUND		:30	7:30-8:00
INTERVIEWS: EMERSON, LAKE AND PALMER (ALEX KING)			
ATLANTIC HELICOPTER DROPS BALLOONS			
HOT-AIR BALLOON ACT			
8. EMERSON, LAKE AND PALMER	ELP	:90	8:00-9:30
POSSIBLE INTERVIEW WITH ELP			
CLOSING: HOT-AIR BALLOON—POSSIBLE "GOOD NIGHT," ETC.			
ON BALLOON AND FIREWORKS FROM GROUND.			
DON B. CLOSES WITH "GOOD NIGHT" AND INDICATES EXITS TO			
AUDIENCE.			

*We had two stages, movable on railway tracts. One stage was called green, the other red. (So many people confuse left and right.)

ACT: <u>EARTH, WIND & FIRE</u> TIME: 11:15–12:00 PM STAGE: <u>RED (SR)</u>

SEQUENCE	TITLE	NOTES		STYLE/MOOD
1.	POWER	LEAD VOCAL:	SPOKEN INTRO STAGE CENTER	
		ASS'T. VOCAL:		
		SOLOS:	KALIMBA/SR GUITAR/SAX/SL GUITAR/ KEYBOARDS	
		NOTE:	"TRAIN" CHOREOGRAPHY/ "MARIONETTE" DANCE AT CLOSE	
2.	EVIL	LEAD VOCAL:	TIMBALES (KALIMBA)	
		ASS'T. VOCAL:	FRONT LINE	
		SOLOS:	KALIMBA	
		NOTE:	RAP	
3.	TIME IS ON YOUR SIDE	LEAD VOCAL:	TIMBALES & CONGAS	
		ASS'T. VOCAL:	FRONT LINE	
		SOLOS:	SAX/SR GUITAR/KEYBOARDS	
		NOTE:	MIME DANCE DURING SAX SOLO	
4.	BASS SOLO	LEAD VOCAL:		
		ASS'T. VOCAL:	FRONT LINE (SCAT ONLY)	
		SOLOS:	UPRIGHT & ELECTRIC BASS	
		NOTE:	FLASHPOTS/FLIGHT?/MIME DANCE AT CLOSE	
5.	KEEP YOUR HEAD TO THE SKY	LEAD VOCAL:	CONGAS	
		ASS'T. VOCAL:	FRONT LINE	
		SOLOS:		
		NOTE:	MID-SONG RAP FOR AUD. PARTICIPATION	

221

ACT: <u>EARTH, WIND & FIRE</u>   TIME: 11:15-12:00 PM   STAGE: <u>RED (SR)</u>

SEQUENCE	TITLE	NOTES	STYLE/MOOD
6.	BUILD YA NEST	LEAD VOCAL: ASS'T. VOCAL: FRONT LINE SOLOS: SAX/DRUMS DUET NOTE: FALSE STOP NEAR END/DRUMMERS EXIT	TIMBALES
7.	COME ON CHILDREN	LEAD VOCAL: ASS'T. VOCAL: FRONT LINE SOLOS: NOTE: "CHORUS LINE" KICKS, BOUNCES, EXIT	CONGAS
8.	MIGHTY MIGHTY	RE-ENTRANCE LEAD VOCAL: ASS'T. VOCAL: FRONT LINE SOLOS: NOTE: BOUNCE OFF FOR EXIT	TIMBALES
9.		LEAD VOCAL: ASS'T. VOCAL: SOLOS: NOTE:	
10.		LEAD VOCAL: ASS'T. VOCAL: SOLOS: NOTE:	
11.		LEAD VOCAL: ASS'T. VOCAL: SOLOS: NOTE:	

222

IN CONCERT/CALIFORNIA JAM CHECK LIST

1. TALENT COMPOUND

1. A	VIP tent	Pacific Presentations
1. B	Motor homes	PP
1. C	Food and beverage	PP Narsai
1. D	Telephones—pay and office	Mel
1. E	Electricity	Tom
1. F	Security	Don
1. G	Radio communications	Mel
1. H	Video monitors	Mel
1. I	Transportation	PP Toby Roberts

2. CREW COMPOUND

2. A	ABC crew tent	Unit Mgr., Canvas, Interview holding area
2. B	Motor homes	Unit Mgr., Luxury Motor Homes
2. C	Food and beverages	Unit Mgr., Narsai
2. D	Telephones	Mel
2. E	Electricity	Mel
2. F	Security	Ray
2. G	Radio communication	Mel
2. H	Video monitors	Mel
2. I	Transportation	Unit Mgr., Crew buses/cars Golf carts
2. J	Production office	Unit Mgr., Kac, Barbara, ABC Management
2. K	Communication center	Unit Mgr/Mel/ABC Pages
2. L	Storage trucks	Off stage right—production services
	Water trucks/rest rooms	Unit mgr.

3. FACILITIES-TV

3. A	Audio	Mel, Wally Heider (2)
3. B	Video	Mel, TransAmerican Video
3. C	ABC videotape unit	Mel
3. D	Crew	Mel

4. SUPPORT EQUIPMENT

4. A	Titan camera cranes	Mel
4. B	Walkie-talkies	Mel
4. C	Video monitors	Mel
4. D	PLS production/lighting	Mel
4. E	Fork lifts/crane	Stan

5. PRODUCTION SERVICES

5. A	Stage crews	Stan
5. B	Lighting crew	Stan
5. C	Lighting trucking	Stan
5. D	Lighting equipmental rental	Stan
5. E	Generator rentals	Stan
5. F	Set construction	Stan
5. G	Scenery Rentals	Stan
5. H	Stage covers	Stan
5. I	Stage wagons	Stan
5. J	Scenic designer	Henry

6. <u>POWER</u>
   6. A Engineering electricity   Mel   audio/video
   6. B Stage electr.   Tom
   6. C ABC compound electr.   Mel
   6. D VIP compound electr.   Tom
   6. E Lighting   Stan
   6. F Generators AC   Mel
   6. G Generators DC   Stan

7. <u>GRAPHIC ARTS</u>
   7. A Crawl   Eileen
   7. B Titles   Eileen
   7. C Labels   Joshua
   7. D Signs   Joshua

8. <u>COMMUNICATIONS</u>
   8. A ABC telephones   Mel
   8. B Promotor telephones   Mel
   8. C Radio communications   Mel
   8. D Intercoms   Mel
   8. E PL's production lighting   Mel

9. <u>PERSONNEL</u>
   9. A Engineering manpower   Mel
   9. B Stage crew   Stan
   9. C Hotel   Unit Mgr.
   9. D Per diem   Unit Mgr.
   9. E Car rentals   Unit Mgr.
   9. F Buses   Unit Mgr.
   9. G Catering   Unit Mgr.

10. <u>STAGE CONSTRUCTION</u>
   10. A Scaffold understructure   IFA   Mike Brown
   10. B Scaffold superstructure   IFA   Mike Brown
   10. C Sound towers   IFA   Mike Brown
   10. D PA mix tower   IFA   Mike Brown
   10. E Railroad track   IFA   Lummus
   10. F Tents and canvas   IFA   Canvas Specialty
   10. G Fences   IFA   Mike Brown

11. <u>PRODUCTION CREW</u>
   11. A Stage managers   Dick Harwood
   11. B Pages   Unit Mgr.
   11. C Gaffers   Unit Mgr.

12. <u>POSTPRODUCTION</u>
   12. A Mix down   Unit Mgr.   Eileen
   12. B Video edit   Unit Mgr.   Josh and Eileen
   12. C Conforming   Unit Mgr.
   12. D Sweetening   Unit Mgr.

13. <u>TAPE STOCK</u>
   13. A Video (location)   Mel
   13. B Audio (location)   Mel
   13. C Video postproduction   Mel
   13. D Audio postproduction   Mel

These examples which we have seen are telescoped samples of what go into planning and into the good producer's production book. They do, I hope, give you some deeper appreciation and respect the next time you see a spontaneous moment on television.

Chapter 10
scripting: form and terms

As a producer or director, you may never write a script, but you will be working with writers and reading scripts all the time. It is important as a professional to know the form of scripts and the very precise terminology used in them.

First drafts of scripts are usually typed on white, 8½-by-11-inch paper, original on bond. Copies are mimeographed or Xeroxed. If changes in the script are extensive and take place before shooting, second and subsequent drafts are submitted in the same manner. However, once a working or shooting script is ready, it is usually bound in a loose-leaf or spring-back binder, so that you can easily take it apart; replacement scenes or pages are typed on different colored pages. Say, the first replacement pages may come in on pink, second on green, third on blue, and so on. This system is a quick and clear means of handling rewrites and making sure that everyone has them. All scripts should have on the title page which draft they are, and the date of completion or submission. For instance, "FIRST DRAFT, 1/1/76." Replacement pages, each and every one, should have similar information. For example, "Page 8, FIRST REVISE, 1/10/76."

As you read through a script and make notes on it for changes, you will want a way to refer back to these notes quickly. My system is to fold down a small triangle of the upper right-hand corner of every page on which I have made notations. Thumbing through the script later, when I am talking to the director or writer or scenic designer, I find that these creased pages are very easy to locate. Sometimes, when I have finished notating a script, I will, on the first page or cover page, list the page numbers where I have made changes and some key word to remind me of what the note is.

Let us define some of the terms you will face as you read and discuss scripts:

CUT TO: You know by now what a cut is—a quick but undisturbing move from one shot to the next.

DISSOLVE TO: An outgoing shot dissolves into an incoming shot.

MATCH DISSOLVE: When an element—say, a person—matches the same position in the frame as an incoming object of like nature, you have a match dissolve.

SFX: This stands for sound effects and will be followed by the sound effects desired. For instance, SFX: Thunder.

PAN: This is an instruction for the camera to turn on a lateral or horizontal line. To simulate a pan, turn your head to the left or right, keeping your eyes straight ahead.

TILT: This is an instruction for the camera to move on its axis in a vertical hinged motion, down or up, as called for in tilt up; or tilt down. If this is still not clear, try leaning over or bending back at the neck and see what this does to the position of your eye. These are tilt motions.

TRACK or TRUCK or TONGUE (LEFT OR RIGHT): This instructs that the camera position, at its base, should move left or right. This should always mean along a horizontal or lateral line.

DOLLY IN or DOLLY OUT: Precisely, this instruction dolly should mean movement in toward the object being photographed or back away from it. Frequently, however, dolly is used instead of track or truck or tongue, in which case it will be followed by the direction desired, such as dolly left.

PEDESTAL DOWN (tape only): This means that the camera will descend on its supporting arm. Sometimes shown as ped down.

PEDESTAL UP (tape only): The opposite of pedestal down.

CRANE UP or CRANE DOWN: This can indicate movement similar to the pedestal moves, but with cranes these moves are usually much more dramatic and can go either higher or lower. The camera is attached to a large arm that balances on a fulcrum, with a giant Chapman crane; the camera movement can also be left or right as well as sweepingly up and down. These movements can be combined and are called for in such instructions as crane up and left. (Many instructions can combine: dolly in, tilt up.)

SMASH CUT: A disturbing cut from one scene to a totally unexpected scene.

RACK FOCUS: This calls for an abrupt or jarring focus change—one that intentionally jerks the eye from one extreme of the lens length to another.

ZOOM: The angle or camera position does not change in a ZOOM. Rather the lens moves. It usually means a fluid movement in or out from wide to close-up or from close-up to wide.

EXT: This means exterior and is usually followed by a designation of what the exterior is in general, and whether it is day or night. For instance, Ext. A country road.—Day.

INT: This means interior and is set up in a manner similar to the example in ext. For instance, Int. George's den.—Night.

SWISH PAN: This indicates a panning movement that is so fast that it causes the image to blur.

WIDE SHOT: This calls for framing that is some distance from the object being photographed and relates it to its surroundings.

MCU: This stands for medium close-up. If it is a person being photographed, an MCU would probably be a waist and head shot.

CU: A close-up, which is maybe head and shoulders on a person.

ECU: An extreme close-up, which includes just the head, or even just the eyes and mouth.

P.O.V.: This is a reverse angle shot. P.O.V. stands for point-of-view. It means a shot which shows a view as though seen by a person who has just been seen in the previous shot.

REVERSE ANGLE: A shot that is 180° around from the shot which precedes it.

2 SHOT: There are two people in the frame. This can be a 3 shot, 4 shot, and so on.

SPLIT SCREEN: Two complete images share the same frame. This can be a vertical split, in which case the line is down the middle; or it can be a horizontal split, in which case the dividing line between the two images runs across the center of the frame.

QUAD INSERT, UPPER LEFT: This calls for dividing the frame into four equal parts. In three-quarters of the frame, you might have Arnold Palmer in a wide shot about to putt. Perhaps in the quad insert, upper left, you would have a close-up of his face.

FADE IN: You are instructed to come up on a scene, gradually, out of black.

FADE OUT: You are instructed to go out on a scene, gradually, into black.

BLACK OUT: You are instructed immediately to go out of a scene into black.

SUPER: Here you are called upon to put one piece of visual information on top of another.

MAIN TITLES: This gives the title of the show and stars, producer, director, and writer credits.

CREDITS or END CREDITS: This indicates the list of job functions at the end of a program and the people's names who do them.

CRAWL: This is a moveable scroll of credits—which crawl across the screen.

BILLBOARD: This calls for the sponsor's logo or company identification.

I.D.: Identification is of either the network or station call letters.

ANNCR.: This indicates the announcer.

ANNC.: This indicates when announcer should speak.

V.O.: This stands for voice-over. It means that someone who is not to be seen should speak.

O.S.: This means off-stage.

S.O.F.: Sound on film. This means that there is sound accompanying what is seen.

M.O.S.: This stands for mit out sound. Many of the early film makers were German, you see. M.O.S. means silent footage or shooting where sound is not required.

STOCK FOOTAGE: This is film which you acquire from libraries, or stock, and do not shoot.

1.: —or whatever number. This indicates the sequential number of the shot from first shot to last shot. This number should precede every camera shot, change of angle, or camera instruction.

MUSIC:

STING: This is a quick, dramatic piece of music.

SEGUE: This is one piece of music going into another, overlapping.

BRIDGE: This refers to suitable music to carry you between scenes.

PLAY-ON: This is bright music, for bringing a person on.

PLAY-OFF: This is bright music for getting a guest off.

VAMP: This is continuing incidental music for ad-lib moments, such as during applause.

RIM SHOT: This refers to a fast drum roll, which is often used to punctuate a comedian's lines.

ESTABLISH: This is to hold long enough to establish a mood, scene, theme.

UNDER: This is a direction to take music below voice or other sound.

UNDER AND OUT: This is a direction to take music below voice or other sound and eventually to fade it completely.

There are two standard ways of setting up a script page. The first, as shown following, is almost always used for the documentary-type show. Then, I will show you the form used for dramatic or comedy/variety shows. This first is the opening sequence of a script I wrote.

SHOOTING SCRIPT 8/8
SECOND REVISE, 8/15/72

PICTURE

SOUND

1. FADE IN: EXT.—DAY. THE SUN FILLS THE FRAME. DURING SPEECH, CAMERA BEGINS SLOW ZOOM BACK TO SHOW PART OF SKY AROUND THE SUN.

    E. G. MARSHALL (V.O.) From the beginning—in the way we learn about such things—only God could command the light: "Let there be light," God said, and there was light. Except—

2. INT.—GLENMONT HALLWAY —NIGHT. E. G. MARSHALL IN DARKNESS ON STAIRS AT GLENMONT, LIGHTS A CANDLE AND BEGINS WALKING DOWNSTAIRS. THE CANDLE SHOULD BE THE ONLY APPARENT SOURCE OF LIGHT.

    E. G. MARSHALL (ON CAMERA)—that there was also night. Again, from the beginning—humankind, never modest in the audacity of its dreams, dreamt of imitating the Lord's order, even into the hours of darkness. Still, for so long in human history that it seemed like always, the dream remained a dream.

E. G. MARSHALL BLOWS OUT THE CANDLE. IT IS DARK. CUT TO:

3. INT.—NIGHT—EDISON LIBRARY. ECU OF MODEL OF FIRST LIGHT BULB ON DESK TOP. BULB IS LIT BY KEY SHAFT OF LIGHT ONLY.

    E. G. MARSHALL (V.O.) That is, until only a splinter of time ago, when one man's tenacious dreaming caught fire in this tiny globe and turned the ancient wishing into a wonderous reality.

ZOOM BACK:
4. WE SEE E. G. MARSHALL IN
SILHOUETTE STANDING AT
THE DESK; HE PICKS UP
THE MODEL OF THE FIRST
LIGHT BULB.

    E. G. MARSHALL
    (ON CAMERA) Today,
because of that man, even
the most thoughtless
among us, with the flip
of a switch—

E. G. MARSHALL TURNS ON
THE LAMP WHICH HANGS
OVER THE DESK; THIS
ILLUMINES E.G., THE
DESK AND PART OF THE
ROOM

Commands the light and
can take the gift for
granted.

CUT TO:
5. EXT.—DAY—GLENMONT
WIDE SHOT OF THE HOUSE
FROM THE SOUTHWEST.
E.G. IS IN FOREGROUND,
AT FIRST WITH HIS BACK
TO CAMERA. ON "THE MAN"
E.G. TURNS TO FACE
CAMERA.

    E. G. MARSHALL
    (ON CAMERA) Here in West
Orange, New Jersey, the
man had his home—called
Glenmont.

CUT TO:
6. EXT.—DAY—LABORATORY
ECU OF E.G. MARSHALL.
CAMERA IS ANGLED HIGH
AND AWAY. RACK FOCUS
BACK TO WIDE SHOT OF
LABS.

(ON CAMERA) But here, a
short distance away, is
where he lived—in his
laboratories.

CUT TO:
7. EXT.—DAY—LABORATORY
ANGLE IS THROUGH STREET
GATE TO E.G. MARSHALL,
WHO IS TURNING FROM
PREVIOUS ANGLE TO FACE
CAMERA. E.G. WALKS
TOWARD CAMERA AS GATE
SWINGS OPEN.

    E. G. MARSHALL
    (ON CAMERA) His name was
Thomas Alva Edison. His
gifts and inventions
were many—and his genius
electrified the world.

SMASH CUT TO:

8. THE ACCUTRON SIGN ON
   TIMES SQUARE. MAIN
   TITLES WILL FLASH ON
   THIS.

MUSIC: THEME: UP & ESTAB-
LISH MUSIC: UNDER FOR
V.O. ANNC. MAIN TITLES,
SUPERED:

A. "AMERICAN LIFE STYLE"
B. "THOMAS ALVA EDISON'S
   GLENMONT"
C. "Your host, E. G.
   MARSHALL"

SUPER BILLBOARD: "U.S.F. &
G."

ANNCR.
(V.O.) American Life
Syle! Thomas Alva
Edison's Glenmont,
starring as your host,
Mr. E. G. Marshall—is
brought to you by—USF & G
and 6,500 independent
insurance agents
representing USF & G.

In this form, the page is divided with camera—or picture—instructions on the left. The sound—or spoken instructions—and words are on the right. Camera directions are in capital letters and the spoken words in lower case.

Certain small visual instructions should be given within the dialogue; for instance, (HE FROWNS), (SHE NODS).

Now, an example of a dramatic script; this form is also used for comedy or variety scripts. This script, finally shot in a largely altered version as a pilot for a weekly hour series for ABC, was written by journalist/dramatic writer Pete Hamill and produced by Herbert B. "Bert" Leonard, a skillful television craftsman ("Route 66," "Naked City"). This particular program failed as a series, but aired as a one-time, one-hour show in the spring of 1973, starring John Cassavettes, Alexis Smith, and June Havoc.

TEASE
FADE IN:

1. EXT. 61ST STREET HELIPORT—EARLY EVENING—   1.
    TITLES OVER

    It is the magic hour in New York, that oddly
    beautiful moment when it is no longer day, and
    not quite night. A frail rain is falling, and
    there are mauve streaks in the darkening sky,
    bringing rumors of evening. We are at the 61st
    Street Heliport, at the base of the Triboro
    Bridge, and a man named CARMINE KELLY waits
    beside a small control building, smoking a
    Cuban cigar. The collar of his coat is pulled
    up tight, and his hands are jammed in his
    pockets. He glances at the sky.

    Kelly has a worn, handsome, urban face, and the
    hour imbues him with a quality of melancholy
    acceptance. The East River lies before him,
    glossy and black, pitted by the rain. The
    lights of Queens are blinking on.

    The sound of a helicopter starts very low, and
    then rises. It is what Carmine is waiting for.
    He steps away from the meagre shelter of the
    building.

                                             CUT TO:

2. EXT. 61ST STREET HELIPORT—EVENING—ANOTHER   2.
    ANGLE

    A woman named VENTURA DAVIS steps out of the
    helicopter, accompanied by a small dandy of a
    man named CHARLIE SHANE. She is wearing a
    smartly cut blue coat and boots. He is wearing
    a smartly cut blue coat and boots. Ventura
    Davis is in her late 40's. There's a sense of
    anacronism about this beautiful face that once
    illuminated a thousand movie screens, and is
    now on the edge of becoming a magnificent ruin.

    Charlie Shane is a 28 year old movie producer.
    He's an energy machine but he wouldn't know
    "Fantasia" from "High Noon."

    Ventura embraces Carmine warmly. Shane steps
    in, to remain part of the act, but Carmine and
    Ventura brush him, and step into a waiting
    limousine. Shane gets in behind them.

                                             CUT TO:

3. EXT. RAMP—EAST RIVER DRIVE—NIGHT   3.

    The limo pulls up on the ramp leading to the
    East River Drive. The city spreads out

downtown, lights blinking like diamonds. The streets are slick with rain.

                                          CUT TO:

4. EXT. PLAZA HOTEL—NIGHT   4.

The limousine pulls around the square in front of the Plaza. The doors of the Plaza are warm with light, in contrast to the drizzling night. The limo stops. Carmine and Ventura step out, followed by Shane, and hurry into the hotel.

5. EXT. PLAZA—ANOTHER EXIT—NIGHT   5.

In an almost matching cut, the trio emerges from another exit. Ventura is now swathed in a lush mink, and Shane has put on his producer's coat. They get back in the limo.

                                          CUT TO:

6. EXT. SECOND AVENUE—NIGHT—TITLES OUT   6.

The limousine moves quickly down the avenue. The neon lights make bands of red across the slick tar. The limo pulls up in front of a place with a canopy marked SMITTY'S. The building seems to stand alone, in isolation, like a town that escaped a war.

7. EXT. SMITTY'S—NIGHT   7.

Carmine gets out and helps Ventura onto the street. She looks smashed. Ventura looks around the entryway and sees that there's a rough board fence plastered with signs that say Gable Construction Company, and behind the vaguely threatening shapes of earth-moving equipment. Three Butter and Egg Types stand under the awning waiting for a cab. They notice Ventura immediately.

As she steps onto the sidewalk, she gestures grandly.

                    VENTURA
My God, Carmine! What on earth has happened around here? There used to be a . . . a button store, yes, a button store, right over there. And an antique shop. And a dry cleaners. What is going on?

                    CARMINE
The neighborhood's got a terminal case of New York, Ventura.

He has her by the elbow now, and is moving to
the entrance. One of the butter-and-egg men
steps forward; he's a little smashed.

> BUTTER AND EGG MAN
> (snapping his fingers)
> I got it! Ventura Davis, right? Right!
> Hey, I saw you in a lot of pictures,
> ever since I was a kid. Ventura Davis!

He turns to the others.

> BUTTER AND EGG MAN (cont'd)
> Was I right or wrong?

> SHANE
> That's right fellas, Ventura Davis.
> Opening soon in "Journey To The Center
> of My Head."

The other guys are less interested. But
Ventura isn't interested at all. She steps
past them, a flicker of fear in her face, as if
afraid of being mauled.

> BUTTER AND EGG MAN
> Hey, Ventura, how about an autograph?
> You know, for my daughter . . .

> CARMINE
> Send your daughter around herself,
> pal.

They go in.

> BUTTER AND EGG MAN
> Goddammovie star.

8. INT. SMITTY'S—NIGHT   8.

Carmine and Ventura followed by Shane step
into Smitty's, which is bubbling warmly. There
is a long bar to their right with three
bartenders pouring drinks for an
extraordinary variety of New Yorkers:
Out-of-work actors, a few second-line
politicians, a couple of off-duty firemen, and
women: Long-legged redheads from the lines of
the Broadway shows, a few expensive hookers
taking a few hours off between calls, a few old
dolls killing loneliness with Cointreau and
young faces, a few cruising stewardesses.

Behind the bar, bottles are piled neatly in
rows against an old Victorian chased mirror;
the diffused light gives the place a burnished
golden feeling, as if it had been there since

before everyone in the room was born. There are
pictures of old prizefighters, forgotten bus
rides and outings, and a picture of Fiorello
LaGuardia in a fireman's hat. To the left there
are tables packed with diners, and more photos
climbing the available walls: pictures of
stars, showgirls, writers, columnists. At one
table, Jimmy Breslin is eating and shouting
something inaudible to his friend Fat Thomas.
At another table, Shirley MacLaine is talking
politics with Howard Samuels. The place feels
very special: safe, boisterously intimate,
speaking of time gone and time present, of
continuity and old standards.

Carmine, Shane and Ventura move into this
scene: Carmine familiar, smiling, at home,
reaching out to shake an offered hand, his
words inaudible in the general hubbub. Ventura
seems more self-conscious, as if she had been
away too long, smiling vulnerably at those who
recognize her.

8A. <u>WIDE ANGLE—MOVING</u>   8A.

The camera is behind the bar, and as Carmine,
Ventura and Shane move through the restaurant,
we move with them. As we follow them, we hear
snatches of dialogue from the customers.

> FIRST CUSTOMER
> She says to me, get a day job. I ses to
> her, I don't like it in the day, it
> hurts my eyes. So for <u>that,</u> she packs
> it in.

> SECOND CUSTOMER
> I knew a broad like that once. One day I
> found her cuttin' her fingernails on
> the rug, so <u>I</u> left . . .

> THIRD CUSTOMER
> Hey, is Bela Lugosi still dead?

> FOURTH CUSTOMER
> (shouting down the bar)
> Listen, I bet this is the first World
> Series Lugosi ever saw, now they play
> at night . . .

> FIFTH CUSTOMER
> Aren't there any broads besides
> hookers that sleep days?

As they reach the end of the bar, ARAM, his back
to the door, is shouting in conversation with
three men.

                    ARAM
So I says to this guy, I says, 'ey,
whatta you some kind of a nut? I am a
police officer, I says to the guy, and____
you are about to go to the <u>slam,</u> and he
starts to say, "ey, I am . . .

                    CARMINE
        (sticking his finger in Aram's back)
. . . . going to eat your liver.

Aram whirls around; he has a rough, hard face,
wears tinted steel-rimmed glasses, but when he
sees Carmine his attitude changes from
hostility to a rough, bear-hugging bravado.
The roughness, in short, of male friendship.

                    ARAM
            (a fake hard guy act)
Stop interrupting.

                    CARMINE
Aram, this is Ventura . . .

                    ARAM
    (breaking in, shaking Ventura's hand,
        ignoring the three men at the bar)
Whatta you kiddin'? You're gonna
introduce <u>me</u> to Ventura Davis. I . . .
                    (MORE)

You will notice immediately a minimum of camera direction.
Most directors honestly prefer the writer to do it this way. "Just give
me the general setting, shot instruction, and dialogue. I'll do the rest,"
they will say.

You will notice several other things: (1) The shots are numbered,
on both margins of the page, and camera instructions are on the right.
They can just as properly be on the left. (2) Characters, the first time
they are introduced, are in caps. It would have been a good idea, and
it is customary, to put significant props, locales, and actions in caps,
such as on page 1, THE EAST RIVER; RAIN; HELICOPTER;
LIMOUSINE. This helps the production manager budget a script and
the designer to design. (3) In this format, the entire page is used for
camera directions and descriptions of characters and action. (4) Dialogue is centered, ten spaces in from the outer margins of the directions. (5) The speaker's name is centered above his lines and his name

appears in caps, as in CARMINE. (6) All internal dialogue directions and the dialogue itself are in lower case. (7) If a speech or action is continued to a next page, it will always say at the bottom of the page going out, (MORE) or (CONTINUED); and at the top of the page coming in, (CONTINUED). (8) Act endings will be spelled out and in caps underlined: <u>END OF ACT THREE.</u> (9) The pages are numbered sequentially. (Frequently, the page numbering will be handled like this, and I prefer it: III-5-47. This means: III is the act number; 5 is the page of the act; 47 is the total running number of script pages.)

Here are the title pages for the two scripts we have examined. Title pages should be set up to include the series title, the episode title, the author's name, the production company's name (the sponsor's name and his agency's name when they have bought the whole show), the number of the draft, and the date of submission.

AMERICAN LIFE STYLE

<u>Thomas Alva Edison's Glenmont</u>

Written By
BOB SHANKS

Starring
E. G. MARSHALL

Sponsored By
U. S. F. & G.

Agency
VANSANT, DUGDALE

Produced By: ANN ZANE SHANKS

For: Comco Productions, Inc.
    850 Seventh Avenue
    New York, New York 10019

FINAL DRAFT
SEPTEMBER 15, 1972

STEFFE PRODUCTIONS

NIGHTSIDE
(Pilot Script)

A VERY SPECIAL PLACE
By
Pete Hamill

Herbert B. Leonard
1701 York Avenue
New York, New York 10028

SECOND DRAFT
DECEMBER 13, 1973

241

Following the title page and preceding the script itself, there should be a CAST PAGE. For instance:

CAST

```
PRINCIPALS:
CARMINE KELLY, early 40's. Worn, handsome, urban,
            romantic, and realistic.
VENTURA DAVIS, late 40's. Fading big movie star.
            Anxiety about aging.
SMITTY, mid 40's. Beautiful, widow, toughened by
            running own business. Needs love.
ARAM, late 50's, tough, ex-detective, loyal to
            friends.
SUPPORTING:
[Here would be listed smaller but important parts,
such as Charlie Shane.]
UNDER FIVE:
[Here would be listed the characters who have fewer
than five speaking lines. This distinction is
important since it is at 5-lines-or-over or at
5-lines-or-under that the performers' unions vary
their pay scales.]
EXTRAS:
[Here would be listed extra players who do not speak,
as to type and numbers, such as BUTTER & EGG MEN, 5
WAITERS, 10 CUSTOMERS, 4 KITCHEN WORKERS and so on.]
[Again, there is another union price scale when there
are no spoken lines. The number is indicated, of
course, so that the producer and production manager
can make quick, sensible estimates as to budget.]
```

The cast page gives everyone concerned a telegraphic feel for the color of the characters, the number of them, and what this means in terms of story, production value, and cost.

On the next page, there should be a sets page.

SETS

EXT.
61ST STREET HELIPORT
RAMP EAST RIVER DRIVE
PLAZA HOTEL
SECOND AVENUE
SMITTY'S A NIGHT-TYPE TAVERN
[and so on, followed by:]
INT.
SMITTY'S THE MAIN ROOM
SMITTY'S THE KITCHEN
LIVING ROOM SMITTY'S APARTMENT
PLAZA HOTEL SUITE
[and so on.]

This sets page again gives everyone interested a quick overview of how many sets there are and thus an idea of what costs and shooting problems may be.

When a script has been accepted, the producer or his associate or the production manager will devise any number of other important sheets and/or pages which will become part of the script book. These are discussed in the chapter on production. For now, I think we have dealt with scripting long enough.

Chapter 11
ratings, or the emperor's clothes

In television, everything depends on the question, How did it do in the ratings? Aside from public television, the ratings will affect the success or failure of every show on the air. Since ratings are so vitally important, obviously, they deserve close attention. What are they? Why do they matter? How are they gathered?

Worst things first. American television is not an art form, but a business; specifically, an advertising medium—Alistair Cooke and an occasional performance of Shakespeare notwithstanding. Commercial television programming is designed to attract audiences to the advertisers' messages which surround the programming, inundate, you might even say. Inherent creative and aesthetic values are important, but always secondary.

When television people speak of attracting audiences they mean mass audiences. The *New York Times* reaches fewer than a million people a day, *TV Guide* perhaps fifteen million an issue, and *Reader's Digest* seventeen million; the National Football League on a given Sunday plays to about nine hundred thousand paying customers. While all of these are venerable and successful American institutions, their impressive audience figures would spell disaster for a prime-time television program. Television must attract mass audiences and that means in prime-time twenty, thirty, forty, fifty million!

When an advertiser invests money in any media purchase, he wants to know how much it is costing him to reach a given number of people. There are refinements of this primary rule which I will come to, but the basic concern is how many people will see an advertisement and how much it will cost. This question is summed up in the term *CPM*. CPM means cost (in dollars) per thousand people seeing the ad. M is one thousand in Roman numerals.

In television, if someone says, "My CPM (or cost per thousand) is four-twenty," he means that he is paying $4.20 for every thousand households who are exposed to his advertisement. (Numbers of viewers per household are also estimated in the ratings services.) This principle applies to print media advertising such as newspapers and magazines as well as to radio and television.

Assume that $4.20 is an acceptable CPM. (It is not a bad one, as a matter of fact, if other factors are favorable.) Assume also that a one-minute commercial on the "Tonight Show" costs $30,000, which approximates the real figure the last time I checked. How then does the advertiser know whether the "Tonight Show" figure is a fair one in terms of his acceptable CPM?

With newspapers and magazines the answers are readily at hand. Publications have definite circulation figures as to newsstand sales and paid subscriptions. An advertiser simply divides the total circulation figure by a thousand to determine the number of thousands. Next, he divides the cost of the advertisement by the number of thousands, which gives him the cost per thousand, the CPM.

Paid events have it easier still. They have ticket and box-office receipts. But what about television?

In the beginning, there was no equivalent way to measure box office or circulation, which in the view of many explains why television had a concurrent Golden Age in the 50s. Another Golden Age theory holds that television sets were owned only by the more affluent and thus better educated citizens, who were more receptive to good programming than the masses who later bought TVs by the millions.

Eventually though, some measurement of audience was absolutely essential to television advertisers if they were to establish acceptable CPMs against what the programmers, networks, and local stations, were charging. And how were the broadcasters themselves to know what they should be charging? Maybe they were overcharging, but they also might be undercharging. Thus, both sides had to establish a box-office measurement. And that is what ratings are.

Let us go on following the "Tonight Show" example for a moment. A one-minute advertisement costs $30,000. According to the ratings (National TV Index, two weeks ending April 6, 1975) the average "Tonight Show" audience was 6,990,000 households; that is, 6,990 thousands, or after computation, about $4.29 as a CPM.

But how does one arrive at the 6,990,000 households figure? The rating?

There are many rating systems—Trendex, ARB, and so on—but only one that finally counts. It is called the Nielsen Rating, put out by the A. C. Nielsen Company, a research firm based in Chicago. Measuring television audiences is only one part of this company's activities, albeit a powerful function and one that gives the company great visibility.

Fifty-two weeks a year Nielsen's national rating book tells broadcasters, advertisers, and creators who is watching what and when. The basic instrument of this rating measurement is a mechanical recording device called an Audimeter (a registered name) which the company attaches to a television set. The Audimeter is known familiarly as the little black box.

The little black box is attached to an estimated 1,170 home television sets. These 1,170 home receivers constitute the base sample for the approximately 68,500,000 television homes in America. Not viewers—homes. The Audimeters are placed in households, that is, homes and apartments. There are no Audimeters in bars, college dorms, military bases, prisons, hospitals, or other institutional and seasonal locations. Nor are there any Audimeters in Hawaii and Alaska.

One thousand, one hundred and seventy is 0.0017 per cent of 68,500,000, a miniscule percentage of the total number of homes in America. It is doubtful, in fact, that ever in history have so few had so much influence over so many.

The Audimeter is attached to a television set and is activated every time that set is turned on. It contains a punch tape which records on a minute-by-minute basis the length of viewing, the time of viewing, and the channel being viewed. The most apparent flaw in this rating system is that the Audimeter can only measure an off-and-on situation. It cannot measure actual viewing and certainly not attention-being-paid or attitudes-being-shaped. While the set is on, perhaps only the family dog or cat is in the room, or the viewer has fallen asleep. Even so, it is this audience that determines which shows get renewed or cancelled. On the advantageous side, however, a viewer being tracked by an Audimeter cannot claim to have watched a program which he or she did not watch, as would be possible in the diary or direct interview techniques of sampling.

Nielsen's literature is quite firm about methodology and cautions subscribers about the flaws inherent in its system.

The Audimeters are placed in the 1,170 homes according to predesignated neighborhoods and geographic distribution. The homes are obviously meant to represent a cross-section of the television audience, according to age, education, economic status, and so on. (All this more refined data will bring us eventually to demographies.) Nielsen never reveals, of course, the identities of Nielsen homes. Curiously enough, only once in the history of television was a producer able to find out this information and try to influence directly what the Nielsen homes viewed.

When the neighborhoods have been selected at random, Nielsen field representatives, working on a probability factor, go to the pre-chosen households in each neighborhood and try to convince their residents to accept Audimeters on their television sets. The field representatives are not always successful. In fact, only about seven out of ten designated households accept Audimeters. This means the Audimeters must be placed in substitute households, which shakes the probability sampling technique at its very base. At least part of the problem in homes rejecting the Audimeters, it has been reported, is that they cause certain interference with television reception and occasionally they cause breakdowns. One ex-Nielsen family reported to me that the Audimeter caused their picture to flop over every minute. (Flop over is the slang term for vertical roll). There have been further reports that Nielsen pays only a small fee for the right to install an Audimeter, and only half of the television repair bills.

What Nielsen pays a householder is a closely guarded secret, but according to the *New York Times* of September 12, 1973, a Nielsen home gets $2 a month for allowing the Audimeter to be placed on a set; it is also widely thought, for this reason, that the sample tends to skew toward lower-class homes.

When the 1,170 households have been chosen, no one knows for certain how long they remain in the Nielsen sample. Nielsen only says that they are a continuing panel, although the company further states that the sample is "systematically updated."

As reported in the same *New York Times* article, Nielsen changes 20 per cent of the sample every year and another 10 per cent are replaced for a variety of reasons, including lack of interest.

I know about one example personally. An unmarried friend of mine (who kindly turned his set on to any show of mine, whether he watched or not) became a young married and then had his second child and several salary increases before the Audimeter was removed from his apartment. All during this time, he was apparently reported as unmarried, at his original age and salary; all of which makes me skeptical about the precision of detailed Nielsen data.

There is a further complication—not all the Audimeters work all the time, even after they have been installed. By way of Nielsen's own disclaimer, the number of usable recorded tapes on any average day is 1,022. One thousand and twenty-two representing the viewing habits of 68,500,000 American homes! Still broadcasters and advertisers do not challenge the results. From time to time, a disgruntled star who has been cancelled will challenge Nielsen; but as often as not, this star will be the same one who swore by the ratings when he was on top.

Why don't professionals complain? We have now come to the

Emperor's Clothes. Everyone in television chooses to see the system as cloaked in the most elaborate robes of truth and precision. In reaction to the occasional outcry for a better way—usually in the wake of a congressional hearing—Nielsen is very reasonable, "We will gladly increase the sample and refine our techniques—and here is what such a new and improved service will cost." At that point the users of the sample rush to re-embrace the old system. The old system is comfortably familiar—and affordable. It is royal raiment. I don't see anyone naked, do you?

In any case, there it is. All who are serious about staying in television simply forget about how ludicrous the system is and accept it. After all, everyone is playing by the same rules, and strangely, backup and deeper research efforts have indicated that Nielsen's thousand are not very far from a true reflection of viewers' tastes and preferences. Very well. When the Audimeter tapes are ready for analysis, what happens to them and how are they reported?

There are four basic reports. We will deal with them in inverse order of their importance.

OVERNIGHTS

In two cities in America, New York and Los Angeles, Nielsen records and publishes rating information on an overnight basis. A certain number of sets in these cities are wired directly to computers in Nielsen offices and the results are recorded immediately. For instance, the viewers of a Monday night program will be known by Tuesday morning at 10:00 A.M. for these two key markets.

It is astonishing what effect these overnights can have. If they are good, you spend the day in a foolish euphoria; if they are bad, you slump through the day, in an equally foolish depression. The overnights are never used to make any important decisions—and they are frequently out of tune with subsequent and more substantive rating information; even so, they are the first matter of interest for everyone in television. Go into any office around 10:00 A.M. and every executive in sight will be asking, "Are the overnights up yet?" "How'd we do in the overnights?" It is an idiotic, meaningless, and masochistic ritual and I participate in it everyday.

If overnights are nearly worthless, why do we bother? There are no very reasonable explanations, only speculations based on experience. Television is a extremely volatile and competitive business, practiced by highly charged individuals. Suppose the Miami Dolphins had to wait ten days to two weeks to find out whether they had won a game or not. Part of the reason for overnights, then, is simply the desperate desire of people in the business to know how they did. Of course, as I have said, the overnights are often wrong in the final outcome. The national rating can be a complete reversal, positively or negatively. The last two (and final) times that I bet with another producer about ratings for a certain show, we paid off on the basis of the overnights. He won the first time. I won the second. When the nationals came in, the numbers were just the opposite. The overnights in New York and Los Angeles are important mostly because nearly everyone in national television lives in New York or Los Angeles. Word-of-mouth in the industry, in the short run at least, always has its source in the overnights. In television, everything is now and ephemeral. Many will remember your good overnight ratings, associating them with the memory of the show itself. Two weeks later, your show might be old news.

Incidentally, as a rough rule of thumb, the Los Angeles overnight is a closer approximation to the eventual national number than the New York figure. But not always. The main thing to remember is that overnights are a temporary source of lift or laceration.

MNAS OR THE 70 CITIES

The next parts of the country heard from are what the industry calls the 70 Cities—the seventy leading population centers in the nation. (Seventy for prime-time programs; sixty-two for daytime.) Nielsen calls these ratings the MNAs, or the Multi-Network Area Report. In the overnights, we are provided with raw data only, the overall rating and share of audience, averaged over the schedule by quarter-hours and households using television, or HUT as it is called. In the MNAs we get total audience, number of stations, and the percentage of coverage of the nation; also included are figures on the age breakdown of the audience and the sex. The MNA arrives a week after broadcast.

The Seventy Cities are those markets in which all three networks compete head to head, minute to minute. This MNA report is particularly important to ABC, the youngest major network, since its true programming strength is reflected here. In smaller markets, where there may be only one or two television stations, these are usually affiliated with NBC or CBS, and ABC is shut out of the market.

The MNAs reveal the relative strength of the three networks and the viewing habits of the largest centers of population where consumers can be reached in their greatest concentration. The MNAs account for approximately 65.7 per cent of the total available national audience.

SIA OR FAST NATIONAL

This is a Nielsen service, inaugurated in September 1973. SIA stands for Storage Instantaneous Audimeter and the SIA provides rating and share of audience data thirty-six hours after a broadcast. Eventually, Nielsen claims, SIA will provide national overnights. All of the reasons I put forth for the overnights have created pressure on Nielsen to provide the SIA. Additionally, it is important for decision makers to know the weak shows as soon as possible so that they can plan scheduling changes and put replacement shows into the works with the maximum amount of lead time, as well as make meaningful their negotiations and contracts about commercial costs.

The SIA system connects all 1,170 Nielsen Audimeters, via telephone wires, to the Nielsen computer headquarters at Dunedin, Florida. This system may eventually replace the NTI.

NTI OR THE NATIONALS

This, finally, is the big pay-off—the national rating, or NTI, which stands for Nielsen Television Index. This book, published every two weeks and covering a two-week period, is the definitive measurement for the time periods and programs covered. The NTI is comprehensive in an extensive and complicated way that wrings statistical wonders out of those 1,170 Nielsen households.

The NTI provides audience by time period; household audience; persons audience, which features seventeen categories of people ranked, among other things, by age, sex, affluence, and education; audience trends, that is, hours and months viewing figures compared to themselves a year ago; ranking of the top fifteen programs for the covered period; in fact, nearly everything, except how many people fell asleep with the set on.

Let us examine the essentials. First, what exactly is a rating? To get the rating for a show, you begin with the gross figure of television homes in the country: 68,500,000. This is 100 per cent. If a show has a rating of 22.3 per cent this means that of all the households in America who could have turned on the program—we say "available to watch a show"—22.3 per cent of them did—15,275,500 households in this case, or, about, 33,606,100 people, since Nielsen figures about 2.2 people per set in prime-time. A 22.3 per cent rating would most definitely give you a hit show. To give you some idea, a superhit such as "All in the Family" plays to some 41,000,000 people.

The three color pages of the NTI which show ABC in blue, CBS in green, and NBC is rosy-pink are the heart of the national Nielsen. These pages begin with Monday evening and go through the week, night by night, reporting data on network programs in the time periods between 7:00 P.M. and 11:00 P.M. Prime-time, this is called. Then come pages for daytime, weekends, and other.

Ratings are provided for every fifteen-minute period in each respective block of time by program name. Thus, if your program is an hour in length, you can see how it did in quarter-hour segments. If your rating starts high and tapers off, it is a pretty good indication that your show generated viewer interest at the start, but lost viewers as it went along.

Four figures are given for each program: The rating, the total audience sampling your program on a minute-to-minute basis, the average audience over the entire program, and the share of audience. Now that we know what a rating is, let us define the other three measurements.

The Total Audience is that number of households which tuned into a program for all or any part of it longer than five minutes. The Average Audience is the audience for a program, averaged over the program's entire length. Share of Audience is that portion of the viewing audience who chose a program over all other programs on at the same time. Share of Audience is very nearly as important as the rating. It is the measurement, not of gross popularity, but of popularity relative to direct competition. A network prime-time show is generally required to get a 30 per cent share of audience in order to survive.

Now come some refinements. Suppose you are an advertiser who has to decide between putting your money into Show A or Show B. Often, there is very little difference in the gross audience for two programs—even if they are on at the same time. Check quantity? About equal. But what about the quality of their respective audiences? What kinds of people are watching these two programs? What age, sex, education, buying power? This brings us to the term *demographics*. Remember the term; it is very important these days.

Demographics is the qualitative analysis of raw rating data, evaluated especially in terms of sex and age. A cereal company, for instance, must know how many children and older people are watching a program, since other market research has revealed that these groups of individuals are primary consumers. Similar rules apply to every other product. Generally, most advertisers are interested in women between 18–34 years of age. Why? Women make the majority of consumer decisions in this country, and the women 18–34 do most of the buying. (Obviously, there are exceptions, depending on the product.)

Let us assume, though, that the aim is to reach these women 18–34. With that as an objective, what can Nielsen reveal about Show

A and Show B? In one section of the NTI, there is a chart evaluating every program by its audience composition, known as audience comp or demographics. Suppose that here we learn that Show B beats Show A in 18–34-year-old women out of every one hundred households viewing and that the overall audience is skewed younger for Show B. As a sponsor, you would prefer to buy Show B.

THE SWEEPS

There are other statistical research tools in use as well. Three times a year, in February, May, and November, Nielsen conducts what it and the industry call sweeps; Sweeps are comprehensive ratings of all time periods for *each individual station in the country.* These are the ratings used by local stations to sell spot and local minutes. These are indirectly but extremely important to the networks. If their national programs do not do well in these sweeps, it means their local affiliates cannot sell their own minutes and thus will become restless with their network affiliations. That is why frequently there have been loaded program schedules during these periods. By loaded I mean the best programs that a network or local station programmer thinks he has available—the best movies, the biggest guest stars, the most provocative themes. All of these appear during the sweeps. Also, damned few documentaries appear then.

Sweep ratings are gathered by a diary technique. That is, our patient probability sample now fills out prepared diaries indicating which shows it watched; and at what times; on what channels; and who in the household was watching. I distrust this technique intensely! I know too much about people to have any faith in the accuracy of this system. Ask trial lawyers or police officers about the credibility of eyewitnesses following an event. Add to this my panic picture of a diary scene:

The week has gone by. The Nielsen field representative comes to pick up the diary. The person who is supposed to fill it out has forgotten to and now to be nice (all probability samples want to be liked) makes up what the household viewed for the week, using the *TV GUIDE* and the field representative's encouragement to complete the diary from memory. The field representative, I am told, only gets paid for completed diaries, so he is very helpful. This is a programmer's favorite nightmare! You are positive your competition is always getting credit for a show the viewer saw on your channel. This is not complete paranoia. There are often wide disparities between the Audimeter numbers and the diary numbers.

The Audimeter figures are not used for the sweeps because that panel of 1,170 is simply too thin to cover each station in each local market. Local markets are what sweeps rate, each station in each market; so extra sample groups are organized for November, February, and May, using the inexpensive, but highly erratic diary technique.

TV-Q

Another research tool rates performers individually. Given a choice of X, Y, or Z stars, is there any scientific method that will help one decide which performer would be selected for a particular part? There purports to be. It is called TV-Q.

The TV-Q makes two measurements of performers, one called familiarity and another called Q (Q for quotient). It works like this: Interviewers first ask members of a sample group, once more allegedly chosen on a statistical probability basis, "Do you know so-and-so?" Let us say the sample group being interviewed is made up of one hundred people. To illustrate further, this question might be asked, "Do you know Bob Hope?" For each person in the sample group who answers yes in a satisfactory way, a way that indicates true knowledge of who Bob Hope is, Hope is given a single point toward his familiarity score. As a veteran entertainer in all media, of course, Bob Hope always gets a high familiarity score.

Let us say that ninety-six of the one hundred people interviewed know who Bob Hope is. Therefore, his familiarity score is ninety-six, a superb score in most cases, but not in all of them.

Now comes the Q. When a person being interviewed has responded by saying "Yes, I know Bob Hope"—or whoever—the person is asked a second question: "Do you *like* Bob Hope?" This question forms the basis for a performer's Q score. The Q represents the percentage of those people familiar with a performer who actually like a performer. (Remember what the butcher said to the lady who was examining the chicken minutely in all its parts? "Tell me, Mrs. Goldberg, could you pass such a test?" Is it any wonder so many performers are insecure and neurotic?)

Carrying our example to its conclusion, let us say that eighty-nine percent of the ninety-six people who knew Bob Hope also said they liked Bob Hope. That is really good: a high familiarity score with a corresponding high Q score. The whole thing is reported this way:

	Familiarity	*Q*
Bob Hope	96	89

Without naming names—and you might be amazed at some of the results about actual stars—let us set up a table of ten performers named A through J.

	Familiarity	Q
Anderson	94	88
Baker	90	70
Case	85	25
Dorn	64	50
Earle	55	40
Farr	43	40
Green	31	11
Hart	29	22
Ingersoll	19	2
Jackson	10	80

In this table you can see that Anderson and Baker are very familiar and widely liked. You would probably take them on your show if you could get them, thereby making everybody happy, most of all the sponser. What about Case? He is almost as well-known as Anderson and Baker, but apparently those who do know him do not like him.

How can that be? If you think about it in terms of your own personal likes and dislikes, there are probably a lot of big names that are familiar to you, but whom you do not like. Stalin is one example who comes quickly to mind. You would think twice about having Stalin on your show, at least as the regular host. I would risk him, given network and sponsor approval, as a guest however, since he has a hot name, or marquee value, though I cannot visualize Stalin holding up the sponsor's product. Villians are attractive on television and sadly we have eliminated most of the real ones, but no advertiser is going to risk using as a spokesperson or program host anyone who is apparently disliked, no matter how familiar he or she may be.

What about Ingersoll and Jackson at the bottom of the list? Chances are that they are both fairly young and unexposed talents since they both have relatively low familiarity scores. But look at their Qs. All right, Ingersoll is somewhat better known, but his Q is terrible. Jackson, on the other hand, is liked by nearly everyone who knows him. All else being equal, whom would you cast? Jackson, of course.

Simply put, in evaluating a TV-Q, it is best for a performer to have a high familiarity and a high Q. It is not so bad for a performer to have a low familiarity and a high Q. That performer could be on the brink of stardom, given the right exposure. But it is disastrous to have a high familiarity and a low Q. Even your agent may start avoiding you.

Do people in power actually use this measurement? Yes, they do. Management may not lean on TV-Q as a compelling factor without regard for other considerations—at least no one I know does—but the TV-Q is used. Let us say Farr and Green are being considered for a second lead in a dramatic series and the character to be portrayed is supposed to be sympathetic and sexy looking (remember those women 18–34). Let us assume that Farr and Green are both sexy-looking. It is also rather safe to assume that Farr will demand a larger salary since he is better known. (Incidentally, TV-Qs can be used effectively on both sides of a salary negotiation.)

Unless there are other overriding variables—maybe Green's father-in-law owns the network—most professionals would pick Farr, even at the higher salary, since he is better known and certainly better liked. That is, with the given proposition that the character is to be portrayed sympathetically, and let us remember that all series leads are sympathetic. This is usually translated as *likability,* a term widely used in television about performers. It is, of course, a cliché, but like most clichés, basically true. There are no antiheroes in television, as there can be quite successfully in movies, plays, and novels. As an audience, you are less receptive to these disagreeable types when they reach you in your home, in mixed company, especially when they come back week after week; and, of course, no sponsor wants to risk his product being associated with a son of a bitch. Not that he is, but Don Rickles has been anathema as a series lead, for instance, since his image is that of a disagreeable, loudmouth, abrasive personality. Don is one of the gentlest and most generous men in the business and, I think, one of the funniest, but I believe he will never be successful as the host of his own series, because of his image, though he remains one of the most sought-after guest stars.

The TV-Qs became very important at one point in my life. When I was producing the "Merv Griffin Show" on CBS and we were fighting for the show's life against the "Johnny Carson Tonight Show" on NBC, the CBS executives were hassling me about the show's rating and share of audience; not only that, they were also combing through my guest bookings to eliminate performers who had low Qs, even relative to their high familiarities. I was urged to stop booking certain performers, though I really fought this. I believe talk shows need villains, and the more familiar the better, to work off the inevitably likable hosts of these programs.

Mostly, TV-Qs, I would say, are used to support one's own prejudices about performers where they can. In this, they are like most statistics. Otherwise, in toss-up situations, they are used as a last resort, in lieu of the rather undignified means of flipping a coin. The good producers and network executives are always aware of performers' TV-Qs, but usually they prefer to trust their own gut instincts when casting. The ones who do this most fully are usually also the greatest showmen. Let the other guys, who rely totally on research, make the Edsel.

There are two further research methods, concept testing and pilot testing. First, concept testing. Let us take a well-known long-running program such as "Gunsmoke" was. Suppose it had not been on the air, but was merely under consideration by a network as an idea for a new show. Once the idea has cleared human measurements—Does the programmer like the man who has brought in the idea? Does he owe a debt to the man's company? And a host of other really scientific things like that—the programmer will have a brief summary of the concept written up and sent to a research company. The research company will put a prepared questionnaire before our old and tireless friend, the probability sample. (Americans loved to be polled, as you may have noticed.)

The concept summary in the case of "Gunsmoke" (titles are also tested for their audience appeal) might read something like this: "Wyatt Earp is a strong, rugged individualist bachelor who is the marshal in Dodge City, Kansas, a raw and raucous frontier town in the Old West. Earp is the only shield in Dodge between civilization and chaos. His good friends are Doc and Kitty—and so on and so on." Characters, plots, situations, and locales are described in about four paragraphs. Respondents, who are given gifts or cash for their cooperation, check a box next to one of three responses: "I would definitely want to watch this program (episode)"; "I might want to watch this program (episode)"; "I would probably not want to watch this program (episode)." The overall sample is again broken down by sex, age, and other demographic categories.

Frequently, networks will themselves make up concepts for shows, test them, and, if certain ones do well, commission shows to be written and produced, based on these concepts. Again, this research is normally used prudently by network executives. Executives who are trained up through law, research, accounting, or sales, generally rely more heavily on this so-called objective evidence; those who have come up through the creative ranks usually rely more on instinct, a sense of actually experiencing what audiences like by having exposed themselves to audiences. I have already referred in passing to a classic example of research versus instinct in another field. The Ford Motor Company researched the introduction of a new automobile tirelessly and expensively and came up with the Edsel. A few years later, Lee Iocacca fought for his instinct that Americans wanted a hot car—and came up with the Mustang, Ford's single greatest success. One sage and veteran television hand observed, "For free you can have the most comprehensive concept testing ever devised—fifty years of box-office receipts of American motion pictures." I tend to agree, since the basic popular concepts haven't changed much since Athens and the Greek Theatre.

In any case, all shows being seriously considered are put through concept testing. But the final proof lies in the execution of a concept. In different hands, a program starring a blue-collar bigot, might well end up as a vulgar, harmful, and unpopular disaster. With Bud Yorkin and Norman Lear producing, writing, directing, and/or supervising, and with Carroll O'Connor starring, you get "All in the Family," with its roots in Jackie Gleason's "Honeymooners" and William Bendix's "Life with Riley." Incidentally, "All in the Family" scored very low in its concept test, was nearly not produced, and came near the guillotine in its first six months on the air. Individuals stuck by it: Yorkin and Lear, of course, and the president of CBS Television, Bob Wood.

To proceed, let us say a network has liked a concept; it has tested well, and they have gone on to set a production team, write a script, cast the parts and make a show—a pilot show, anyway. What happens then? I won't describe the whole process now, but will simply continue with the research aspects.

A pilot is a sample episode of what a program is supposed to be like when it is on every week. It is a test model. At least, it used to be. Nowadays, as much money is spent on a pilot as might be spent on two regular weekly episodes of the same program. Everyone involved tries to make it superperfect.

For ABC, a company called ASI, Audience Survey Index, tests the pilots. All pilot programs at all the networks are put through similar kinds of evaluations. ASI puts two hundred people, the probability sample, into a theatre and each of the two hundred has in front of him a dial, marked 0 to 100. He is told to turn the dial up or down to record the intensity of his interest, involvement, or enjoyment of every second of the program he is about to view. The closer to 100 a program gets, the better. The results of the viewers' reactions are charted on a graph and produce peaks and valleys like a seismograph. A good score for a program, in an overall average, would be in the 70s. Higher peaks at particular moments within the show are studied very carefully.

To determine if the current two hundred is a typical audience, ASI first shows the two hundred-member audience a Mr. Magoo cartoon, on which there have been countless scorings and thus a reliable standard established. If the two hundred react in any atypical way to the Mr. Magoo cartoon, this is noted and the pilot is usually shown again to another audience.

Once more, I must caution that no sane network programmer relies absolutely on such research results. However, it is not unimportant and in toss-up situations, the program with a higher ASI will get the nod to go on the air.

When I was producing the daytime "Merv Griffin Show" on NBC, Merv and I were called in by the research department. They showed us a graph of one of these pilot-type tests. The line was going along at a fairly regular frequency with only minor variations, when suddenly it shot up to 100. "Quick," Merv said, "tell me what I did there, so I can do it some more."

The researcher, in deadly earnest, replied, "Florence Henderson punched you in the stomach."

So much for research. While trying always to keep it in perspective, we have been forced to live with it, and to take it seriously. Especially the ratings, that wrathful God who sits in judgement on all of commercial television. As a pro, one learns soon enough to say, "My, isn't the emperor well dressed today."

Chapter 12
technology and equipment

The more you know about technology and equipment, the better, I suppose; yet there are producers-cum-millionaires who barely know their aspect ratios from a hole in their sound and technical geniuses who cannot make thirty consecutive seconds of interesting film. My own technical knowledge is both extensive and severely limited.

The technology and equipment that I understand best are my eyes, my ears, and my brain; again, not so much in how they work, but in what they perceive. Since my personal interests are of a more general nature and more directed toward ideas and people than engineering and technical expertise, I have always relied heavily on technical specialists. Furthermore, I have always worked on the premise that if I can imagine something, the technicians can reproduce it. I have often been disabused of this idealized notion; but when I am honest and the technicians are proud of their skills and have respect for the ideas, seemingly unattainable dreams sometimes come true.

My technical ignorance has been such a mixed blessing over the years that even now I hardly know whether it is a virtue or a liability. Often, in making grievous rule book errors, I have hit upon surprising creative solutions to sticky situations. And, up front in situations, not knowing that I cannot do something, I have done it—with agreeable results. On the other hand, I have also bobbled opportunities to enrich a production through ignorance of how to achieve certain desired effects.

One thing is certain, however, and it is an ironclad rule: *Do not fake it.* When you do not know how to achieve what you are seeing or hearing inside, ask. Ask someone who does know. Most technicians will be helpful—perhaps even flattered to share their knowledge. If you try to fake it, your general credibility will be tarnished and your specific needs put in jeopardy. The game will begin, as the expert toys with your pseudo-knowledge to test you. Also, you are tempting him to cheat you and loosening his own inner restraints against doing so.

There is, to be sure, a specific phenomenon I should warn you about—a base antagonism—that exists between people who produce, direct, write, perform, design, choreograph, and those on the technical side.

I think this exists fundamentally because two completely different psychological archetypes are involved. The psychic characteristics required to be an artist—for want of a better term—are dramatically different from the equally valuable characteristics required to be a technician. Viewpoints, attitudes, thought processes, actions and reactions, are all shaped on these diverse foundations. For instance, generally, the artist proceeds in a spherical or lateral thought process, subject to and needful of his emotions and his senses. He is abstract, a dreamer; he imagines. The technician thinks in a straight line, sequentially, sublimating his emotions to the logic of machines and cause-effect constructions in order to accomplish his ends.

Next, society at large rewards the artist and penalizes the technician, because it is easier to understand art than science. Artists are more visible, more glamorous, and frequently better paid than their technical counterparts.

In other words, to choose an obvious example, Elizabeth Taylor is "bigger" than her cameraman. Another clear example lies in the fact that artists receive their Emmy Awards in public and on television before the millions while the craftsmen are given theirs more privately and off-screen; I deplore this double standard.

A further aggravation between artists and technicians in television is the galling truth for both sides that they are absolutely dependent on each other. This alone breeds resentment. And not only are they dependent, but also they are together physically. As I write this book, I am dependent on the technician who made my pen or typewriter, as I will be on the printer and binder who will put it in final form. They in turn are dependent on writers. Yet, none of us has to see the other. Our various functions take place separately. Just the opposite in television. We cannot work alone. In television production, actors must be in physical relationship to technicians to achieve their ends and the technicians must likewise share the arena with actors. They are locked together and must accommodate their various skills.

The work of technicians is more tangible and objective, and therefore more concretely adjudged than is the more subjective work of artists. It follows that artists are more vulnerable and therefore, generally, must work harder at the accommodation. It is usually the producer, director, writer, performer, or his brokers who must persuade, cajole, and inspire (occasionally terrify) the technicians to get the interdependent relationship to function and the final product to be realized. It works out, since the artist's heightened need to please or to reach out for approval and communication is what drew him to art in the first place.

Lastly, since we and our machines are imperfect, our realizations always fall short of our expectations. How easy it becomes to blame the other guy.

At its best, however, when both sides value their own skills and, equally, the skills of the others, show production is a superb experience, enriching to all. At its worst, when one or the other side is energetically pursuing its contempt or hostility, the struggle is exhausting and the results stillborn.

You must strive unceasingly to create a positive psychological atmosphere around the show. It is when this collapses that you need working knowledge of technical matters—in self-defense. Again, if your knowledge is shaky—and it will be sometimes, no matter how much you know—you are vulnerable. At those times, when a technician may be causing you trouble or you suspect he is cheating you, confront him.

For example, the first day I worked with John Murray, a mountain of a man physically and a superb West Coast craftsman (he works as a film gaffer mostly, but he is knowledgeable in all the categories), he felt I, as the director, did not know for sure what I wanted or how to achieve it. That time, he was right. I was trying, however, and I had written the script and organized the production as well. I was taking all the risks and was paying him for his best, not for the negative vibes he was putting out. His turn-off to me was so apparent that even when I did things right, they were adjudged negative. The production was in jeopardy.

I stopped shooting, called a break, took John aside, and said, "Look, John, so I'm not Fellini. I'm taking the risks and you're taking the pay. It's no good for either of us, working the way we are. If you think I'm screwing up, don't poison things by turning the crew off or sighing and making faces and muttering under your breath. Help me, for God's sake. I welcome it. I'm not a bad guy. Let's make a good picture—together. If you know things I don't, can see ways things can be done better, tell me. I want to know. We're not enemies—or shouldn't be. Now what the hell am I doing wrong? Tell me."

He told me, that's for sure, but in a positive, constructive way. He read the script, saw the goals and came up with innumerable technical solutions that aided the production. He came through even with a number of creative or aesthetic suggestions that enhanced the picture, which incidentally went on to win awards. (If this approach does not work, take Elia Kazan's advice —"Fire the bastards.")

Television, as we have seen, uses two basic systems of technology: visual electronics and film, both augmented by sound.

ELECTRONIC

Television was not invented by Thomas Alva Edison (although much of his work made it possible) or any other single genius. It was a group invention, with people in various parts of the world and at different times contributing to the ultimate phenomenon. E. F. W. Alexanderson, John L. Baird, Heinrich Herz, Guglielmo Marconi, Lee DeForest, Vladimir Zworykin, Charles F. Jenkins, Philo T. Farnsworth and Paul Nipkow, among scores of others, all played significant roles. These pioneers, working in the late nineteenth and early twentieth centuries, discovered basic electronic facts that made television practical as early as 1923.

Television is a system of electronic inventions. Let us begin with the camera. A black and white, or monochrome, television camera (much of this applies to color cameras, which I will come to) has built into it an electron tube which, on its faceplate, has a photoconductive layer of chemicals arranged in 367,000 microscopic but individual dots. The lens of the camera focuses the image it is aimed at—let us say it is you—onto this photoconductive layer.

You are read by the photoconductive layer, each dot of which gives off an individual electrical charge. These charges vary in strength depending on the amount of light hitting each dot. The more light, the stronger the electrical charge in the dot. In other words, if your hair is dark, those dots on which the lens has focused your hair will produce weaker electrical charges than those which are reading the white shirt you may be wearing.

The varied electrical charges in the dots of the photoconductive layer establish themselves as a mosaic of gradations from black-black to white-white. This range from black to white is known as the tonal scale, or the gray scale.

At the base, or back, of the electron tube there is an electron gun which shoots a beam of electrons at the rear side of the mosaic and reads, or scans, it. The electron gun fires simply by getting hot, which creates the ability to throw off electrons. These electrons are shaped into a beam.

The beam is aimed or controlled by wire coils which surround the electron tube and create magnetic fields. These magnetic fields steer the beam from left to right (horizontally) and from top to bottom (vertically). The beam moves over the dots in this configuration and translates the variations of electrical charges it sees in the dots into variations (in frequency) of electrical voltage output. This electrical output is known as the camera's video signal.

In North American television, the beam scans 525 horizontal lines of the photoconductive layer of dots. The beam scans in a pattern beginning at top left which then goes left to right, top to bottom, through all of the odd-numbered lines. When it reaches bottom right, it goes back to scan or trace all the even-numbered lines, right to left, bottom to top. This alternate horizontal line scan system is called interlacing, and it happens sixty times a second. Each complete scan, or picture, is called a frame and there are thirty frames per second.

Having been hit by the beam of the electron gun, the individual dot gives up its charge to the beam and creates a new charge, that is, reads the next impression it receives from you, your hair, or whatever is focused toward it by the lens.

Converted now into a video signal, or electrical output, the picture travels via cables in a directed manner toward receivers, tape machines, control rooms, whatever; a live picture would travel directly to the stations' transmitter and antenna and be put into the air. When the video signal does go into the air, it is caught by a receiving antenna, fed into a television set, or receiver, and translated back into a picture in a process that reverses what I have just described. That is, the video signal is translated by a receiving electron gun which shoots it at the back of a photoconductive surface on the home screen and puts it back into dots of light and shadow. Again, there are 525 horizontal lines of dots. The afterimage retention factor in the picture tube and in the human eye make it appear, not as flickering dots, but as a series of whole and stable, though moving, pictures; this effect is also active in film motion pictures.

In color cameras (and receivers) there are three electron guns—blue, green, and red—instead of one, and the photoconductive layer is treated with phosphorous particles of blue, green, and red.

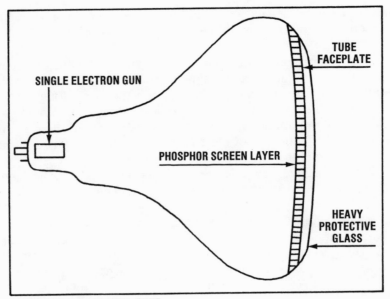

MONOCHROME PICTURE TUBE

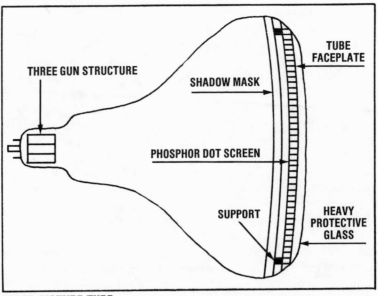

COLOR PICTURE TUBE

Television pictures are transmitted through the air on assigned bands in the radio frequency spectrum. In the United States and Canada, these are 6MHz in width. (M is megacycles and Hz is the internationally used symbol for cycles per second. It is named in honor of Heinrich Rudolph Herz, a German physicist, who discovered how to rapidly vary electrical current so as to put it into the air as waves.)

The channels on your set numbered 2 through 13 are located on the spectrum between 54 and 216 MHz and are defined as VHF (very high frequency) bands. (Channel 1 is assigned to land mobile or two-way radio users.) When more television stations were wanted, thus creating the need for more channels, additional bands of the radio spectrum, UHF (ultra high frequency) were allocated to television. UHF uses frequencies from 470 to 884 MHz. These appear on your set as channels 14 to 83. Picture, chrominance, or color, and audio are all carried in each band of 6MHz width. Each 6MHz width equals one channel. The video signal portion of a channel uses 4.5MHz of the 6MHz width. Sound uses 0.75MHz. Color uses 1.5MHz in an overlap with video.

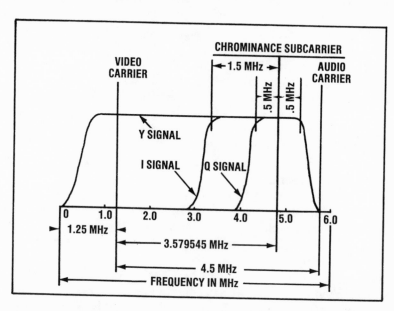

As color transmission was perfected, a system of color compatability was required to insure that black and white receivers would not be outmoded and that black and white material could be received on color sets. This color compat system was achieved technically by RCA in the United States and was adopted in 1953 as the national standard by the Federal Communications Commission, on industry recommendation by the National Television System Committee.

All of the technical information that follows will perhaps be outmoded before you read it. Generally, however, the principles will remain.

ELECTRONIC CAMERAS: Mostly, you will encounter electronic cameras made by three major manufacturers—RCA, Norelco (Phillips), and Fernseh. The trend in design and manufacture for all is toward miniaturization and compactness. The cameras are getting more portable and they are capable of acceptable picture quality with less light and they are also capable of more stable color.

RCA is offering two models currently: a Type TK-44B, which is a descendant of the first color camera to dominate the American market. The TK-44B is twice as light-sensitive as its predecessor and can shoot at under one hundred foot-candles (as low as five foot-candles, it is claimed) without video lag, depth of field loss, or picture noise. It is designed for studio or field use. It is not a hand-held camera.

The RCA TK-630 is less expensive, lighter in weight, trimmer in line, and not quite as complex or deluxe. It, too, is sold as a studio/field camera, though it is probably best for the field. It cannot be hand-held. Both cameras are equipped with ten to one zoom lenses with manual zoom control (it can be equipped with electric zooms) and twist grip handles to follow focus. If the smallest image area which the zoom lens is capable of producing is "one," then the largest image area will be ten times larger.

Norelco's studio/field camera is a PC-100A. It has a built-in zoom lens and uses the new, thin triaxial cable. It, too, can work in low-light situations. With Plumbicon tubes, it is particularly adept at eliminating video lag, or comet-tailing, as it is also called. Video lag is particularly noticeable in panning shots, where color seems to bleed or leave tails from one image as the scene goes on to a new image.

The Norelco PCP-90B, while it can be mounted on a pedestal or tripod, is most desirable for its hand-held capability. The PCP-90 is currently the most popular hand-held video camera in the country. When it is working on triax cable, the camera weighs only eighteen pounds. The PCP-90 can operate in conjunction with a self-contained battery backpack or can transmit, without cable, live by microwave feed.

Fernseh makes a range of video cameras, but the one that I particularly like is the KCR-40 which is the closest electronic camera yet to the 16mm hand-held film camera in terms of weight and mobility—and, of course, it gives you instantly replayable pictures, eliminating the costly and time-consuming laboratory processing which film requires. *This is the future.* The KCR-40 fits snugly over a cameraman's shoulder and can work in a self-contained backpack setup or on cable runs up to three hundred feet for quarter-inch cable, or twenty-five hundred feet for half-inch cable. The camera itself weighs eleven and a half pounds.

CBS is putting its faith in two new cameras: The Ikegami hand-held color camera which weighs twelve pounds, its support backpack twenty-two pounds. It can videotape record self-contained or transmit live. The other CBS order went for the Thompson CSF, a new lightweight, durable mounted field camera that weighs only eighty-eight pounds and works on half-inch triaxial cable on a maximum run of five thousand feet to the control truck. The traditional coaxial or multiwire cable is 1¼ inches in diameter. There are various pedestals, camera heads, tripods, lens mounts, and other accessories for all of these cameras.

VIDEOTAPE MACHINES—TWO INCH: The standard broadcast videotape is two inches wide and this tape is used for initial recording, final editing, and transmission. The machines are mostly from two manufacturers—RCA and Ampex. These days, I see the Ampex 2000 as the workhorse. The Ampex 2000 can take on a lot of sophisticated accessories—color corrector, drop out compensator, and so on—and is a high-fidelity band machine, or high-band, as it is called. High-band is merely a technical advance, in terms of better reproduction of material, over its forerunner machines, which are now called low band. It is a little like having gotten a stereo system to replace your phonograph.

The Ampex 2000's little brother is the Ampex 1200, used most frequently in remote trucks. The kid of the family is the Ampex 3000, a backpack videotape machine designed for use with a hand-held video camera, that can record up to twenty minutes per reel. While it records in color, it can play back in the field only in black and white.

VIDEOTAPE—TWO INCH: The most commonly used professional broadcast tape is two inches wide and on its coated side—coated with magnetic oxide particles—can be stimulated electronically to store electrical pulses and give them back as picture and sound. The dominant manufacturer is the 3M Company. The content of videotape can be erased—this is called burning—and it can be used about a thousand times before serious deterioration sets in. This process is also called degausing (pronounced like "housing").

VIDEOTAPE EDITING: Manual edits of videotape that is, physically cutting the tape, may be made, and still occasionally are, but the more common and more desirable way is electronic editing. In its simplest form, electronic editing requires two tape machines. One to record and one to play back. On the record machine, you set up a tape (crystal black, ideally) which will become your edited master. On the playback machine you are setting up and knocking down various other tapes which contain the recorded material you want to assemble into one final program on the edited master. In this two machine setup, you cannot dissolve or fade in and out between scenes or elements. Only straight cut edits are possible.

It is best to have a third machine—a second playback machine and a switcher. This will permit you to *A* and *B* edit and to make dissolves and fades. In some editing rooms, there is a switcher built in. Other setups require going through a control room to get a switcher capability.

Let me take you through the first part of the electronic editing of one of my "Great American Dream Machine" shows. We used to assemble the shows at Teletronics in New York City. We had the three-machine setup with a built-in switcher capacity. Also, we had a vidicom camera that could super in graphics and titles. In this particular show, I had at least thirty different pieces of material that had to be assembled into one show. This assembly process was actually a final edit session. I had taken much of the material—the major stories at least—through pre-edits. Many of the segments had been edited first on film and then transferred to tape. Many of the tape pieces—shot stop-and-start—had been pre-edited to make finished packages. When I had these packages ready for the final assembly edit, they were all on videotape, but they were on a lot of different pieces of videotape.

Again, we set up our record machine tape (crystal black) which would become our edited master. (An edited master is one generation down from the original master. The original master is that piece of tape on which an image is initially recorded. Since I had taken some of my video pieces through a pre-edit; that material would now be third generation when it got to the edited master.) The editor lay on bars and tone. He set the digital read-out at zero hours, minutes, seconds, frames. On playback machine number one, the editors put up the take that had the NET (National Educational Television) logo on it. This piece of tape ran five seconds, with an open end for fading or dissolving. On playback machine number two, we put up the second piece of tape material I wanted to go into the show. I liked to open my "Dream Machines" with fast comedy blackouts—cold openers—before going into the show's main titles. For this show I had found an actor named Jan Leighton, who was a dead ringer for George

Washington. He dressed in a powdered wig, satin breeches, and all. Shooting with an electronic camera, I placed him as the Father of Our Country before a full-length mirror in a television studio, looking mighty pleased with himself, and after a bit, breaking into song: "You've got the cool, clear eyes of a seeker of wisdom and truth—I believe in you!" (Frank Loesser's song from *How to Succeed in Business*).* Then, into the main titles. The editors rehearsed the sequence. It would be an *A* and *B* edit; that is, taking a piece from playback one—*A*—and joining it to a piece from playback two—*B*—without stopping. The sequence required a fade-in on the NET logo, a fade-out of it, a fade-in on George Washington, a cut out of it, so that when the next edit of the main titles came, it would come in as a smash cut and give George Washington a black-out ending.

The editor set the cue mark where he wanted the incoming material to hit on the tape. He gave this number to the editor on playback machine number one, who then set his machine accordingly, and the same for the editor on playback machine number two. Now each editor backed up his machine ten seconds to allow the rolling machines to get up to speed and lock picture. The editor on the record machine first rehearsed the edit by simulation in the rehearsal mode, that is, we could view the edit without it actually being recorded. If all of us looked at it and it worked, we went back to the original marks and this time recorded. When the editor hit the record button, the record machine went forward; at the right moment, playback machine number one rolled and—in this case—on my call, the editor, using the switcher, faded in the picture from playback machine number one. There was the NET logo. The editor watched for his digital read-out to hit five seconds. I watched the monitor. At five seconds (and a feel of it), I called for a fade out. Playback machine number two had already been activated and on its preview monitor, we could see George Washington just before the point we wanted to take him. I called fade in two, and the feed from that machine—George Washington—was being laid onto the tape on the record machine. When it got to the end, or the point that I thought should be the end, I said, "Cut" and the editor hit the edit point button. This does not erase anything, since I might have missed "the magic moment," but it does lay down an audio edit cue on the control track of the videotape. You can, as an option, just stop recording and make the fine edit point later when you rehearse this outgoing scene against the next incoming scene. In

---

*"I Believe in You," by Frank Loesser © 1961 Frank Music Corp. All Rights Reserved. Used by permission.

any case, when you have finished your edit, you stop recording. You roll back on the record machine and then play it forward again to see if the edited material has gone together the way you want it to. If it has, you go on to the next edit. If it has not, you go back and do it again, making the adjustments as you think necessary.

In this case, we went on. We knocked down the tapes—NET logo on playback one and George Washington on playback two—and put up the next two pieces of tape that were to go into the show. On playback one we put up the main title tape of the "Dream Machine" and on playback two we put up the pre-edited tape of a production number which featured a chorus of singers dressed as various American types. They were singing the title song, the "Great American Dream Machine," written by Steve Katz of "Blood, Sweat and Tears." The process here was similar to what I have described, except that between George Washington and the main titles I wanted a straight cut and between the main titles and the chorus piece I wanted a dissolve, so when we got to that point we needed to use the switcher again. Proceeding this way, it took us one eight-hour day to assemble a sixty-minute show, even though I always know before going into an edit session the order in which I want pieces assembled and which effects I want to use.

TIME CODE: This is an electronic pulse laid down on videotape that can be translated into a visual read-out of frames, seconds, minutes, and hours, and which is stored on the tape itself. If you have logged the time-code numbers of particular scenes, ins, outs, cuts, actions, and what-have-yous, you can go to these points quickly by referring to the visual read-out or character generator. Ideally, time code should be put onto the tapes at the time of original recording. It can be added later.

Time code has given rise to the invention of CMX and other computerized editing systems. In CMX, all of the various materials for assembly are stored in a bank of one-inch tapes on machines. By referring to the time-code numbers and hitting appropriate buttons on a console panel, these scenes are instantly retrievable. All of the edit choices are punched into a computer tape rather than actually edited. This computer tape is later played back and orders the two-inch video-tape machines to start, stop, start, and keep in effects. Everything is assembled into the edited master automatically—while you are out having a martini.

With the advent of one-inch, three-quarter-inch, and half-inch tape and tape machines, many producers transfer their original two-inch material to one of these narrower widths and do their initial editing on it, later conforming their two-inch material. This saves considerable expense, since two-inch editing costs anywhere from $100 to $300 an hour. One-inch (or three-quarter-inch or half-inch) is particularly advisable when one must play with edits, as in unscripted documentaries, for example. This is frequently referred to as slant-track editing.

Another thing you should be aware of: You can strip or erase audio from a tape, while maintaining picture. Conversely, you can keep the audio portion and strip or erase video or picture. This is good when you want to add voice-over or similar audio effects to a picture or you want to put in cut away pictures without losing the audio portion.

Following are a few more brief explanations of some of the terms which will also be useful for you to know when dealing with the electronic media:

AUDIO TRACK: That portion of the two-inch tape which carries sound. The audio track is divided into two main parts: the program track, which carries the audio content of the recorded material; and the control track, which carries a synchronous electric pulse which locks audio to video. A second portion of the Program Track is called the cue track, which is used to record electronic cue marks for editing, or for slates—identification of content. The cue track can also be used for lesser level audio recording separable from the material recorded on a program track—audience reaction, for example.

BANDING: Caused by oversaturating colors which break down the picture so that you begin to see horizontal bars.

BREAKUP: When the picture falls apart. Can run from minor to massive.

CHROME KEY: An electronic matting device. Removal of one of the three colors from a camera's guns, let's say blue—so that when the camera is aimed at a blue area, it will read it as black. This black area may then be filled by the visual information from another camera. You see this mostly on the news—when the commentator is sitting in front of, say, a raging forest fire. Actually he is sitting in front of, say, a blue panel, and the forest fire is coming from the feed of another camera, probably a telecine film chain.

COLOR BARS: You will see these a lot, and they have nothing to do with Apartheid. Color bars are electronically produced vertical stripes of red, green, blue, cyan, magenta, and yellow, plus black and white. They are made by a color bar generator which can make these colors by shifting the phase of the 3.5MHz frequency in a timed sequence pattern. You can get yellow, for instance, by a shift of 12 degrees or red by a shift of 76.5 degrees— and so on. Color bars are used as a means of adjusting color encoders, tape machines, picture monitors, and receivers, to achieve a single standard of color.

CRYSTAL BLACK: Obtained by passing a videotape through a recording machine and recording only black on it, establishing a solid synchronous signal (the crystal) on to the tape. This is to smooth out the tape (electronically) and minimize any irregularities which may be in it.

DC POWER: Direct current power—all television cameras and machines run on it.

DEGAUSING: Removing any magnetizing that may have gathered on videotape (and consequently, all prerecorded audio and video information is erased).

DROP OUT: Dots of the picture drop out and appear as white dots or spots. This can be caused by faulty oxides on the tape, by a dirty recording or playback head on the tape machine, by recording head tip penetration of the tape stock.

EDIOPHOR: This is an electronic system which provides a technique for blowing up electronic television pictures to larger, direct projection screen size. The ediophor can be used as front or rear screen projection and can project any video source: the output of another camera, a videotape playback, slides, film, remotes.

ELECTRIC GENERATOR: A direct-powered electric plant used to supply power in the field or at remote locations when it is impossible or too expensive, because of the long cable run, to tie into a local utility power system. Generators are usually noisy and must be parked at a considerable distance from any microphones. (Also used for film).

ESU: Engineering setup. This is the period in which the video man fires up the cameras and makes certain that they are balanced or matched with the same electronic signal strength—so that color and luminance are the same in each camera.

GEN LOCK: An electronic device for locking all elements in one facility or operation into one stable source of regulated pulses. Without it, you get picture roll-over.

NOISE: This is video noise, caused by peaking white levels which cause graininess, or loss of picture detail.

OFF-LINE EDITING: Various systems—slant track, Sony, one-inch, half-inch.

ON-LINE EDITING: Editing on two-inch system.

OUT OF PHASE: Can apply to a camera, a tape machine, a monitor.

It means that when you see it, color is not balanced with the other elements in the system. The color is not true. Back to the vectorscope to set it right.

SWEETENING: This term is used to describe the final audio composite mixing of a videotape program: Where dialogue, narration, applause, balanced music, train whistles, gunshots, laughter, bird calls, wind, rain, and the voice of the turtle are all blended together. The equipment to accomplish this feat is called a McKenzie cartridge machine. The McKenzie is loaded with all the needed effects each on its own library, or stock, cartridge or on especially prepared cartridges. The McKenzie comes as a basic five holer; multiples can be added as needed—ten or twenty holers.

SYNC GENERATOR: An electronic device which governs the electronic beams in cameras, videotape machines, and TV receivers to stay in step. It does this via a steady stream of timed and shaped electrical pulses.

TONE: Tone is laid onto videotape to do for sound what color bars do for video. Tone is also used as a cue device, when you are editing or fast-forwarding, to alert you to when you have arrived at the next take.

VECTORSCOPE: A round oscilloscope—it is green—to show the video man what the color phase relationships are compared to the phase reference. Each color can be determined by comparing it to the phase reference in degrees of rotation.

VIDICON: The small stationary cameras used in telecine chains. External vidicons can be mounted in a studio or postproduction setup to shoot graphics, title cards, or other insert material. Vidicons are usually preset and unmanned.

VIEW FINDER: The small picture screen in the rear of an electronic camera which the cameraman looks at to determine picture composition and luminance. This screen is always in black and white, so the cameraman does not make value judgments—and changes—in color.

VIEW-FINDER SHIELD, OR SCREEN: A protective brim which shades the view finder and keeps out light reflections or distortions. Its ancestor is the black cloth which early still photographers put over their heads.

VTR: Videotape recording.

WAVE FORM: A correct video signal is a wave form of precise characteristic with standard black level and peak white level. This can be read on a wave-form monitor that has a graph face on it, with an outline of the proper wave form. It also shows the sync pulse. The video man matches his wave form to the one shown on the graph face.

All right. That is some of what I know or can explain and really all one needs to know about electronic television to get started or to begin to appreciate how little one does know. If you feel you have to know more, you will find it, and you will probably be better off as an engineer or technician than a program maker. For the time being, you have learned enough to get yourself in trouble.

FILM

In television there is no direct projection of film. Film is used as a subsidiary technique that is always converted to electronic material and transmitted electronically. However, film is used extensively as an original shooting form in television and it represents nearly half of the three commercial networks' programming output.

Film is converted to electronic images via a system called telecine. In a telecine setup there is a film projector, but instead of the film being focused onto a screen, it is directed at a specially designed television camera called a vidicon, which is locked into a stationary unit. The vidicon camera reads the film much as does an ordinary television camera. Usually, though, this process is more sophisticated, with the single electronic camera in the telecine chain able, through an arrangement of optics—mirrors really—to take the feed of two film projectors and one or more slide chains. This setup is called a multiplexer. There are thirty-five mm film and slide telecine chains and sixteen mm film telecine chains. (Sound is converted in a similar manner, as we will learn later.)

Once the film has been converted by the telecine process, it can be aired or it can be transferred to videotape and aired later. These days, the networks transfer all film material—programs, theatrical motion pictures, and commercials—to videotape before airing them.

Because there are different tolerances and densities of light and color between film and electronics, the telecine chain is set up for the maximum and minimum of white and black levels of electronic video. The telecine attempts to compress the film densities into the tolerable electronic range. On a straight transfer of film to electronic tape, there are usually terrible distortions of color and picture definition. These can be minimized by a color corrector or through step-transferring. A color corrector is an electronic device which alters the film/video differences so that the truer colors of the original film are maintained or more closely approximated in the video. Step-transfers require more stop-and-start and have a more arbitrary system of correction.

Each film scene is tabbed for its maximum transfer truth, as judged by a technician who assigns it a number on a staircase slide that calls for a range from maximum to minimum color value and light density.

The best way to get good film to video transfers is for the film to be shot originally within the known light and color tolerances of video. This, of course, works best in controlled filming situations, but is frequently undesirable or impossible in news or documentary situations.

Aside from this exposure control problem, all film equipment that has been designed and used for direct projection film making is used for the making of films for television.

The two most universally used film widths and technologies are 35mm and 16mm, which describes the width of the original film stock: 35mm is thirty-five milimeters wide; 16mm is sixteen milimeters wide.

Since 35mm is a larger canvas, so to speak, it provides more picture detail and clarity. Less definition of image is provided by 16mm, but it has its own advantages in terms of portability of the equipment used to shoot and lower cost factors in each step of production.

Both 35mm and 16mm are normally exposed and projected at twenty-four frames a second, the standard speed acceptable to the human eye, and they are driven by sixty-cycle motors (in Europe it is twenty-five frames a second with fifty-cycle motors) to achieve natural motion. By varying the motor speed to more than twenty-four frames a second—overcranking—you can achieve the slow-motion effect. By varying the motor speed to less than twenty-four frames a second—undercranking—you can achieve the fast-motion effect, similar to the old silent movies. In 35mm, sixteen frames are exposed in every foot of film and ninety feet of 35mm film are one minute of playing time. In 16mm, forty frames are exposed in every foot and thirty-six feet of 16mm film are one minute of playing time. Thus, a half-hour 35mm film is twenty-seven hundred feet long; a half-hour 16mm film is a thousand and eighty feet long.

Every motion picture camera actually takes still pictures. This still picture is called a frame. It is the rapidity with which the shutter opens and closes, and the film starts, stops in the aperture opening, and starts again that provides the illusion of motion (coupled with the persistence of vision factor).

Film is perforated (sprocket holes) on either one side (single perf) or on both outer edges (double perf). These perforations are used to move the film through all stages—original manufacture, in the camera, in the labs, in the editing process, in projection. In the motion picture camera the film is pulled along by claws and it is held in place during its stop—one frame at a time at the aperture opening—by pilot pins. These pilot pins control the vertical stability of the film. The film is held in a steady flat plane by two plates which keep it from wobbling or flapping. These are called the aperture plate and the pressure plate. The aperture plate backs the film. The pressure plate closes over the opposite or part side of the film. Here is where most film negative scratching takes place. Scratching can be caused by faulty or worn plates, but it is frequently the result of dirty plates, that is, emulsion particles from former film running between the plates have created a build-up which then rubs or scratches against the currently running film. (Insist that your cameraman clean these plates each time he loads a new roll of film.)

Loops above and below the aperture, or picture window, are required to compensate for the fact that the same piece of film is running at different speeds when it is at different points within the camera. This is called intermittent motion. It is going very fast when it is controlled by the pull-down device, which positions the individual frame for the stop at the aperture opening. When that frame has been exposed, the pull-down device quickly removes that frame and positions the next. The slower speed is the sprocket motion. In a straight-line motion and speed, without the slack which loops provide, the film would tear, be unsteady, or simply blur. Loops that are too small tear the film. Loops that are too large wobble the film, and thus the picture.

Film, called raw stock in its unexposed form, has a base side and an emulsion side. The base side is the translucent foundation material —plastic—called cellulose acetate. The emulsion side is a layer of chemicals which is photosensitive and stores the latent image which the lens has focused on it when the film is exposed. These latent images are later made visible by the development and printing process. Black and white film, generally, has a single layer emulsion consisting of silver-halide crystals which alter when exposed to light. In development these latent images are turned into visible images through an alteration of black and silver grains in the emulsion.

Color film emulsions have three layers of photosensitive chemicals to produce the basic colors—red, green, and blue.

There are two basic types of film stock—reversal and negative. Reversal film produces positive images after the first lab process and is good for news situations, for instance, where quick airing is important and where the original film will be projected or only a few prints will be needed. Negative film is nearly always used in 35mm feature work, and in 16mm where immediate projection is not required and larger numbers of prints are needed. Negative film must go through additional lab processes before producing a positive image, but it does have much sharper definition and better color resolution. It has more grain and it requires more light. The speed of film defines its sensitivity to light and is expressed by an assigned number. The faster the speed of the film (fast film or slow film), the less light is required to get an acceptable, or truthful, image.

There are many film stocks designed for various specific purposes; these stocks can sometimes be altered by the use of filters in the lenses. You must consult the manufacturer, supply house, or other experts for advice as to which type will best serve your particular purpose on a particular job. (Eastman Kodak is very responsive in providing this information.) Incidentally, when you are purchasing raw stock, buy it direct from Kodak rather than supply houses, which add a mark-up cost.

CAMERAS: Most of the cameras today are reflex type. This means that what you are seeing through the eyepiece is what the lens is seeing. Earlier cameras had eyepieces which offered a parallax view; roughly, what you saw was parallel to—and dangerously unlike—what the camera lens was seeing. Reflex view is achieved through a mirroring effect which bounces off the shutter blades to a ground glass positioned so that the distance light must travel between it and the lens is the same as the distance light must travel between the lens and the film.

In 33mm film production the most frequently encountered cameras are made by the Mitchell Company. The standard 35mm studio camera is the Mitchell NC reflex camera. It is encased to run silently (blimped) for sound shooting and has a turret mount for four different lenses. The film magazine is external and fits onto the top of the camera.

Its cousin, the Mitchell BNC, is also blimped, but has a single-lens bayonet mount instead of the four-lens turret. Both of these cameras must work off a power source, rather than a battery.

Arriflex makes a range of 35mm cameras. One that is effective for hand-held shooting is the 2C/B model. It has a three-lens turret or it can take a single-lens bayonet mount, and it has a quick-change modular magazine capability in two-hundred- or four-hundred-foot rolls. This camera is not silenced, however, and must be enclosed in an extra Arriflex sound blimp for synchronous sound recording. It can be battery operated. Variations and accessories are epidemic, as with most cameras and manufacturers.

The most advanced models in 35mm for mounted and/or hand-held use are the Mitchell MKIII and the Arriflex 35BL. The MKIII weighs twenty-two pounds without the lens, runs quietly for sound takes, has a variable-speed motor which can run at eight, sixteen, twenty-four, twenty-five, twenty-eight, or thirty-two frames per second, with either a fifty- or sixty-cycle motor or on a battery. It has a cable synchronizing signal for sound recordings, but it can also run synchronous sound without a cable (on sixty cycles), and it slates by fogging a few frames of the film and sending simultaneously a radio beep signal to the sound recorder. The magazine attachment is a modular design for preloading and fits to the camera externally by a spring release bayonet lock. It can handle only four-hundred-foot magazine loads (4.4 minutes of film). It has a lens mount to accommodate various lens sizes. It can come with an electric zoom device built into the left-hand grip.

The Arriflex 35BL, with motor and four-hundred-foot magazine, weighs about twenty-five pounds. It has a rather good self-blimping for sound takes, a twelve-volt DC motor which can vary from ten to one hundred frames per second at fifty or sixty cycles, and it can be battery powered. It slates automatically without umbilical cord for cordless sync sound, and can handle four-hundred- or one-thousand-foot magazines. Of course, it has a reflex view finder and can be fitted with various lenses.

In 16mm, I have worked on a variety of films that used at least eight different makes of camera: Eclair, Arriflex, Bolex, Beaulieu, Auricon, Cannon, Bell & Howell, and Frezzolini. I have worked mostly with the Eclair and think of it as an old and trusted friend.

The traditional Eclair is the prototype Eclair NPR which came onto the market in 1961 and did a hero's work in making 16mm respectable. There is now a new, improved NPR on the market. It is self-blimped with quick-change modular magazine loading (an Eclair innovation) which holds four hundred feet, or about eleven minutes; it can work mounted, but it became a star as a hand-held camera. Because of its design, most of the camera weight is balanced on the cameraman's shoulder, with the motor fitting against him as would a rifle butt. This relieves the extraordinary muscle tension and fatigue that are endemic to most hand-held cameras and, in fact, it frees the hands for focus changes and zoom work. The Eclair NPR's standard motor is constant-speed at twenty-four frames per second and it employs a sync pulse system which requires a sync cable, or umbilical, between the camera and the sound recorder. As an option, you can get a universal crystal control motor that allows you to shoot without a cable between camera and recorder and at variable speeds or frames per second, from one to forty.

The view finder has a full-aperture frame line built into it and within this, a TV cutoff; that is to say, you can see by this engraved frame line what portions of the image will actually be seen on a home screen, which always cuts off the outer perimeter of the actual television image.

The Eclair NPR, usually equipped with an Angenieux 12 to 120 zoom lens, does have a two-position lens turret: a Camerette bayonet-type mount to handle heavy, wide-angle, and zoom lenses and the standard C mount. The NPR can run off a power source or on battery. Again, there are numerous additional features and options.

The newest model is the Eclair ACL, which weighs in at seven pounds, seven ounces—its chief claim to fame. It is well suited for those situations in which you want to be unobtrusive or maintain a low profile. The ACL also has quick-change modular magazine design and can handle film loads of two hundred feet (about 5.5 minutes) or four hundred feet. The lens mount is a threaded C that can take a variety of lenses. The camera is self-blimped and its standard motor is crystal control which allows cordless sync sound recording and is constant-speed, twenty-four frames per second. The standard battery weighs just over a pound, can run for an hour of filming without being recharged, and will fit into a back pants pocket. There are any number of accessories.

Arriflex makes three 16mm models: The 16 S/B, the 16 M/B, and the 16 BL.

The 16 S/B is a mirror-shutter reflex camera with a one-hundred-foot internal film load capability, which is best suited for silent filming. It is designed for interchangeable motors which can run on power supply or battery. The 16 S/B can accommodate two-hundred- or four-hundred-foot external magazines, but these still must be blimped for noiseless sound takes. The camera weighs five pounds, fourteen ounces. It has a three-lens turret mount.

The 16 M/B has all of the features of the 16 S/B, but has only an external magazine capacity with loads up to twelve hundred feet. It, too, must be blimped for sync sound recording. The accessory system is copious and extends to animation, time-lapse, and micros-copy capability.

The Arriflex 16BL has all of the fine design features of the 16 S/B and 16 M/B but adds self-blimped sound recording capability as its foremost feature, with external modular magazine (four hundred feet) loading. I am not sure, but my educated hunch is that this camera is a direct competetive response to the Eclair. The Arriflex 16BL has a universal lens housing, but was made primarily to handle zoom lenses. It can be fitted with a range of motors, constant speed and variable speed (one to forty frames per second), and is capable of fifty or sixty cycles and cordless sync sound. It weighs sixteen pounds, four ounces, with lens and magazine. Here, too, accessories and optional features are manifold.

Auricon, which makes several models, has traditionally been famous for its single-system camera used for newsreel sync sound. Single system means that the sound is recorded on the film—that is, a magnetic sound recording stripe is built right onto the edge of the film itself and the microphone plugs directly into the camera. At first, this seems easier and more sensible. But you will realize shortly why single system is mostly not desirable. The Auricon is motor driven off either power supply or battery. It has a lens turret but is used most frequently with ten to one zoom lenses.

While Bolex and Bell & Howell make motor-driven cameras—and again in a maddening array of types and accessories—they are mostly thought of for their spring-wind (yes, you wind them up manually) models. The Bolex H16 Rex 5 is widely used for one-hundred-foot (can handle four-hundred-foot) loads for silent shooting or wild shooting. It is a three-lens turret reflex camera that has variable-speed capability from twelve to sixty-four frames per second and it is popular as a stop-action or single-frame camera.

The Bell & Howell work horse is the 70DR spring-drive motor: seven speeds from eight to sixty-four frames per second; three-lens turret. It is most often used by newsreel cameramen—silent and on one-hundred-foot loads.

LENSES: The lens of the camera functions essentially as its eye, both in electronic and film cameras. No lens made, of course, is as flexible or as well-engineered as our human eyes. In every manufactured lens there are compromises and limitations. Thus, a range of lenses has been built, first to simulate the various ways we see ordinarily and then to achieve certain abnormal but highly effective ways of seeing.

I will not attempt a complete description of lenses or optics here. I simply will try to describe some fundamentals to provide you with a basic comprehension of how and why they work.

A camera lens is made up of several elements, chief among them the arrangement of convex and concave curvatures of optical glass, which have varying refractive (light-bending) powers. These are contained in what is called a barrel. Lenses also have built into them an iris, or diaphragm, which can be externally manipulated to allow more or less light to pass through. Nowadays they have antireflective coatings (thin layers of transparent magnesium fluoride) which are designed to reduce reflected light.

Since the canvas—16mm or 35mm film size, for example—always remains the same, it is the relationship between the focal length of the lens and its aperture size (how much light is let in) that determines a lens's aperture speed; the focal length of a lens also determines its range of view (the human eye can see along an arc of 120 degrees), its depth of field, and its magnifying power.

In 35mm, lenses with focal lengths in the 25 to 35mm range are wide-angle, 40 to 50mm lenses are normal (normal being roughly how we would see the object at the same distance and angle with our own eyes), and 75 to 500mm are long lenses, or telephoto.

A lens perceives objects circularly; the film frame is a rectangle within that circle. Thus, there is always some image cutoff between what the lens sees and what is shown to the film. Since a diagonal line drawn across the frame rectangle is also the diameter of the lens circle (if the line were extended), the length of the diagonal determines the magnification of the lens at any given focal length.

Since 16mm frames are approximately half the diameter of 35mm frames, wide-angle lenses in 16mm are in the range of 12 to 18mm; normal, 20 to 25mm; and telephoto, 35 to 250—with more dramatic telephotoing the higher up you go.

No lens has a perfect plane of focus, though this has been practically assumed and established because our eyes will forgive small distortions, which even the finest lenses have. The depth of focus of a lens, then, is defined as twice the distance the film can be moved from the perfect plane of focus before points on the image become noticeably blurred.

The focal length of a lens is noted as f and it is followed by a number to indicate what that length is: $f/2$, $f/11$, and so on. This f-stop is commonly used to measure the speed (how much light comes in) of a lens. An $f/2$, for example, allows four times the light of an $f/4$ stop. (It is an inverse measurement.) Thus, the more external light available, the smaller your $f/$number stop must be. Standard $f/$number stops are 1.4, 2, 2.8, 4, 5.6, 8, 11—and sometimes 16, 22, and 32.

Depth of field in a lens means the relative sharpness of focus over the entire image, especially at points closer and farther away than the object being focused upon.

Aimed at a fixed point from a fixed distance, different lenses will provide different sizes of images on the film frame. You must know the size of the image you want in order to pick the right lens. For one instance, in the "American Life Style" series, I was nearly always confronted with filming in large rooms and I wanted to establish in the audiences' eyes and in their emotions a sense of the imposing space of these rooms. The camera position might be a hundred feet away from the opposite end of a room and might have to encompass lateral widths of twenty-five feet on either side. This required, of course, extensive use of wide-angle lenses—an Angenieux 5.9 mostly—in order to embrace this feeling of granduer. The 5.9 was not so wide-angle, however, that it caused a disturbing linear distortion (unless the host, E. G. Marshall, got very close to the camera), as would a fish-eye lens. Of course, I also wanted to show the art objects or pieces of furniture in the rooms in more detail, so we would change to more normal size lenses for these shots. Frequently, to save time and money, we would keep the wide-angle camera setup, put on a telephoto lens, and be able to see an object in close-up detail that might be fifty or seventy-five feet away.

Lenses can play a powerful role in the aesthetics of filming—in making editorial story points, in deliniating character, and in stirring emotions. You can establish a villian quickly by distorting him close-up with a wide-angle lens or you can emphasize the beauty of a young heroine by shooting her telephoto, so that everything around her is in soft focus and she becomes the center of the universe.

The choice of lens is also affected by the distance from which you want to or must shoot. If you are at a presidential press conference for instance and are trapped a long way from the president, you will obviously need a long, or telephoto, lens to get a close-up.

It is the relationship of the values between image size, focal points, and distance that must determine the lens choice. If you are producing or directing, make sure that you have discussed fully with your cameraman the look and the emotional feel you hope to evoke in particular scenes. He can then choose the appropriate lenses and distances between camera and object to achieve what you want.

Some rough rules of guidance: (1) Wide-angle lenses show a wider degree of a scene and present everything in the frame in relative focus. They have more linear distortion. (2) Normal lenses encompass a smaller area and begin to lose focal definition in depth (but in relatively mild linear distortion) out from the epicenter of the frame. (3) Long, or telephoto, lenses provide sharp central focus, but have blurred foreground and background detail. Overall, the wider the lens is, the greater will be the depth of field; and the longer the lens, the shallower the depth of field.

ZOOM LENSES: Zoom lenses provide within one lens the ability to change focal length even during shooting, although it is usually necessary to change your f/number stop as you go. This is called follow focus. They come in varying focal lengths—minimums and maximums. The zoom lens can be operated manually by moving a handle or turning a crank that is attached to it, or it can be operated automatically by an electric zoom control which you activate by pressing a button provided with it.

The zoom lens was an aesthetic Caliban at first and was frowned upon by structured film and television makers. Now, however, through frequent use, it has established its own aesthetics. Most of us have developed a taste for it, even in the middle of shots, and certainly we have reaped the practical benefits of it for eliminating multiple setups for close, medium, and wide shots, thus cutting both shooting and editing time. In the beginning, it was used mostly by low-budget film makers or electronic program makers. It has been extremely valuable for coverage of one-take situations—sports, news, or documentary events. In planned shots, moreover, the zoom lens can achieve surprise and declarative editorial viewpoints. For its electronic cameras, ABC recently has purchased fifteen Varotal sixteen to one R, zoom lenses—eight for 30mm format cameras and seven for Norelco PC-100A cameras. The Varotal lens has a viewing angle of from 30 degrees to 0.7 degrees and a focal length that ranges from 22mm to 1,000mm. They are manufactured by Rank Precision Industries, Inc.

LIGHTING

As with cameras and lenses, lighting is scientific knowledge and application in pursuit of art. The quantity and quality of lighting in electronic television and film are essential ingredients for achieving satisfying audience viewing results. Lighting can affect emotional mood, altering our feelings from happy to sad to terrified, for instance, and can clarify or distort the meaning of content.

There are two types of light: sun and artificial. It is tricky, though possible, to mix them. Sunlight can vary widely, of course, in intensity and mood, but when people speak of it they generally mean what it is between two hours after sunrise to two hours before sunset. Cloud cover, overcast, geography, time of day, angle of scene, and so on, however, can all alter sunlight. You will need much more instruction and experience to really know how to use it.

There are two basic kinds of artificial light applications: spotlights and/or key lights; and floodlights or fill lights. Simply put, spots and keys are lights which are projected through lenses and thus are focused on a particular subject—person or object. Floods and fills are used to establish general illumination and mood in scene. Both categories come in various sizes and intensities of illumination.

There are four basic means of achieving artificial light: (1) A tungsten filament lamp which can range anywhere between a 100 watt inkie lightbulb to a 10,000 watt brute; (2) an overrun filament lamp, commonly known as a photoflood; (3) The arc lamp, which produces high intensity light by establishing an electrical current across the gap between two carbon rods; (4) The recently developed quartz crystal bulb, high intensity in a small package, and with a longer burn life. Lighting is powered by variously plugging into established power systems, by field generators, or by batteries.

Again, lights come in a diverse range of sizes and designs which to detail are beyond the purview of this book. Support accessories for lighting a show are also profuse—reflectors, relay boxes and circuits, silk screens, scrims (metal and fabric), cookies (for projecting various light patterns), barn doors, flags, filters, gels, stands, C clamps, Lowell attachments, reostats, miles of cable and gaffer tape, and on and on and on. There are entire books on lighting for electronic television and film production and you must seek them to know more.

Basically, a scene or subject should be lit from three sources: (1) front lighting, for general illumination; (2) back lighting, to provide separation of the subject from the background and to suggest dimension or depth; (3) slide lighting, to cast shadows which emphasize the relative shapes of objects and provide a more natural look.

Painting or sculpturing with light is a fusion of art and science. The best practitioner I know is a gentle and talented man named Imero Fiorentino who says about our business, "It is experience that matters, not tradition." I would want him or his consultation for any lighting I might need for a show—and, I would hope for all our sakes that he will write *the* book about lighting.

SOUND

Sound, unfortunately, is too often a low priority in the making of television programs; yet it plays a role virtually equal to that of the picture. If you do not believe me, turn the sound down and try to watch a television show without it. For a few moments, the novelty may be rewarding and you may even get a few laughs, but soon the picture becomes nearly meaningless (granted, many of them are in any case) without it. There is a considerable history in the evolution of sound technology that I am going to have to ignore. But I will describe the current technology in use.

In discussing electronic television, we have seen where the sound track actually fits onto the channel of the videotape; and you will recall that the real sound waves are either converted into immediately transmitted electrical impulses or stored through capture by magnetized oxides on the videotape for later transmission (although this is changing rapidly, with many programs now being recorded on separate sound tracks which are then mixed down to one track and then relaid onto the videotape).

In film production, sound is also converted into electrical impulses at certain stages and this is achieved by magnetic means, or by being photographed optically and printed on the edge of the frame next to the picture portion. When one of these composite optical prints is projected, the projector aperture is always smaller than the aperture of the frame; thus, the optical sound track is hidden from view. In many projectors it is possible to remove this aperture cutoff, called an academy mask, and see the sound. Every real sound makes its own characteristic visual pattern, since the translated electrical impulses vary in intensity and frequency and thus form different photographs. When this pattern is read by the sound bulb, or exciter bulb, as it is called, the continually changing visual pattern is reconverted into the real sounds.

The exciter bulb is positioned opposite and focused on a phototube. The film runs between these, and the visual pattern on the film track alters or modulates the quantity and character of the light hitting the phototube, which in turn gives off varying electron charges which are then amplified to reproduce the various original sounds. The reconstituted sound is fed through a larger amplifier (an electrical devise for maintaining or increasing the strength of the sound wave signal) and finally through a loudspeaker (a conical shaped device with a reverberating diaphragm) that throws the sound back into the air for us to hear.

Not really explained? Well, as one television friend of mine said, after failing to explain the technology of our industry, "Actually, God never intended for pictures and sound to go through the air."

Most original sound recording in film is now made on magnetic audiotape a quarter-inch wide. This audiotape has a base side and an emulsion side consisting of thousands of magnetized metallic particles sealed onto it. The particles on the tape, when passing the magnetic head of a recording machine, are altered when hit by sound-as-electrical-impulses and they thereby capture and store the impulses. In a reverse procedure, they surrender, or spend the impulses in playback. Magnetic sound recordings require no processing and can instantly re-create, or playback, the sound.

It is also possible to record on perforated magnetic stock of a 16mm width which is fully coated with the metallic particles, or on perforated and transparent 35mm stock which has a magnetic surface bonded onto part of it. (We will run into both of these stocks at later stages of sound production.) The raw stocks and equipment to handle them, however, are much more expensive and cumbersome than quarter-inch capability, without justifiable compensations of quality, so they are seldom used in original recording situations.

Let me mention one other means of original recording before I describe in detail the quarter-inch, separate-track, original recording process. When I described the Auricon single-system camera, I mentioned film that has a magnetic strip sealed directly onto it, making it possible to record simultaneously with picture taking. Fine, if you are in a hurry and do not worry about constructed sound or having to edit the material, or if you do edit, do not care that a person talking may be heard out of sync with his visual lip movements, use it. The cause of these flaws in single-system sound recording is that light travels faster than sound. In order to record in sync, sound in single-system must be twenty-six frames ahead of picture. Thus when you make a correct picture cut across the single-system film, you have made a wrong sound cut and have destroyed the sync. I am sure you have seen such butchered edits on newscast film footage.

Correcting sound flaws, eliminating boring extraneous sounds, or mixing in additional sounds or sound effects are also impossible with single-system recording. Avoid it, except for news coverage that must be used within a few hours.

Let us now go on to double-system sound recording; that is, where picture and sound are originally achieved (and are played) independently of each other, albeit in sync.

Accurate and easy sync sound recording at the time of shooting has been made possible by a number of technical advances. The most important of these is the sync pulse system. On a quarter-inch roll of audiotape it is possible to record the content sound on only the bottom half of the tape—or an eighth-inch of it. Recorded on the top eighth-inch is an electrical pulse transmitted by the camera, either via cable (or syncronous AC motors in both camera and recorder) or, cordless, via crystal. This pulse provides a guide for keeping the picture and the sound in syncronization even when the motor speeds of the camera and the sound tape-recording machine are different, which is frequently the case. For example, in 16mm, the camera is running at 7.2 inches a second, whereas the audiotape (for the best quality) may be running at 15 inches a second. These variable speeds can be adjusted in the sound transfer process, since the audiotape has stored an exact speed record of the camera movement via the sync pulse. The sound transfer equipment can modulate the sound speed to sync with picture. If the camera speed has been constant, there is no difficulty at all. Within certain prescribed tolerances, a varying loss or increase of speed in the camera can also be reconciled—more easily with spoken voice than with music or singing.

If the sync is there, it is always there, but it is more difficult for an editor to find it and lock picture and sound together if he has not been provided with easy visual and audible sync points. Rudimentary sync points, or slates, can be provided by a snap of the fingers in front of the camera and within hearing distance of the microphone. You can clap your hands together in a single definite clap with the hands in a vertical plane for easy reading by the camera and within hearing range of the mike. However, a more sophisticated slating system for providing sync points has been devised. It has various forms, but basically a "bloop" or "beep" is put on the audiotape and a fogged (light-exposed) frame is put on the film at the same time. Later, when an editor aligns these, the picture and the sound are in sync.

The traditional way—and the one I prefer—to slate picture and sound is to use a clapstick board. The clapstick board has a rectangular solid frontal surface on which you can write pertinent information (the early ones were actual pieces of slate, hence the term, or black-wood written on by chalk) such as the name of the show, the production company, the director, the cameraman, the film roll number, the scene number, the take number of the scene and the sound roll and take number. All of this information is important for later identification of the film. On top of the wooden rectangle are two sticks, one stationery, the other hinged so that it can be raised and then clapped down on the opposing stick.

This clapstick board is held up to the camera to be shot and is close enough to the microphone to be heard. The person holding it reads the information on the board aloud so that there is audible as well as visual record of the information. Then he claps the two sticks together. Where the clap is seen in a single frame of the film and where it is heard on the tape is the sync point.

Sometimes it happens that a subject is miked and too far away from camera for a slate to be seen (or to be heard if it is near to the camera). In such cases, it is possible, given two microphones and a sound mixer, to have a slate mike. Here the two mikes would be in sync with the camera through the sync pulse and the slate mike can be kept in close proximity with the camera. The camera merely has to shoot the visual slate first before refocusing on the subject.

Let me take you through a simple picture sync sound scene in 16mm film. Suppose you have Alistair Cooke delivering a speech directly to the camera. He is wearing a lavalier microphone. (A lavalier is a microphone designed to hang or attach directly to the person speaking.) When you have chosen your scene location, established a mark (a fixed position) for Mr. Cooke, and placed him on it, and when you have established your lighting exposure and lens focus and taken a voice-level test, you are ready to shoot and record. First, you roll sound (turn on the recorder) and wait for the sound man to call, "Speed" (machine is turning at normal operating speed). Now you roll camera (turn on the camera) and wait for the cameraman to call, "Rolling" (camera is turning at desired operating speed). Next, you slate the scene with information describing it—visually to the camera and audibly for the recorder. Next you make your sync point—with a clapstick, bloop-fog, or handclap or finger snap. Then, you let everyone settle for a moment (stay quiet and stop moving), after which the director yells, "Action," and Mr. Cooke begins to talk. When the scene is finished, the director will usually take a beat—a pause in time—and then yell, "Cut." Camera and sound recorder stop turning at that instruction.

If you get into situations where it is awkward or impossible to get a head slate (at the beginning of a scene), then you should always get a tail slate (at the end of the scene) before you cut. When this is necessary, the director or cameraman should yell out, "Tail slate it," ahead of time so everyone knows not to turn off before the slating is completed.

Now that we have filmed Mr. Cooke and recorded his voice, the first thing we should do is to play back the sound immediately to make sure that it is all right. (Also, even in this simple sound situation, I like to have a second mike that is mixing in ambient sound—that is the tone or sound atmosphere of the location indoors or out, since the one-voice mike on Cooke will give you a very flat or dead sound.)

When you have heard the sound and it is acceptable and when that particular audiotape is used up, it is sent, usually at the end of the shooting day, along with all the other recorded tapes, for sound transfer. (The day's exposed film is sent to the lab for processing.) In the Alistair Cooke example, the original quarter-inch audiotape will be transferred to 16mm magnetic stock (full-coat) which has perforated sprocket holes on it, just like film does. When the transfer is completed, the 16 mag will be sent to a film editor who, when he has also received the printed film dailies, or rushes, will sync the picture together with the 16 mag sound track. These two stocks—picture and sound—will be run at exactly the same speeds now, both pulled along by their sprocket holes. The editor, using the sync point will line up the film and 16 mag track and mark both stocks with sync start marks. Then he will, before edit marking or cutting, send these synced dailies for edge numbering, or coding.

Edge numbers are sequential numbers printed onto the edge of the negative, the first print (or work print), and the 16 mag sound track, at regular intervals along their entire lengths. The numbers at any given footage count will be always exactly the same on all three materials and now make cutting possible without losing sound sync or picture frames. When the work-print picture is assembled, the original negative can be matched-cut, when the negative cutter follows the edge numbers. This process is the same for any film width, including 35mm.

Not all sound, of course, need be recorded syncronously. Sound as well as picture may be recorded wild—that is, independently. The process of adding sound to picture after shooting is called dubbing. Dubbing is justified by any number of reasons—uneven sound at locations, putting on voices in another language, extraneous sounds at the time of shooting (such as jackhammers, airplanes, and so on), bad acting or accents, bad singers for musicals, voice-over narration, or such impracticalities as taking a hundred-piece orchestra on location with you.

Sound dubbing can be utilized for adding on-screen dialogue, music, voice-over narration or dialogue, and sound effects. As you arrive at your final sound mix you might have as many as ten or more separate sound tracks. At the final mix these are all run in sync with the picture, which is now seen on direct projection, and they are mixed through a sound mixing console onto one sound track, which is called a composite sound track. (Usually at this point the sound is still on magnetic recorded material which is then sent for an optical, or photographed, transfer.)

The mixing console is an electronic board of volume and tone controls which are wired to receive the various track feeds which can be integrated and blended into one. Most of your sound will be on separate tracks (usually *A, B, C,* and so forth) for blending of sounds and these are slugged with blank (silent) stock in those places where they are silent so as to maintain equal length (and thus sync) with all other picture and track lengths. The person who operates the sound console is called a sound mixer. The sound mixer works from footage counts written on large sheets of paper called cue sheets. He knows when to bring in or take out or mix or cross-fade the various sound tracks. Additional sound may be mixed in from what are called loops. For instance, you want bird whistles behind a scene between two actors and when you shot their dialogue there were no birds to be heard. You make a loop of bird whistles, usually purchased from a stock sound library, and mix this sound in under the dialogue. A loop is made by joining or editing together the two ends of an audiotape, so that the tape then plays in a continuous cycle, over and over and over. In our example, if you listened carefully, you would hear the same bird whistles repeatedly.

MICROPHONES: How programs are miked is critical in telling the sound story of what takes place. In many shows—particularly electronic variety shows—more than one microphone is used. In a program such as the "Tonight Show," as many as twenty microphones may be used, and all of these must be fed into a single mixing console to end up with one track of recorded sound.

For "In Concert," we frequently had as many as thirty to forty microphones. Each musician's instrument had at least one mike, the singers had mikes, and there were several microphones in the auditorium to pick up audience reaction. There was an announcer's mike backstage. Each of these various sound sources was recorded on a separate track and we mixed them together later in two forms: We made a stereo mix-down which ends up in two tracks, continuous *A* and *B,* dividing the sound in order to approximate the way we naturally perceive sound with our two ears. These were then broadcast—simulcast—by radio stations which have stereo transmitting capability. We sent each station the separate continuous *A* and *B* tracks which were put in sync with the picture on the videotape and on the stereo audiotapes. This pulse is transmitted by telephone cable from the television station to the radio station. We also made a monaural mix-down of the "In Concert" sound, in which we ended up with a single sound track. This track, which had been built separately from the videotape, is then laid down on the tape replacing the poorly balanced sound that is on the videotape from the time of original recording and which is never thought of as more than a guide, or reference, track for syncing the mix-down. This monaural sound is transmitted and received by the home set in the usual manner. Sound buffs will realize that this monaural mix-down provided "In Concert" with the best television sound being transmitted, but it is still wanting, since television sets have very inadequate speakers for quality sound.

A sound mixer may also be used at the time of original recording. It may be as simple as a two-mike imput affair or it may be a giant console capable of taking the feed of fifty microphones and sound sources (pretaped or prerecorded material may be mixed in with live). Especially for music, it is better to record separate sound elements at different times on different tracks when possible. There is usually too much distraction at the site of recording and not sufficiently capable equipment to get a good mix;

however, most show sound is still balanced and mixed at the time of original recording.

There are many different kinds of microphones designed for varying purposes and every manufacturer has his own design characteristics for the basic types. Current microphone technology is also trending toward portability and miniaturization. The newest mikes are RF, that is radio frequency, microphones which are cordless. An RF mike has its own transmitter and transmitting antenna which sends the sound directly through the air to the tape recorder. An RF mike may be not much longer or thicker than the filter on a cigarette. It is powered by a battery not much larger than a cigarette case, which is carried on the person of the man or woman who is miked. An RF mike is most reliable at relatively small distances from the recorder, though most are claimed to be capable up to a half-mile. A receiving antenna plugged into the recorder is required. RF sound is vulnerable to other radio frequency signals—you may get a call for a taxi or for airplane landing instructions right in the middle of your big dramatic scene— and extraneous electrical sources—car engines and the like. RF mikes are suitable for voice recording but are inadequate for music.

Another fairly recent microphone development is the shotgun mike—designed to record sound at more than average distance from the microphone. It is a familiar and favorite tool of the young documentary film maker, since it can be hand-held, thus offering great mobility; but it should be used more discriminately than it is because of its ability to reach out for sound—it reaches out for all sounds in the direction in which it is pointed. Overreliance on the shotgun mike is the principal reason for such poor sound quality in so many documentaries—"An American Family" for example.

There is a complete range of engineering advances in more traditional microphone usage, and recorded sound is better for these. The mikes I see most these days are made by three manufacturers—Sennheiser, Sony, and AKG. All of these companies can provide you with overwhelming detail on what they have available. But again, explain fully what you intend to do and your sound man, supply house, or other expert will know which kind of mike is best suited for the job and what auxiliary equipment is needed.

Among professional syncronous tape recorders my favorite is the Nagra line and I like especially the Nagra 4.2 model which weighs only eleven pounds, nine ounces without tape or batteries. It can also work on a power source. Nagra has put out a new recorder that is only 5.8 inches by 1.02 inches and can fit in your jacket pocket. It is known

warmly by some as the G. Gorden Liddy model. The newest model
of all, the Nagra SL and SD can record in stereo. And the technologcal
explosion goes on: Is it any wonder that film crews, on breaks, lunches, dinners, spend most of the time talking about equipment and
filming situations. It's hard to keep up.

THE CUTTING ROOM

The cutting room, or editing room, is where it all comes together. The
most rewarding and deeply satisfying moments—and some of the
most distressing—of my professional life have taken place in film
cutting rooms. There are few experiences in life more thrilling than
being in a cutting room with all the disparate pieces of film and sound
tracks waiting to be assembled into a finished motion picture or television show.

There are more overt energy vibrations in a video control room,
perhaps even in a videotape editing room, but these can never equal
the intense focus of concentration and the wonderous isolation I have
experienced in the cutting room. Also, film cutting rooms are friend-
lier, usually more cluttered, more eccentric, and humanistic in their
personalities and atmospheres than the more futuristic and bloodless
video rooms.

Ideally, a cutting room should have adjacent to it an area for
screening the film on direct projection, but within it, the following are
basic:

There should be a machine for screening and marking the film
and sound. The traditional piece of equipment for this purpose has
been the Moviola, currently produced in the Series 20 models, which
has a four-inch-by-five-inch viewing screen and a magnetic and/or
optical sound head. There is a speaker built into the face of the
machine. Such a machine can be threaded with the film and sound on
separate stocks, which can be run forward, backward, at varying
speeds, and locked in sync or moved independently. The film can be
marked by lifting the hinged viewing screen, but without opening the
film gate. Each single frame can be stopped in the viewing screen. The
standard Moviola machine comes with one-reel film and one-reel
sound capability but can be modified with modular units to run multiple picture and sound tracks.

This Moviola is a homely but trusted old friend of a machine and
I take this opportunity to apologize publicly for literally punching
mine in its viewing screen face one night when my frustrations at not
being able to get a desired sequence cut could no longer be contained.
Obviously, the fault was not in my Moviola, but in myself. Although

this incident turned out to be a crime of passion. I did actually give it a shot with my fist—cleanly, thankfully, or I might be bleeding still —and knocked the viewing screen glass completely out. (Haven't you ever been tempted to punch out your television set?) This clattery, but honorable, old upright machine is being replaced by recently developed console machines. The forerunner in this console, or table, design was the Steenbeck Company, followed by Kem and then by the Moviola Company, with its M-77. Several innovations are included: Reels are no longer necessary, since the film and sound can spool out from and be taken up by cores. The film and sound material lie flat on modular (interchangeable) metal flanges or plates. Threading is simplified. There is table space for splicing. (With the traditional model, splicing is usually done at the editor's table which I will describe later.) Viewing is on a large television-size screen, although the picture tends to flutter and illumination is not so bright. Two tracks of sound can be played simultaneously on standard models. Film and sound tracks can move faster forward and backward. A counter computes and displays frames and footage numbers or minutes and seconds. It can be modified by additional modules to handle multiple picture and sound tracks, and either in total or partial 16mm and 35mm. It is easy to sit at. Some producers report that films can be edited together in 25 to 50 per cent less time on these horizontal machines than on the traditional models.

Some other basic cutting room equipment can usually be found on the editing bench or table. These should include:

MOVISCOP: A small-screen machine, sometimes with a built-in sound head, which allows an editor to run quickly through film rolls to find particular shots or edit marks for cutting.

AMPLIFIER, OR SOUND READER: When the Moviscop does not have a sound head, this allows the editor to hear sync scenes.

MULTIPLE-TRACK SYNCHRONIZER: Keeps multiple picture and sound tracks locked in absolute sync as cuts are made.

SPRING CLAMPS: Hold multiple reels in one motion on the rewind spindles.

REELS: Needed in various sizes.

SPLIT REELS: With one side which can be screwed off to facilitate transferring rolls from reels to cores.

PLASTIC CORES: For rolling film and sound on.

REWINDS: Arms with cranks to turn rotating spindles on which film reels are placed and used for quick moving of the film and sound tracks backward and forward and for rewinding reels after projection.

(There are automatic electric ones available as well as the manual ones.)

TAPE SPLICER: Allows the making of quick mylar or cellulose tape splice edits.

MYLAR OR CELLULOSE SPLICING TAPE

HOT SPLICER: Used for making liquid cement-welded edit splices which are smoother and more long-lasting than tape splices.

FILM BINS: Hold "out" scenes by their sprocket holes on small pins extending from the top of the metal frames. These must be lined and scratch-proof.

RACKS: Needed to store reels and cans.

FLANGES: For handling film or sound tracks on cores.

Additional miscellaneous items include: a HOLE PUNCH, a MAG-NIFYING GLASS, SCISSORS, FILM CLEANER, FILM CEMENT, EDITOR'S ADHESIVE TAPE, a STOP WATCH, GREASE MARK-ING PENCILS, PENS for making notes or labeling scenes or takes, EDITOR'S SOFT COTTON GLOVES, and a specially designed EDI-TOR'S CHAIR. Finally, depending on your personal style, a cutting room should also include a small REFRIGERATOR and a FIFTH OF SCOTCH.

Sadly, as I read back over this entire chapter on equipment and technology, I realize it is finally unsatisfying—rather in the way of showing photographs of food to a starving person. A lot is missing.

One last comment about equipment and technology: With all of the advances of the technical revolution in film and television, these remain but tools and it is still the depth and wonder of one's human imagination and talent and vision that can finally stimulate a viewer's mind or stir his heart. Content is supreme and Griffith and Einstein, Mozart and Shakespeare are not diminished in their powers for having lacked the latest framus or whatzit. Protect and celebrate the human spirit; the machines can only serve it.

Chapter **13**
public, pay, cable, and cassette

Anyone interested in television should be aware of public television, pay television, cable television, and video cassettes and discs. These forms are present fact and potential future giants, if Congress and the fates are benevolent.

PUBLIC TELEVISION

In the beginning it was called educational television and it was best typified by four tweedy, briar-piped professors sitting around a coffee table putting almost everyone, and occasionally each other, to sleep. It is better today, of course, though at its best, decidedly produced by British television.

Educational television began almost as soon as television itself, when the FCC declared that 639 channel allocations should be reserved for this purpose. In 1947, in Ames, Iowa, WOI-TV,* owned by Iowa State College, became the first. By 1955 there were still only 15 stations. From that time, however, growth has been steady and, since 1967, rapid. Today there are 246 public television stations throughout the country. These stations are owned variously by state and local educational systems or schools, universities and colleges, and nonprofit community organizations. I got my early television experience and education through one of these stations owned by Indiana University.

Public television's present shape is based in large part on recommendations set forth in a landmark study of public television potential published in 1967 by the Carnegie Commission on Educational Television and entitled "Public Television—A Program for Action." The Congress passed and President Johnson signed into law in November 1967, the Public Broadcasting Act, which incorporates many of these recommendations.

* Yet another exception to W east of the Mississippi and K west.

The act established the Corporation for Public Broadcasting, which was mandated to develop programs and a system of distribution and to encourage local station activity. It was to provide these services in a manner that would permit the stations freedom to make their own decisions and pursue their own actions.

Congress was stingy, however, and kept a tight rein on the money it did allocate by making the allocations one year at a time and at its discretion. Congress chose to ignore the Carnegie Commission's more practical recommendations for long-range and self-sustaining funding through a form of license fees on television sets, which would have served the long lead time requirements of quality television and removed public television from the inevitable political pressures of congressional funding.

The CPB, headed by men with absolutely no television experience, set up an independent organization called the Public Broadcasting Service—PBS—to handle the distribution of programs. PBS's sole function is to network, or interconnect, programs which it does by means of simultaneous long-line and microwave interconnection or through the bicycling systems of mails and messengers.

It had been a further recommendation of the Carnegie Commission to establish national production centers concurrent with the strong support of individual local stations around the country. NET—National Educational Television—in business since 1954, had been evolving over the years until by 1970 it had become a national production and distribution service, funded in very large measure by the Ford Foundation. NET seemed a natural to become the commission's recommended national production center. But, as we have seen, PBS took over the distribution role, and next, NET was destroyed completely—by politics. As James Day, its innovative president, who was purged, said, "This is the sad thing. This history of public television is politics."

The Nixon Administration—suspicious of all media—particularly any that smacked of "Eastern Elitism"—came down lethally on NET, which was headquartered in New York City. The administration voiced its fear publicly that NET was becoming a centralized fourth network and a liberally biased one at that.

Clay Whitehead, Nixon's director of the White House Office of Telecommunications, itself a Nixon invention unauthorized by Congress, made it clear that the administration would oppose public broadcasting's dream of long-range financing unless the system became a structure of "bedrock localism." There would be no national production centers and no investigative reporting.

This wrought chaos in the ranks of public television. Divided, they appeared to be conquered as an effective programming source. CPB, with its Nixon appointed board, took over program decisions (the "Great American Dream Machine" fell victim, among other fine programs), and such federal funds as were available went to local stations. These thinly spread dollars, coupled with insufficient talent pools, made local stations impotent in the production of significant programs.

The local stations quickly realized that this fragmented funding and scattered talent doomed their hopes of making good programs, so what has emerged is a Rube Goldberg administrative invention put together by the local stations acting in concert. With priming funds from the Ford Foundation, they organized the Station Program Cooperative.

Here is how it functions at present: Local stations who wish to make programs present these program ideas, along with the budgets, to the Cooperative. All the program ideas from all the stations get printed in a catalog. If enough local stations—through a staggering and bewildering computerizedbidding—are willing to buy a particular show in the catalog with their own money, the show gets produced and placed on the national schedule. Again, according to James Day, of the 246 public television stations, perhaps 15 reach 50 per cent of the public television audience and yet, "all of them have one vote . . . so you have a situation not unlike that of the United Nations. The smaller station . . . the more vulnerable station . . . has a tendancy toward caution."

Roughly half of the nationally televised programs are chosen by this system. Think of the millions of dollars that are squandered in the elephantine administration machinery of this process—money that should be going on the air, not to mention Mr. Day's point about the watering down of program ideas that is an inevitable consequence.

The best of the other 50 per cent of national shows we see come from outside financing—more and more from corporations who "advertise" their participation with on-air mentions and make the same subtle program demands as they do in commercial television. What do they fund, for instance? Bold, innovative, minority interest, or even for the most part American programs? No, and let it resound. They import prestigious and well-made, but safe, programs from the BBC: "The Six Wives of Henry VIII" and others in the "Masterpiece Theatre" series (including the American novel, *The Last of the Mohicans*), "Civilisation," "The Ascent of Man," "Upstairs, Downstairs," and anything with Alistair Cooke in it.

I do not mean that these splendid programs should not be seen in the United States; but, when they are seen in lieu of American programs that could be of equal quality and perhaps more relevant impact, then we are faced with a culturally scandalous and creatively bankrupt system of public television.

The Nixon policy of localism is a naïve understanding of television realities at best, and, at worst, cynically suffocating to the wholesome flowering of public television in America. The locals themselves acknowledge their programming anemia through the fact of their crisis-created Program Cooperative. Local stations, of course, should have adequate funds for local programs and services. They should not and cannot produce national programming of quality.

As I have alluded, talent is scarce at best, but exists where it exists at all, in concentrated centers of the nation. In America, this means New York City and Los Angeles, with special resources available in Boston and Washington, D.C. These cities should get the national funds for national programs, since they have the enormous concentration of skills—performers, writers, directors, producers, technicians—required to make quality television.

Imagine French culture without Paris or suppose the BBC were located in one hundred cities and towns instead of being in London, Great Britain's concentrated cultural heart. Its programs would be sterile and undistinguished, rather than being the pride of American public television.

In the spirit of a new American Revolution, the present system should be repudiated. Safeguards to assuage grass-roots fear of the East and West Coast liberals (and who are these but the sons and daughters of the entire nation?) and to protect grass-roots thinking could easily be provided in a system which would establish a board composed of local and regional representatives. Furthermore, a $5-a-year license fee per television set would guarantee politically independent funds, in sufficient amount to make distinguished public television programs possible.

As for the program makers in public television, my own experience offers a case study of their creative waste and frustration in the current setup. I proposed in the late summer of 1970 a ninety-minute program featuring the American Ballet Theatre in location performance and documentary off-stage life. Because of a prize-winning television film I had made of Agnes DeMille's "Fall River Legend" (financed ironically by commercial broadcast interests), I had the Ballet Theatre's blessings for the project.

With that I went to Channel 13, the public television station in New York, to get them to submit the program for networking. They said they would, if I could raise the money. They did say they would put up $50,000 of my $150,000 budget, if I could raise the first $100,000.

With that agreement I went to the National Endowment for the Arts, in Washington, D.C. First, they doubted that the program could be made for $150,000, based on their experience. As gently as possible, I told them that perhaps my experience as a producer of over two thousand television programs was more relevant and realistic than theirs. As a convincer, I said I would find an underwriter to pay any budget overages. After a year—six trips to Washington and a landfill's worth of forms to submit—they gave me $50,000 (Channel 13, actually).

Next stop was the Mellon Foundation. The prospects looked good, but they could promise nothing until the fall. About that time, I had a good offer from ABC and went to work for them—on September 25, 1972. On October 1, 1972, the Mellon Foundation agreed to put up the remaining $50,000.

Another producer/director, Jerry Schnurr, was assigned my Ballet Theatre project. It was produced (for $200,000), highly acclaimed, and won a number of awards. I like it at ABC. But is it any wonder that so many of the best of us opt for the more efficient, if less soul-satisfying realms of commercial television? If one program takes two years and considerable personal financial sacrifice, who good can or will want to endure such a process?

PAY TELEVISION

So far, the most successful pay television has been the kind you leave home for—the theatre or arena big-screen, closed-circuit television of championship fights; and, on one occasion, Evel Knievel's abortive Snake River Canyon jump. Muhammed Ali is the star attraction of this television form and, while millions of dollars have been made this way on his fights, widely expanded use of this medium seems doubtful. (I think even the fights would not have been so profitable without Ali's superb showmanship.)

Of course, other highly popular one-time events such as the Super Bowl would draw, but it is unlikely that the handful of entrepreneurs in this field can compete with commercial free television in acquiring such exclusive rights. Various promoters have tried in vain to organize major rock star shows for presentation in this form—ABC and I among them—but until now the sound qualities have been inadequate and frustrating. Look for this to happen, however.

Various home pay television schemes have been attempted since the middle 1950s, but none has been able to overcome the powerful

opposition of movie theatre owners and commercial television interests—or the public's apathy. All along, the pay television people have
insisted that they want to bring to special-interest audiences such
rarely available fare as opera and ballet, but indeed they, too, have
been in there scrambling for the major attractions—popular first-run
motion pictures and sports events.

This battle is fierce and complex and involves the combating
parties, the courts, Congress, the White House, the FCC, state and
local governments, and the telephone companies. The war is nowhere
near being over. Since pay television is now almost exclusively delivered by cable, the issues also will determine the fate of cable television, as we will see.

In its present form, let us call pay television paycable. It began
in late 1972 and today there are forty-seven systems in operation,
which reach a modest television audience. Nearly all the systems offer
six to eight feature films a month that are less than three years old and
others that are over ten years old that have not been shown on free
television for three years. They also offer a wide-ranging mix of
shorter nonfiction films and entertainment shows as well as whatever
sports events they can get.

To receive paycable a person must have already subscribed to
cable television service. If one has, then there are two basic forms of
the additional paycable service. In one system, a special tuning box is
installed in the subscriber's home to permit unscrambled viewing of
the pay channel and the subscriber is charged a flat fee of between
$6.00 and $8.00 for a monthly programming package. In the other
system, the subscriber activates the unscrambling of the pay channel
himself by turning a key or inserting a specially coded card and is
charged on a per-program basis; and is billed as for telephone use.
(Coming soon are over-the-air subscription stations. The signal will
come through the air as in free television, but will be scrambled and
available only to paying subscribers equipped with unscrambling
equipment.

The major establishment television industry arguments against
paycable contend that it will fragment audiences and thus weaken the
current programming capabilities; and that it will syphon off programs
and events that are presently available to the audience of free television. Paycable advocates respond that these arguments are based on
illusory fears if they are sincere; and that, if they are not, they camou-
flage a protectionist point of view that works for restraint of trade and
that the citizenry is the victim. They say audiences have a right to
choose. For instance, if people want to see a movie on free television,
fine. But if they want to see the movie on paycable, without deletions

and commercials, nothing and no one should prevent it.

The FCC is heavily involved. Among its rulings so far: No network may own a cable or paycable system. No paycable system may offer any movie that is more than three years old and no more than one a month that is more than ten years old—"the three and ten ruling." There are no restrictions on foreign films. Paycable is restricted in obtaining sports events presently offered on free television.

This is a vigorously contested and evanescently held battleground, with millions of dollars at stake. Conventional television interests and movie theatre exhibitors are allied on one side; major movie makers and paycable owners are on the other; in between, the FCC is an irresolute and nervous Solomon. Facts, rulings, and arguments are fluid and will be for some time. My hunch is, however, that paycable will win enough ground in the coming years to establish itself as a major entertainment entity, without seriously effecting the profitability of *status quo* television.

CABLE TELEVISION

The underlying technology of paycable is cable television, which itself, in a way, is pay television, since one pays a monthly fee for the service. This service, depending on the market, costs from $5.00 to $9.00 a month. You are not, of course, theoretically, paying for the programs, but for the technical advantage of improved picture quality.

Cable television—CATV or Community Antenna Television, as it is called—came into being in Astoria, Oregon, in 1949. Since this particular community was cut off from receiving ordinary television signals, because of surrounding mountains, a local group formed a company to build an antenna on one of the mountains, from which the signal was picked up and fed into individual homes by wire—pencil-thin coaxial cable. Other communities followed suit. Not all of them because of mountains. Some were plagued by man-made objects. Other communities were too sparsely settled to have any more than one television station nearby. Today, CATV systems are widespread—over three thousand systems serving more than six thousand communities and eleven million subscribers. The United States Commerce Department's annual *U.S. Industrial Outlook* projects that CATV systems by 1980 will be serving twenty million subscribers and taking revenues of $1.55 billion.

Cable television is a wide-band (most often, 54MHz to 216MHz), low-gain RF signal distribution system. It distributes broadcast signals from a single antenna site simultaneously to multiple terminals. The major components are: antenna, head end, coaxial cable, and distribution amplifiers.

The major obstacles confronting CATV's growth are copyright problems, particularly when television signals are imported by the antennas from distant markets; access to telephone company poles and underground conduits for placing its wires; multilayered government regulation; conventional television's strong opposition; and the immense capitalization required to generate its own attractive program resources, as well as to endure until there are subscribers in sufficient numbers to make operations profitable.

But CATV was born to conquer mountains. I foresee a vigorous and profitable large-scale cable industry for America in the 1980s. Program makers can only benefit from this additional outlet for their wares. Already, through the public access channels that CATV systems are required to provide, young television makers have unprecedented opportunities to get on, to learn, and to experiment and grow.

In addition to offering the more traditional program forms, cable television, with its multichannel and two-way communications capabilities provides heady prospects for future enterprises—talking back to your set, for instance, or we may vote this way eventually, or shop by television. These are only a few examples futurists point to. With it all, there is yet another future hardware system for program suppliers.

VIDEO CASSETTES AND DISCS

In 1970, we were promised a video revolution in the form of cassettes, cartridges, and discs, not by wild-eyed kooks and tinkerers, but by such sober and solvent folks as CBS, RCA, Sony, Phillips, British Decca, Telefunken, Ampex, Panasonic, and Avco. I, like hundreds of others, rushed out and optioned all the ballet companies, story sources, chefs, doctors, auto mechanics, golf, tennis, and sewing instructors I could find. I even flew to Memphis and tried to talk Kemmons Wilson of Holiday Inns into putting them into his two hundred thousand guest rooms.

The revolution died aborning and the corporate giants blew over a $150 million on the way to this video funeral. I lost almost as much in my fantasy paper profits. Most decided, that was that, but a few hardware giants wiped the tearstains from their financial ledgers and pressed ahead.

Video cassettes, using magnetic technology, have hung on—Sony is the leader—in limited use by established television entities as a storing and screening convenience, and through some modest acceptance in the institutional fields—school, hospital, military, and corporate training use. But the major thrust of activity and the most hope are invested in video discs. The technology is definitely here and the prices are coming down, though what the buying public's response will be is still uncertain. Any meaningful market place for video discs depends on mass consumer buying and the prognosis is not immediately cheerful, when weighed against the history of color television penetration, which took over twenty years to reach 50 per cent of set ownership in the United States.

Still, people made money in color television—and continue to— and this experience has whetted the appetites of the video disc makers.

Leading those who remain in this field are RCA which offers a grooved disc which turns at 350 revolutions per minute and is activated by a stylus; and North American Phillips and MCA, who, in a joint venture, offer a disc turning at 1,800 revolutions per minute and which uses laser beam technology to activate.

In an echo of the great struggle between CBS's 33 and a 1/3 long-playing phonograph record and RCA's 45 rpm disc, these two video discs systems are incompatible. No major consumer response can be reasonably expected until people are assured that they are not buying outmoded equipment. A victor or compatibility must emerge in the state of the art.

Why buy at all? The reasons put forth are: So you may have available to you in a convenient form and at any time you choose any video material you desire—just as we now enjoy our record players and audio cassette players.

The video playback units attach to one's currently owned television set and the viewing is in this television form. Programs can be purchased, rented, or recorded off-the-air.

If and when the video player business is a pervading reality, the need for software—program material—should be a boon to program makers. The more halls there are to put your shows into the better. But, for now, conventional television remains the best economic hope for reducing my mortgage and for putting my children through college.

Chapter 14
summing up

I cannot forget them or make them vanish from my inner vision.

The bark-skinned man at 7:00 A.M., in the dark, in the cold, in the fragile wooden box of a Maine farmhouse, who cannot see even the smoke from any neighbor's chimney in any direction, but who lights the cool fire of his television set and connects himself to Ho Chi Minh City on the opposite side of the earth.

The woman at 9:30 A.M. on Long Island in the split-level modern, who does not tell the truth about being thirty-five and worries if her thighs are waffling, who sips her coffee before the cool fire of Barbara Walters discussing important things and wonders why she never did something with her B.A.

The widow in Chicago at 11:00 A.M. (Central Standard Time) who asks her daughter on the phone with real problems to call back later because she is engrossed now with the flickering problems of a soap opera.

The out-of-work aerospace engineer at 2:00 P.M. in Wichita who has just answered all the questions correctly on a quiz show and who in his mind has been asked to come back tomorrow. He is available.

Then it is late afternoon in Texas and a preacher is wearing make-up and introing a rock group for Jesus.

In Los Angeles, on "Sesame Street," they are counting from one to ten, and a black boy, five, is watching it in Watts and is storing it; he may, by a few, be liked even less someday for being smart.

Then, it is nighttime and news and game shows and situation comedies and cops and crooks and docs and made-for-television movies. Here a lawyer, there a comic—and the family is together; the nation is together.

Late news follows—not different from the evening news at 7:00 or 6:00, except for the ball scores, and unless someone famous has been assassinated in-between. Then come the talk shows and the old movies, watched more, they say, by younger adults than older, richer than poorer, smarter than dumber, femaler than maler.

And then, finally, in most towns, no matter how many clicks you make on your remote control roulette wheel, there is nothing. Except the snow and the sizzle. Unless you live in New York City or Los Angeles or other big towns where it goes without ceasing and Bette Davis or George Brent are always there to help you through the night. Until, until—once more it is "Today" and "Good Morning, America." The images are pervasive—and frightening.

The cool fire is always there now, every hour, every day, everywhere. What does it accomplish? Does it ease the chill—of loneliness? Of facing reality or relatives? Of sapped energies? Defeated dreams? Of being godless or jobless or four years old and unattended? To be sure. But does it not also remove the chill of ignorance and provincialism and false authority?

In other cultures and in other times, politics, quality art, entertainment, and education have been the private perquisites of the privileged class and have been often used, not simply for personal pleasure and pride, but actively, willfully, as weapons to suppress or exploit the larger population. I meet lots of people today who would draw the cultural line at Ingmar Bergman's Movies, and who condemn television as the successor to Marx's vision of religion as "the opiate of the masses." Of course, if you have been educated in an upper-middle-class home, a prep school, and Harvard, most of television must strike you as sterile, wasteful, and banal. But if you have been raised in a sharecropper's shack and systematically denied formal quality education, television will nourish your mentality through a bountiful harvest of knowledge and possibilities. Distribute the American population between these two poles and see toward which it skews and you will begin to see why I think of television as a force of enlightenment rather than an electronic anesthesia.

To be sure, there is a surfeit of cops and detectives and killings and car chases and other assorted cultural obscenities, but I believe America gets the television it wants, and largely needs, and the wonder to me is not how bad it is, but quite regularly, how extraordinarily good it is. There is no compelling national or social issue that has not been touched on by at least one of the three networks' regularly scheduled entertainment programs in any given season; and the specials, the sports, and news coverage are the best in the world.

What do you get in the rest of the world? I saw an hour show on the history of scissors at 8:00 P.M. on Saturday night in Denmark. At the same hour, another time, I saw a yawning thirty minutes on the vaunted BBC of Princess Anne reviewing the corps at Sandhurst. In

France, not too long ago, the people rose in open protest against their state-run television system because it was boring and heavily censored. In the Soviet Union there are the Disneylike fantasies of the news broadcasts and the endless tours of heavy machinery factories. Small wonder that American programs are in demand around the world and, when they are permitted, clobber the competition.

American television is as erratically eclectic as a bright and curious child, and it weighs in just as modestly in its depth and attention span. But its all-consuming randomness and restlessness and availability are what will get you. Not forever will you be able to view suffering in Bangladesh, or homosexuals revealed as human beings, or women's lib truths in soap operas without effect. This unblinking vision from around the corner and around the world may for a time yet either cause protective calluses on your senses or polarize your traditional views to the boiling point. But not forever. Television will get you and change you, and that can change the world. It has begun.

I sincerely believe that American commercial television hastened —however slowly—the end of the Vietnam tragedy. I believe it spurred the civil rights movement of the Sixties. When it showed one black head getting busted on that bridge at Selma, it did more than a thousand print editorials or sermons to pass redemptive legislation. Television commercials, also, did not say, "White Only." The goods and seductions were available to all, it seemed, and when they said, "Get," "Be," it raised the expectations of black Americans as well as white.

The unremitting revelations about Watergate and the persona of Senator Sam Ervin restored vigor to our Constitution and forced the conclusion of Nixon's resignation.

I believe in American television. And I believe that it will get better. I am glad and proud to be part of it.

Especially if you have come this far in the book, I hope you have enjoyed it and have learned something. It is so hard for me to know if I have gotten through to you, particularly in light of one recent experience. After one of my lectures at the New School, when I thought I had been particularly trenchant, I was reinforced in the belief by the large number of students who stayed after class to ask good and provocative questions. I took the time to answer each in detail, one at a time. Finally, when the last young man stepped up, I was about to commend him for his obvious dedication and patience —and myself for my good works—when he said, "I hate to burden you with my question—it's so late."

"No, no, that's all right," I said. "That's what I'm here for."

"Well," he said, "I really like—uh—could you tell me where you got your suit?"

index